THE LITERARY REPUTATION

OF

MARK TWAIN

FROM 1910 TO 1950

PUBLICATIONS DE
LA FACULTÉ DES LETTRES DE L'UNIVERSITÉ DE CLERMONT

FASCICULE HORS-SÉRIE

ROGER ASSELINEAU

THE LITERARY REPUTATION

OF

MARK TWAIN

FROM 1910 TO 1950

A critical essay and a bibliography

GREENWOOD PRESS, PUBLISHERS
WESTPORT, CONNECTICUT

The Library of Congress cataloged this book as follows:

Asselineau, Roger.
    The literary reputation of Mark Twain from 1910 to
1950; a critical essay and a bibliography. Westport, Conn.,
Greenwood Press ₍1971₎

    240 p. 23 cm. (Publications de la Faculté des lettres de l'Uni-
versité de Clermont. Fasc. hors-sér.)
      Reprint of the 1954 ed.
    Originally presented as the author's thesis, Université de Paris.

    1. Clemens, Samuel Langhorne, 1835–1910—Criticism and interpre-
tation.   2. Clemens, Samuel Langhorne, 1835–1910 — Bibliography.
I. Title.   (Series: Clermont-Ferrand, France. Université. Faculté
des lettres et sciences humaines. Publications, fasc. hors-sér.)

PS1338.A8   1971   016.818′4′09   73–98744
ISBN 0–8371–3069–7   MARC

Library of Congress   71 ₍4₎

PS
1338
.A8
1971

Originally published in 1954 by Librarie Marcel Didier,
Paris

Reprinted from an original copy in the collections of the
University of Southern Illinois

Reprinted in 1971 by Greenwood Press,
a division of Congressional Information Service, Inc.,
51 Riverside Avenue, Westport, Connecticut 06880

Library of Congress catalog card number 73-98744
ISBN 0-8371-3069-7

Printed in the United States of America

10 9 8 7 6 5 4 3

ERRATA

Please, read :

P. 15, l. 18 .... In Germany, Mark Twain was regarded...

P. 25, l. 14 .... of life in the Mississippi valley...

P. 30, l. 2 .... set of values...

P. 32, l. 29-32. ..... *The Mysterious Stranger* (1916), *What is Man ?*
and Other Essays (1917), and *The Curious*
Republic of Gondour and Other Whimsical
Sketches (1919).

P. 36, l. 16 .... as we shall see, against himself...

P. 40, l. 6 .... the best boys' books...

P. 49, l. 20 .... bucolic activities...

P. 50, l. 10 .... expressions or statements...

P. 57, l. 11 .... he undertook...

P. 65, last l .... that he should ever...

P. 70, nᵒ 11. .... O'Rell...

P. 74, nᵒ 56. .... *Book News Monthly*...

P. 93, nᵒ 213. ...... claimed that he never had...

P. 100, nᵒ 267. .... Lehmann und Fink...

P. 102, nᵒ 287, last l. Introduction, p. 55.

P. 105, nᵒ 313. .... Brooks's thesis...

nᵒ 314. .... Inner Sanctum...

P. 108, nᵒ 334. ..... « Huckleberry and Sherlock »...

P. 122, nᵒ 546, l. 4.. ... Mississippi...

P. 131, last line .... silent...

P. 137, nᵒ 575, l. 3.. ... to make fun...

P. 138, nᵒ 591. ..... " Mark Twain's First Published Effort. "

P. 142, nᵒ 628. ..... SMITH, Anabella...

P. 157, nᵒ 771, l. 4.. Twain's relations...

P. 158, nᵒ 776, l. 3.. " It is not always easy to bear prosperity... "

P. 162, nᵒ 810. .... *Commonweal*...

nᵒ 819 .... " A Silent Celebrity. "...

P. 186, nᵒ 1003, l. 3. ... against De Voto in a review...

P. 188, nᵒ 1023, l. 2. ... crystallization...

P. 189, nᵒ 1034, l. 3. ... famous joke...

P. 211, nᵒ 1207, l. 2. ... di tutte le letterature...

P. 212, nᵒ 1221 ..... " Mark Twain, premier classique de l'Amérique. "

P. 226, nᵒ 1330. .... " Tom Sawyer and Don Quixote. "...

TO MY WIFE

TABLE OF CONTENTS

FOREWORD [1]

This work consists of two parts : on the one hand, an introductory essay in which we have tried to describe the evolution of Mark Twain criticism in the United States since the great humorist's death, and, on the other, a critical bibliography of Mark Twain criticism in the United States as well as in Great Britain, France, Germany, Italy, Spain and Latin America.

The more important part is the latter, which we hope will be of help to all critics and scholars interested in Mark Twain. It is the most complete bibliography of this author ever compiled so far, and, to make it more useful we have summed up in a few lines all material books and articles, overlooking only insignificant contributions or books and articles which are discussed in the introductory essay. Besides, the index will enable the reader to find quickly all the information he needs.

In the bibliography we have preferred to follow a chronological rather than an alphabetical order. It is thus easier to follow the evolution of Mark Twain criticism through the years. Thanks to this method our bibliography is something more than a mere list of books and articles. It offers a complete picture of the reactions provoked by Mark Twain's works and a graph of the progress of research during the last forty years. It can be read in connection with our introductory essay which it illustrates and complements. However we have not thought it necessary to follow the chronological order for the articles written in a given year. Such a classification would be more confusing than enlightening. In particular, it would make the task of following the production of the different critics more difficult by scattering the references to their contributions. It might help to trace derivations and influences. But, whenever necessary, we have called the reader's attention to such facts in our notes. Besides,

1. The numbers in the footnotes of the introductory essay refer to the entries in the Bibliography ; e.g. cf. n° *1272*.

the more important polemics are studied in our introductory essay.

The biographical and critical production of each year is divided for clarity's sake into a certain number of categories : Bibliographies, Biographies and Books of Criticism, Introductions and Prefaces, Other Books Dealing with Mark Twain, Periodical Literature, and lastly, Unpublished Theses. This disposition enables the reader immediately to find the different bibliographies which have been compiled so far and the more important books on the subject. The listing under a separate heading of the Introductions and Prefaces to Mark Twain's works reveals the growing interest of the public and the critics in *Tom Sawyer* and, above all, *Huckleberry Finn,* and the decline in popularity of such humorous tales as " The Jumping Frog " on which his early reputation was based. In the category Periodical Literature, reviews are listed separately. It is thus possible to study the reception and repercussions of the major biographies and books of criticism, which is especially interesting at the time of the Brooks-De Voto controversy.

We have devoted a few pages of our bibliography to the period preceding 1910, but, of course, the list we give is merely selective. We have compiled it only to give the American reader some information about European books and articles rarely mentioned in the United-States [1].

Each book and article listed in the bibliography bears a number, and the alphabetical index of authors at the end refers to these numbers. So, the reader can find all the contributions of a given critic as easily as if the items had been alphabetically classified in the bibliography. The index also contains, under the name of Mark Twain, the titles of those of his works on which separate studies have been written.

The compilation of this bibliography would have been impossible without the Fulbright and Smith-Mundt grants which we were awarded in 1950. These enabled us to do the necessary research in the United States in 1950-51. So, we owe particular thanks to the administrators of these foundations and to the authorities of Harvard University who generously gave us the freedom of their libraries — an invaluable privilege. We must express our

1. More complete bibliographies of Mark Twain criticism prior to 1910 will be found in Robert Gilkey, *Mark Twain Voyageur et son Image de l'Europe* (cf. n° *1272*) and Cyrille Arnavon, *Les Lettres américaines devant la Critique française (1887-1917),* Annales de l'Université de Lyon, III, 20 (Paris, Les Belles Lettres, 1951, 153 pp.).

thanks to the officials of Widener Library who helped us on many occasions and to the librarians of the Library of Congress, of the Boston and New York Public Libraries, and of the British Museum, and the Biblioteca Nazionale in Florence in which we completed our investigations.

Many thanks are also due to Professor Louis Landré of the Sorbonne under whom this thesis has been written. We are very grateful to him for his critical guidance and helpful suggestions. We must also mention our debt to Professor Albert Farmer of the Sorbonne who has read our manuscript and corrected several errors.

In closing we have to thank Mr. Blair Wilkie, " lecteur " at Clermont-Ferrand University who has been kind enough to read over our introductory essay.

Clermont-Ferrand, May 1st 1952.

A CRITICAL ESSAY

INTRODUCTION

It may seem strange that we should have limited our study of Mark Twain's literary reputation to the United States, whereas we have tried to cover as broad a field as possible in our critical bibliography and included books and articles published in Great Britain, France, Germany, Italy and Spain as well as in America. But the reason for this apparent inconsistency simply is that no major book of criticism has been written on Mark Twain outside his native country.

In his lifetime, he was even more popular in England than in the United States. While most of his compatriots, much to his indignation, insisted on seeing only a jester in him and forced him to play a clowning part, the British thought him worthy of the highest academic distinction and the University of Oxford conferred an honorary doctorate on him in 1907 [1]. Yet, no English critic has dared to write about him, probably because he was too typically American and it was felt that only an American could fully appreciate all the implications of his works [2].

In Germany [3], Mark Twain was regarded almost as if he had been a native German writer. According to the Viennese philosopher Leon Kellner, his works read " precisely like a German original " [4]. However, only studies of secondary importance, like F. Schönemann's thesis [5], have been published on Mark Twain in Germany.

One finds the same dearth of critical material in Spain and Italy where people seem to be perfectly satisfied with enjoying Mark Twain's humour without trying to analyse it.

---

1. Cf. n⁰ *113*, pp. 1376-1404.
2. On Mark Twain's reception in Great Britain, cf. n⁰ *1089*.
3. On Mark Twain's reception in Germany, cf. n⁰ *837*.
4. Quoted by A. Henderson, n⁰ *57*, p. 607. Cf. also what F. Schönemann wrote in 1936 : « Endlich hat auch sein durchaus germanisch gefärbter Humor vielfätiges Echo in unserem Volk gefunden ", n⁰ *759*, p. 260.
5. Cf. n⁰ *362*.

In France, the case has been different.   Mark Twain was never popular there in his lifetime.   As his daughter Clara later remarked : " With the exception of France, he seemed equally famous in all countries [1]. "   The French readers of those days failed to appreciate his humour in spite of the fervour of Michel Epuy who had translated some of his tales [2].   In 1911 someone wrote in the *Figaro* : " It is as difficult for a Frenchman to understand Mark Twain as for a North American to understand La Fontaine [3]. "   Régis Michaud in 1918 was hardly more encouraging : « Quand on n'a pas le privilège d'être Américain, les livres de Mark Twain souvent irritent et étonnent... [4] »   As late as 1935 Gabriel de Lautrec still treated him with marked condescension : « ... les États-unisiens de tout âge, à un certain point de vue sont des enfants... la moindre plaisanterie les fait rire aux éclats, enfantinement... [5] »   So M. Le Breton was right to conclude in the same year : « On ne lit guère Mark Twain en France, on ne l'a jamais beaucoup lu... son humour a paru trop gros pour avoir droit a une place dans la littérature qui se respecte... [6] »   Yet, there have been a few French critics who have not let themselves be put off by the specific Americanism of Mark Twain — M. Le Breton in particular, who in the centenary year wrote for the *Revue Anglo-Américaine* a balanced and searching study in which he tried to reconcile the different interpretations so far proposed [7].   Léon Lemonnier followed suit and in 1936 published a lively little book which gave a picturesque description of Mark Twain's life and personality [8].   More recently, in 1950, Simon Hornstein competently summed up for the general public the conclusions reached by transatlantic experts [9] and Jean Kanapa, a communist critic, has drawn the attention of his readers to the anti-imperialist writings of Mark Twain's old age [10]

However interesting these books and articles may be, they

1. Cf. n° *504*, p. 96.
2. Speaking of *Eve's Diary* he wrote for instance " ... il a atteint la perfection d'Homère ou de La Fontaine ... c'est à Voltaire ou à Anatole France que l'on se sent contraint de comparer le spirituel humoriste américain " (n° *41*, p. 28).
3. Quoted in *Bookman*, 1911 ; cf. n° *111*.
4. Cf. n° *200*, pp. 136-137.
5. Cf. n° *688*, p. 76.
6. Cf. n° *690*, p. 401.
7. *Ibid.*
8. Cf. n° *725*.
9. Cf. n° *1233*.
10. Cf. n° *1145*.   Here is a sample of this strange criticism : « Il a fallu que la critique soviétique soulève récemment la question avec une indispensable vigueur pour qu'enfin on se décide à amener au jour ces écrits des dernières années de Twain... Scandale ! Ces écrits, articles ou projets manuscrits sont en majorité des pamphlets anti-impérialistes » (p. iv).

cannot be considered original contributions to Mark Twain criticism. The work could be done only by American critics, and they did not fight shy of it. For the last forty years, as our bibliography shows, there has been a steady flow of critical literature on Mark Twain. He has been presented successively as a picturesque personality, a psychic and social problem, a projection of the American frontier and finally as a great artist.

We shall study these different metamorphoses of Mark Twain's reputation since 1910, which we have chosen as the starting-point of our study because it is the year of his death. Generally speaking it is always difficult to appraise an author before he dies. Biographical information is lacking, his personality keeps changing. There is always the danger that some unpredictable move should suddenly upset our conception of him. Only death can put a stop to this unpleasant uncertainty by turning his erratic existence into a well-determined essence. This is precisely what happened in the case of Mark Twain. A full appraisal of his genius became possible only after his death, when the 25 volume edition of his complete works was brought out and when Paine, his official biographer, published the first complete and coherent story of his life. Besides, the reception of Mark Twain's major works in his lifetime has already been thoroughly studied in the United States [1] and there is no point in going over the subject again and recapitulating the conclusions of American scholars.

1. Cf. our bibliography, Henderson (n° 57), Peckham (n° 248), Hoben (n° 1077) and Vogelback (n°ˢ 877, 881, 956).

CHAPTER I

MARK TWAIN'S REPUTATION IN 1910

The contemporaries of Mark Twain were content for the greater part to enjoy him [1]. His popularity was as instant as it was vast, but as Howells pointed out in 1910, " it must be acknowledged that for a much longer time than in England polite learning hesitated his praise... In proportion as people thought themselves refined they questioned that quality which all recognize in him now, but which was then the inspired knowledge of the simple-hearted multitude. I went with him to see Longfellow, but I do not think Longfellow made much of him, and Lowell made less [2] ". In other words, the power of the genteel tradition was so great in such circles that he was thought of as hardly a man of letters at all. There was a cleavage between his fame and his critical reputation. His books won popular acclaim, the intelligent reading public regarded him as a literary artist of the first rank, but for at least thirty-five years most reviewers during his lifetime rejected him altogether.

The reason for this lack of appreciation by the cognoscenti was that criticism of American literature was embryonic in those days and everything too strongly American was frowned upon and considered vulgar. Emerson's declaration of independence in *The American Scholar* (1837) did not take full effect before the beginning of the XXth century. In Mark Twain's lifetime American literature was not yet studied in American universities. Education in English literature meant education in British literature, and the canons of good taste were extremely narrow.

So it was only when the colonial complex broke down in the rising tide of nationalistic impulse that Mark Twain became

---

1. Cf. n⁰ *709*, p. 472. On the critical reception of *The Prince and the Pauper* and *Huckleberry Finn*, cf. two excellent articles by A. L. Vogelback (nᵒˢ *877*, *956*).
2. Cf. n⁰ *33*, p. 46.

appreciated for what he really was. But in 1910 many critics still looked down on him and viewed him merely as a " funny man " and a clever humorist. Thus Ada Foster Murray in a farewell poem to Mark Twain extolled him as the

" Great master of the jester's bells,
The crowned and sceptred king of mirth. [1] "

Alden in the *Bookman*, though enthusiastic over *Huckleberry Finn* and *Tom Sawyer*, denied Mark Twain the title of artist : " The art which premeditatively determines the scope of its venture so that one sees at every step the curvature of its rounding up — in a word the literary art, — was foreign to Mark Twain's nature... [2] " In the *Independent* the anonymous author of Mark Twain's obituary was not even sure that his works would live :

" To the older men these writers [Irving, Holmes, G. W. Curtis] will still seem supreme, while the younger generation will give their loyalty to Stockton and Mark Twain. Only Stockton can compare with Twain, and he was less *outré*, and his loss was a very sad one for American letters. Probably in the future, as in the past, each generation will give its homage to its own popular writers of the day, while the next will put their collected works on the shelf for occasional reference and only three or four of a century will compel familiarity as well as lessening homage. Whether Mark Twain will be one of these few, the next century will decide... [3] "

The point of view of Mark Twain's disparagers was pretty well summed up by Barry Pain who wrote : " ... Mark Twain's artistic endowment was very slight, but he was a successful funmaker [4]. "

Often in those years Bret Harte was rated higher than Mark Twain. In 1912, in their *Great Writers of America*, Trent and Erskine devoted 12 pages to the former and 7 only to the latter — though they acknowledged that, " had he no other qualities, he might even now begin to take his place with the jokers out of fashion, like Josh Billings or Artemus Ward [5]. " Such an open-minded scholar as Bliss Perry, who had written an extremely sympathetic book on Walt Whitman a few years before, hardly mentioned *Huckleberry Finn* in 1912 in *The American Mind* [1],

1. Cf. n° *67*.
2. Cf. n° *49*, p. 366.
3. Cf. n° *87*, p. 935.
4. Cf. n° *69*, p. 107.
5. Cf. n° *119*, p. 248.
6. Cf. n° *116*.

and as to W. B. Cairns, he went so far as to say in his *History of American Literature* :

" It would be unduly rash to predict at this time the future place of Mark Twain in American Literature. It already becomes evident that in his later years and since his death he has been overrated. Little of his ambitiously serious work appears to have the elements of permanency, and it is probable that with change of taste his purely funny writings will seem less and less interesting. "

However, after delivering this oracular judgment, he concluded somewhat more cautiously :

" He has left... a considerable amount of truly genuine work in which the humor is more than cleverness and the seriousness is without affectation ; and it will be strange if American readers willingly let this die [1]. "

His caution was fully justified, for, in spite of all these detractors and half-hearted admirers, Mark Twain's cause was championed by a small band of enthusiastic critics. When he died, they loudly sang his praises and acclaimed him as much more than a mere humorist :

" Mark Twain has won unquestioned primacy among us as a humorist, but he was ever much more than that [2]. "
" ... his best was so very good that his popularity has become fixed and general and there is no doubt that he will continue to be read both here and abroad for many years to come [3]. "

Wilbur D. Nesbit rapturously proclaimed :

" He is Cervantes and Carlyle and Hugo and Dickens all in one. He has the humor and the sarcasm and the philosophy and the gentleness and the brilliancy and the patience and the brother-love of them all [4]. "

The founder of the American Federation of Labor, Samuel Gompers, among other tributes to Mark Twain published by the *North American Review*, asserted that " Mark Twain was more than a humorist. He was a deep student of men and events, a profound philosopher [5] ". Hamlin Garland expressed the same opinion :

1. Cf. nº *115*, p. 452. The passage was unchanged in the 1930 edition of his book.
2. Cf. nº *96*, p. 663.
3. Cf. nº *90*, p. 972.
4. Cf. nº *84*, p. 832.
5. *Ibid.*, p. 831.

" He was much more than humorous. He was a great fictionist and a rough-hewn stylist uttering himself in his own way, which was a large, direct and forceful way [1]. "

Walter Jerrold claimed that " *Tom Sawyer* and *Huckleberry Finn* were at once recognized as additions to the gallery of the immortals of fiction [2] " and Clarence H. Gaines very clearly brought out the special quality of Mark Twain's humour :

" ... he uses humor to make things *real*, instead of employing it, as so many writers do, to make matters appear more grotesquely improbable than they are by nature ",

and so he predicted that his works would live while those of Petroleum V. Nasby, John Phoenix, Artemus Ward, etc., would be forgotten [3].

Two well-known college professors who had long been admirers of Mark Twain joined in the chorus, thus making up for the short-sightedness of the majority of their colleagues : Brander Matthews of Columbia and William Lyon Phelps of Yale University. Brander Matthews wrote in the *North American Review* :

" Mark Twain was great in many ways and especially in four — as a humorist, as a story-teller, as a stylist, and as a moralist... As a master of English prose he has not received the appreciation he deserved, for he could call up an unforgettable picture with the utmost economy of stroke. *The Man That Corrupted Hadleyburg*, a masterpiece of stern irony which Swift would not have disowned and which is free from the corroding misanthropy that Swift might have bestowed upon it... A great artist in humor and in narrative and in style — and a great man in himself [4]. "

As to W. L. Phelps, he ranked Mark Twain with the greatest humorists of all times :

" ... there are not wanting good critics who already dare to place him with Rabelais, Cervantes, and Molière. Others would regard such an estimate as mere hyperbole, born of transient enthusiasm. But we all know that he was more than a fun-maker ; we know that his humor, while purely American, had the note of universality [5]. "

But the most authoritative champion of Mark Twain's cause was his fellow novelist, William Dean Howells who had been his friend ever since he wrote a favourable review of *Innocents*

1. *Ibid.*, p. 833.
2. Cf. n° *63*, p. 116.
3. Cf. n° *56*, pp. 585-586.
4. Cf. n° *84*, p. 835. He will express the same opinion in 1920 ; cf. n° *246*.
5. Cf. n° *73*, p. 702.

Abroad for the *Atlantic Monthly*. After Mark Twain's death he published a little book containing some reminiscences and all the articles in which he had commented on his books. He placed Mark Twain very high :

" He is not only the greatest living humorist, but incomparably the greatest, and without a rival since Cervantes and Shakespeare, unless it be that eternal Jew, Heinrich Heine, who of all the humorists is the least like him. "

" Emerson, Longfellow, Lowell, Holmes — I knew them all and all the rest of our sages, poets, seers, critics, humorists ; they were like one another and like other literary men ; but Clemens was sole, incomparable, the Lincoln of our literature [1]. "

All this shows that the more discerning critics had become perfectly aware of Mark Twain's greatness by 1910 and did not make the mistake of considering him merely a public jester. An anonymous contributor to the Chicago *Dial* defined this evolution of critical opinion in very clear terms :

" The attitude of criticism toward Mark Twain as a writer has undergone a slow but complete change during the past thirty years. From being thought of simply as a " funny man" of the kin of Josh Billings and Artemus Ward, he has gradually come to be recognized as one of our foremost men of letters... The recognition has been unduly delayed, partly because so much of his output has been utterly unworthy of his best self, and partly because his work in its totality is of so nondescript a character... [2] "

Yet, however high the claims Mark Twain's champions made for their hero, none of them — except B. Matthews [3], — dared to praise his artistry. Even Howells made reservations :

" What you will have in him is a style which is as personal, as biographical as the style of any one who has written, and expresses a civilization whose courage of the chances, the preferences, the duties, is not the measure of its essential modesty. It has a thing to say and it says it in the word that may be the first, or second, or third choice, but will not be the instrument of the most fastidious ear, the most delicate and exacting sense, though it will be the word that surely and strongly conveys intention from the author's mind to the reader's. It is the Abraham Lincolnian word, not the Charles Sumnerian, it is American, Western [4]. "

Arnold Bennett summed up brilliantly what most of Mark Twain's admirers felt when he said : " Episodically, both *Huckle-*

1. Cf. n° *33*, pp. 161, 101.
2. Cf. n° *92*, p. 307.
3. Cf. above n. 4, p. 22.
4. Cf. n° *33*, pp. 169-170.

berry Finn and *Tom Sawyer* are magnificent, but as complete works of art they are of quite inferior quality. Mark Twain was always a divine amateur... [1] " His reputation had to undergo several metamorphoses before he finally came to be considered a " literary artist [2] ".

1. Cf. n° *85*, p. 118 B.
2. Cf. the title of one of the latest books on Mark Twain *Mark Twain as a Literary Artist* by G. C. Bellamy (1950).

CHAPTER II

THE GROWTH OF THE LEGEND —
MARK TWAIN AS A PICTURESQUE PERSONALITY
AND A GREAT AMERICAN

In 1912, two years after Mark Twain's death, there came out three thick volumes of more than 1,700 pages in all, entitled *Mark Twain — A Biography. The Personal and Literary Life of Samuel Langhorne Clemens* by Albert Bigelow Paine. This impressive monument to the glory of the deceased humorist was the work of an obscure author whom Mark Twain himself had commissioned to write his life in Jan. 1906 [1]. From that time on Paine had practically shared Mark Twain's life as his official Boswell and had had access to all his manuscripts and papers. The result was this bulky biography which purported to be " history rather than eulogy [2] ".

Unfortunately the book did not fulfill this alluring promise. It was a romantic biography which glossed over the squalor of life in the Mississipi valley and the Far West, and dwelt complacently on Mark Twain's wooing of Olivia Langdon and happy married life. It offered the idealized portrait of a perfect hero who could do no wrong. According to Paine, even as a boy, young Sam Clemens in spite of his pranks, was already on the side of the angels, for he and his friends " were not vicious boys ; they were not really bad boys ; they were only mischievous, fun-loving boys — thoughtless and rather disregardful of the comforts and the rights of others [3] ". He was a devoted son and later in life became a perfect husband, who gladly submitted to his wife's refining influence [4], and a perfect father. Such

---

1. Cf. nº *113*, pp. 1257-1265.
2. *Ibid.*, dedication of vol. I.
3. Cf. nº *113*, p. 55.
4. Cf. this passage for instance : " She became his editor during those happy courtship days — a position which she held to her death. The world owed a large debt of gratitude

shining virtue deserved a reward. Success crowned all his enterprises. He became rich and prosperous, but prosperity did not spoil him.

" Men are likely to be spoiled by prosperity, to be made arrogant, even harsh. Success made Samuel Clemens elate, more kindly, more humanly generous. Every day almost he wrote to Webster, suggesting some new book or venture, but always considerately, always deferring to suggestions from other points of view [1]. "

He resisted age and misfortune with the same fortitude as prosperity :

" It is interesting to note that age and misfortune and illness had a tempering influence on Mark Twain's nature. Instead of becoming harsh and severe and bitter, he had become more gentle, more kindly [2]. "

Is not such perfection unheard of, superhuman ? But precisely, according to Paine, " he was not only human, but superhuman ; not only a man, but superman [3] ". No wonder then that " the contemplation of the drama of the skies always meant so much to him, and somehow always seemed akin to him in its proportions [4] ".

Such a hero could have little oddities — plenty of them, even ; Paine multiplied them for the entertainment of the reader, — but no faults, however venial. He was even made to bear with equanimity the crotchets of Cable during the reading-tour on which they went together :

" Clemens and Cable had a pleasant enough time, and had it not been for the absence from home and the disagreeableness of railway travel, there would have been little to regret [5]. "

The letters which Mark Twain sent to his wife during this tour — and Paine must have read them, — show on the contrary that his nerves were constantly frayed by the exasperating peculiarities of his partner, a Bible-reader and fanatical Sabbath-observer on whom he finally passed the following judgment :

to Mark Twain's wife, who from the very beginning — and always, so far as in her strength she was able — inspired him to give only his worthiest to the world... " *Ibid.*, p. 380.

1. *Ibid.*, p. 836. Charles Webster's son has since then published the business correspondence which passed between Mark Twain and his father (n° *1057*) ; it shows that Mark Twain was an exacting, tyrannical employer, not the kindly and considerate relative that Paine depicts.

2. Cf. n° *113*, p. 961.

3. *Ibid.*, p. 1328.

4. *Ibid.*, p. 1542.

5. *Ibid.*, p. 784.

" His body is small, but it is much too large for his soul. He is the pitifulest human louse I have ever known [1]. "

But there was no place for such a fit of temper in Paine's biography. Everything had to be perfect. Unpleasant details — such as the fact that Mark Twain once contemplated suicide while in California [2], — were relegated to foot-notes.

Though Paine's purpose, theoretically, was to give a true picture of Mark Twain, he constantly felt called upon to set him up as a model. So, when he had to mention some unsavoury aspect of Mark Twain's personality — his love of profane language for instance, — he immediately apologized for it :

It seems proper to add that it is not the purpose of this work to magnify or modify or excuse that extreme example of humankind which forms its chief subject ; but to set him down as he was — inadequately, of course, but with good conscience and clear intent [3]. "

His primness was such that when telling the story of the Whittier Birthday speech he could not help siding with the New England prigs against his hero [4], nor could he bring himself to quote in full the title of the obscene speech Mark Twain once delivered before the Stomach Club in Paris [5].

But he was guilty of still more serious distortions. As he wanted above all to edify his reader, he did his best to minimize the heterodoxy of Mark Twain and prove that he believed in the immortality of the soul [6] and leant to pessimism in his old age for accidental rather than philosophical reasons [7].

This uncritical biography which described all Mark Twain's books indiscrimately as masterpieces — even *1601*! — achieved immediate success in spite of its obvious defects [8] and fairly numerous factual errors [9]. Perry F. Bicknell declared in the *Dial*:

" The result is a book so filled with the spirit of Mark Twain as to vie in interest with his own works and to furnish an extent and variety of interest hardly to be found in any other recent biography [10]. "

1. Cf. n⁰ *1205*, p. 237.
2. Cf. n⁰ *113*, p. 291, n. ; cf. also p. 390, n., in which Paine quotes a rather coarse joke.
3. *Ibid.*, p. 214.
4. *Ibid.*, p. 610.
5. Cf. n⁰ *113*, p. 643. The title of the speech was " Some Thoughts on the Science of Onanism ".
6. *Ibid.*, p. 1431. Cf. also the chapter on " Mark Twain's Religion ", pp. 1581-1585.
7. *Ibid.*, p. 1021.
8. Its lack of balance in particular. More space is given to the later than to the earlier years in inverse ratio to their real importance, but Paine knew Mark Twain's old age best.
9. A few of these errors are corrected by Samuel Charles Webster in the book quoted above (p. 26, n. 1) and by Dixon Wecter in *Mark Twain to Mrs. Fairbanks* (n⁰ *1204*), pp. 36-37 and *Mark Twain's Love Letters* (n⁰ *1205*), pp. 48, n., 153-154, 165, 178, 302.
10. Cf. n⁰ *121*, p. 290.

As late as 1923 Brander Matthews could still write :

" ... Mr. A. B. Paine whose life of Mark Twain I believe to be the best biography of an American man of letters which has yet been written [1]. "

The reason for this extraordinary enthusiasm is to be found in an anonymous review contributed to the *Nation* :

" This is not the biography of an author ; it is the prose Odyssey of the American people ; and it will continue to be read when half of Mark Twain's writings are forgotten [2]. "

The book was popular because it flattered the patriotism of the public. It glorified not only Mark Twain, but the American character, of which he was supposed to be the supreme incarnation, being, in Paine's own words, " the foremost American-born author — the man most characteristically American in every thought and word and action of his life [3] ".

Thus, to use Lewis Mumford's phrase, Mark Twain found himself " enlarged into a myth without being appraised as a man [4] ". He became a great American hero, the champion of the American way of life against the European, a patriot whose heart beat faster whenever he caught sight of his native land from the ship that brought him back home — irrespective of the fact that he chose to spend nine years of his life in Europe rather than in America [5].

During the First World War, he became the great native writer that every good American citizen should read in preference to the " exotics " :

" To a generation fed upon exotics, this correspondence [*Mark Twain's Letters*, ed. by Paine] comes like a breath out of the continent's heart, out of a generation that knew not and cared not for the exotics, for Maeterlinck, Wilde, Strindberg, Ibsen and the Russian gloom artists [6]. "

Even W. D. Howells now reacted in this moral-sentimental way :

" The reader who is of the same make, the good average American make, will be, first of all, glad of the letters which Mark Twain wrote to his mother in his boyhood when he left home and until he had grown a gray-haired man [7]. "

1. Cf. n⁰ *308*, p. 23.
2. Cf. n⁰ *123*, p. 458.
3. Cf. n⁰ *113*, p. 12.
4. Cf. n⁰ *589*, p. 374.
5. Cf. n⁰ *1272*, p. 292.
6. Cf. n⁰ *205*, p. 50.
7. Cf. n⁰ *204*, pp. 602-603.

Mark Twain's fame then completely eclipsed that of Bret Harte [1]. In 1914, Irving Bacheller, the novelist, named as " the six great men who had done all the big things accomplished in America since 1850, Commodore Vanderbilt, businessman, Abraham Lincoln, statesman, Thomas A. Edison, inventor, Horace Greeley, journalist, Walt Whitman, poet, and Mark Twain, novelist [2] ".

Other critics had joined Paine in his hero-worship — J C. Underwood in particular, who declared in *Literature and Insurgency* :

" Mark Twain was consistently the typical American pioneer, the typical American journalist, who keeps his hands clean and remains his own man to the last, till he reached an eminence where he was enabled to speak as the first great prophet of democracy and of literature, of the people, by the people and preeminently for the people, in this country and in the modern world [3]. "

G. H. Fitch in *Great Spiritual Writers* exalted the self-made man whose success proved the excellence of democracy :

" In no other country could Mark Twain have reached such eminence as he enjoyed during the last ten years of his life. It is a far cry from the barefooted boy of Hannibal, Missouri, to the first citizen of New York... The life of Mark Twain affords a good example of the splendid opportunities in America open to those who have the ability to grasp them [4]. "

Stuart P. Sherman in his book *On Contemporary Literature* (1917) represented Mark Twain as the champion of Democracy and American optimism [5].

As late as 1920 Gamaliel Bradford praised " A. B. Paine's monumental and very human biography " and claimed that Mark Twain " was not to be defined or judged by the ordinary standards of mere writers ", but he added :

" It is on this lack of depth in thinking and feeling that I base my reluctance to class Mark Twain with the greatest comic writers of the world. His thought was bitter because it was shallow... His writing alternates from the violence of unmeaning laughter to the harshness of satire that has no laughter in it. And Mark Twain's place is rather with the bitter satirists, Molière, Ben Jonson, Swift, than with the great, broad, sunshiny laughers, Lamb, Cervantes, and the golden comedy of Shakespeare [6]. "

---

1. Cf. n° *178*.
2. Charles B. Willard, *Walt Whitman's American Fame* (Providence, R. I., Brown Univ. Press, 1950, 269 pp.), pp. 206-207.
3. Cf. n° *161*, p. 8.
4. Cf. n° *176*, p. 112.
5. Cf. n° *186*, p. 49.
6. Cf. n° *240*, pp. 463-469.

The times were changing. The First World War was over. A new generation with a new outlook and a different set of value was beginning to make itself heard. Its spokesmen called in question the opinions of their elders and often reversed their judgments. Mark Twain was soon brought up for trial.

CHAPTER III

THE "DEBUNKING" OF A HERO —
or MARK TWAIN AS A PSYCHIC AND SOCIAL PROBLEM

A reputation created with such superlatives of judgment and vocabulary was bound to suffer diminution sooner or later, and the moment came when the Younger Generation entered the Post War scene.

The First World War remained unreal for most Americans — and seemed to them more remote and less interesting than the Civil War. But it had a tremendous moral effect. It shattered ideals, shook beliefs and dispelled prejudices. Its aftermath disillusioned the American public, but at the same time gave it increased self-confidence now that the United States emerged from the War as a dominant World Power. The result was boisterousness and gaiety on the one hand and a bitter critical mood on the other. The War had brought the Americans into contact with a more sophisticated and less naïve world. They had realized their provincialism and discovered the shallowness of the conventions on which they had been brought up. So the literature of criticism and revolt which the realists and muck-rakers had begun to build before the War was given a new vigour by the restlessness that followed it. Many brilliant young writers with joyous pride in their liberation from tradition launched savage attacks on the shams which their elders had stupidly venerated in spite of the mocking taunts of H. L. Mencken. The Younger Generation came into power.

Their *bête noire* was the Genteel Tradition, that American form of Victorianism, with its fear of sex and elemental forces. They rebelled against puritanism in all its forms and attacked all its American by-products from Prohibition to Comstockery. They also hated the "Herd", the masses, who stupidly believed everything they were told. But they were especially contemptuous of the middle-class, Mencken's " booboisie ", with its mania for wealth and comfort. They held it responsible for the stifling of so many American artists in the past : Hawthorne, Melville, Emily Dickinson... and accused it of having driven others, like Henry James, into exile. They wanted to liberate the artist from the hostile society that cramped his genius. As Matthew Josephson will later put it :

" The eternal drama for the artist becomes *resistance to the milieu*, as if the supreme prerogative were the preservation of the individual type, the defense of the human self from dissolution in the horde [1]. "

One form which that resistance took was an attack on the idols of popular worship and in particular on the official myths about great men which had been taught to them in school. In their childhood, these brilliant young intellectuals had shared the common illusions, but they had outgrown such naivety and finally discovered that there were no great men at all — and so they joyously started " debunking " and deriding.

They were especially attracted by one period of American history which they thought very similar to the one in which they lived, the eighteen seventies, eighties and nineties, what Mark Twain had called the Gilded Age. It seemed to them both periods were characterized by an outrageous materialism and a scandalously acquisitive spirit which produced nothing but a tawdry culture from which true artists could only fly. If they stayed they were morally destroyed. The temptation was great to make Mark Twain an honorary member of the Lost Generation.

Another factor also came into play. A new Mark Twain was revealed just at that time by the posthumous publication of three of his books : The Mysterious Stranger (1916). *What is Man ? and Other Essays* (1917) [2], and *The Curious Republic of Gondour and Other Whimsical Sketches* (1919) Paine had hardly mentioned the second in his biography and completely overlooked the others, though he had had access to all Mark Twain's manuscripts [3]. All these books showed that Mark Twain had been less of a jester than his contemporaries had thought, and much more of a pensive, bitter and pessimistic observer of men and manners. A selection of his *Letters* edited by Paine was also published in 1917 [4], and

---

1. Quoted by Alfred Kazin, *On Native Grounds*, Overseas Ed., 1942, p. 162.
2. This book had been privately and anonymouly printed in Mark Twain's lifetime (1906), but caused no stir. Cf. A. B. Paine, *Mark Twain — A Biography*, pp. 1321-1323.
3. He merely mentioned *The Mysterious Stranger* rather slightingly as an unfinished and very uneven piece of work existing in three versions.
4. Cf. n° *182*.

equally contributed to change the perspective. It was impossible now to call him a writer of funny books ; as Carl Van Doren remarked :

" Gradually his accomplishments as a humorist are being reduced in the ratio they bear to his accomplishments as a commentator. The world which knew him in the flesh too often failed to distinguish him at many points from its favorite clown... The more reflective world, which alone keeps alive the fame of a writer after his death, finds more and more in Mark Twain to remember him by, as more and more of his posthumous work sees the light [1]. "

It became incontestable that he was a deeper, more complex character than his most fervent admirers had suspected. He had chiefly pleased an uncritical public so far. He now deserved to engross the attention of critical readers as well. His bad taste, his lack of a sense of proportion, the rougher and balder aspects of his humour could no longer be counted against him. They were more or less overlooked as the appreciation of his intelligence grew deeper. When *The Mysterious Stranger* came out, it was acclaimed as a masterpiece. H. E. Woodbridge wrote in the *Nation* that it was

" ... the book which the future may perhaps regard as Mark Twain's greatest work. If he had written nothing else it would have given him an assured fame. No American writer, not Hawthorne or Poe, has surpassed *The Mysterious Stranger* in imaginative intensity ; in breadth and virile sweep it is beyond the range of those masters of exquisite miniature... As a satire it is more terrible than *Gulliver's Travels* [2]... "

Besides, as Carl Van Doren pointed out, the fact that *What is Man ? The Mysterious Stranger* and *Captain Stormfield's Visit to Heaven* [3] were published posthumously makes one suspect that " many of Mark Twain's earlier books... said less than was in their author's mind... in most of his works he appears to have considered long before vexing any large body of current prejudice [4] ".

So it became more and more imperative to proceed to a new appraisal of the serious writer whom everyone had until then mistaken for a mere buffoon.

1. Cf. nº *337*.
2. Cf. nº *220*, pp. 424-425.
3. *Captain Stormfield's Visit to Heaven* was actually published for the first time in 1909, one year before Mark Twain's death, but Carl Van Doren and other critics thought it was a posthumous publication.
4. Cf. nº *390*.

Since he had not dared to publish his more serious works in his lifetime, the obvious course for the Younger Generation to take was to represent him as a great artist degraded by a narrow, prudish, greedy environment and obliged to repress his genius to cater for the low tastes of the society into which he happened to be born.

The first critic who tried to " debunk " this literary idol of the pre-war era was Waldo Frank, who in 1919 published a volume entitled *Our America*[1]. It attempted an interpretation of American life and literature, but it had a purpose : it was an attack on materialism, a hymn to the idealistic and poetic spirit which American society too often destroyed. He gave two examples of American writers to whom a crude and oppressive environment had proved fatal : first, Jack London " corporeally mature, innerly a child ", and then Mark Twain, for,

" the land of the pioneer has had a more heroic victim " he said. " Jack London was a man of talent : Mark Twain was a man of genius. The mind of Jack London was brilliant : the soul of Mark Twain was great [2]. "

According to him, the proof of Mark Twain's genius was *Huckleberry Finn*. For, though his life was a failure, he produced at least one masterpiece :

" Out of the bitter wreckage of his long life, one great work emerges, by whose contrasting fire we can observe the darkness. This work is *Huckleberry Finn*... In it for once, the soul of Mark Twain burst its bonds of false intruction and false ideal and found voice [3]. "

But unfortunately,

" Mark Twain was fifty when this book appeared. The balance of his literary life before and after, went mostly to the wastage of half-baked, half-believed, half-clownish labor. And underneath the jibes and antics of the professional jester, brooded the hatred and resentment of a tortured child [4]. "

" His one great work was the result of a burst of spirit over the dikes of social inhibition and intellectual fears [5]. "

In other words, Mark Twain's personality was double. The real, deeper Mark Twain was a great writer capable of producing immortal books, but he was superseded and defeated by a clownish

1. Cf. n° *212.*
2. Cf. n° *212,* p. 38.
3. *Ibid.*
4. Cf. n° *212,* p. 40.
5. *Ibid.,* p. 40.

Mark Twain who truckled to the society of his time and lost his soul in the process. This pattern of a dual Mark Twain was to be followed by all later " debunkers " of the humorist. But Waldo Frank, who was sentimental and fond of pathos, insisted on the intense sufferings undergone by the unhappy victim of social repression :

" Mark Twain went through life, lost in a bitter blindness that is far more terrible than the hate of men like Schopenhauer or Jonathan Swift... in his later days, he wrote a book entitled *What is Man ?*... It is the profane utterance of a defeated soul bent upon degrading the world to the low level where it was forced to live, whence came its ruin [1]. "

When a young man, Waldo Frank had once heard Mark Twain at a Benefit Performance for an Association for the Blind in New York, and, instead of laughing at his jokes, he had been terribly upset. The sight of this old man clowning before a stupid audience had made him very sad [2]. He obviously had no sense of humour at all, even at that early age. No wonder he later turned Mark Twain into a serious writer and a tragic character.

But Waldo Frank's ideas about America were not wholly original. He had borrowed them from Van Wyck Brooks whose friend and disciple he was. *Our America* reflects opinions which Brooks had already developed in *America's Coming of Age* (1915). Unlike Frank, Brooks was not a Jew or a New Yorker corrupted by alien influences, but a Yankee of Protestant descent who had graduated from Harvard College. However he had turned against the spirit and traditions of New England and rejected the puritanism of his ancestors, which, according to him, had led to two *impasses*, bloodless transcendentalism, on the one hand, and practical materialism, on the other.

He soon proceeded to apply his theories to specific cases and first chose Mark Twain to illustrate his thesis. His analysis was much more thorough than that of Waldo Frank. He devoted a whole book to it : *The Ordeal of Mark Twain* which came out in 1920 [3]. It was a critical biography, but, as the title itself showed, it was biased, for it aimed at demonstrating that Mark Twain's life had been an ordeal, and not the success story Paine had so naïvely told. According to Brooks,

1. *Ibid.*, pp. 42-43.
2. Cf. n° *212*, p. 41.
3. Cf. n° *224*.

" That bitterness of his was the effect of a certain miscarriage in his creative life, a balked personality, an arrested development of which he was himself almost wholly unaware, but which for him destroyed the meaning of life [1]. "

And to prove his point, he laid emphasis on Mark Twain's despair and took objection to " the opinion of his loyal biographer, Mr. Paine, " according to whom " he was ' not a pessimist in his heart but only by premeditation ' " [2]. For Brooks, on the contrary, Mark Twain's pessimism was not a pose, but a deep philosophical conviction from which he could not escape. So,

" From his philosophy alone... we can see that Mark Twain was a frustrated spirit, a victim of arrested development, and beyond this fact, as we know from innumerable instances the psychologists have placed before us, we need not look for an explanation of the chagrin of his old age. He had been balked, he had been divided, he had even been turned, as we shall see against himself ; the poet, the artist in him, consequently, had withered into the cynic and the whole man had become a spiritual valetudinarian [3]. "

Brooks accounted for this arrested development by two sets of factors — psychological and social. On the psychological plane, his personality was oppressed by the excessive influence of his mother and, later, of his wife and his daughter Clara as mother-substitutes, while on the social plane his creative life was stifled by the false standards of gentility of the Gilded Age and its demand for mere entertainment literature.

It was an extremely ingenious and penetrating book. After the fashion of psycho-analysts, Brooks made capital out of the smallest biographical details. For instance, the fact that young Sam Clemens swore to be a good boy when his father died, and walked in his sleep for several nights after the event, was in Brooks's opinion the sign and portent of all Mark Twain's subsequent career :

" One thing... we feel with irresistible certitude, that Mark Twain's fate was once for all decided there. That hour by his father's corpse, that solemn oath, that walking in his sleep — we must hazard some interpretation of it all... It is perfectly evident what happened to Mark Twain at this moment : he became, and his immediate manifestation of somnambulism is the proof of it, a dual personality... His ' wish ' to be an artist, which has been so frowned upon and has encountered such an insurmountable obstacle in the disapproval of

---

1. Cf. n° *224*, p. 14.
2. *Ibid.*, p. 2. He devotes a whole chapter to " Mark Twain's Despair ".
3. *Ibid.*

his mother, is now repressed more or less definitively, and another wish, that of winning approval, which inclines him to conform with public opinion, has supplanted it. The individual, in short, has given way to the type [1]. "

Mark Twain's use of a pen-name [2], his drawl [3], his dreams [4], were similarly interpreted by means of Freudian or other methods. And, of course, Brooks finally came to the conclusion that he was a pathological case :

" ... he poured vitriol promiscuously over the whole human scene... that is pathology [5]. "

Unfortunately, many of these deductions were vitiated by Brooks's complete lack of humour. He again and again misinterpreted Mark Twain's meaning — as in the following passage :

" ' There has always been somebody in authority over my manuscripts and privileged to improve it ', he wrote in 1900, with a touch of chagrin [6]. "

Now, the " touch of chagrin " is entirely Brooks's invention, for the rest or the passage in the original shows that Mark Twain was merely joking.

With such a cast of mind, it is only natural that Brooks should despise Mark Twain's achievements as a humorist. He reverted to " the assertion of Henry James that Mark Twain's appeal is an appeal to rudimentary minds [7] ". Unlike Waldo Frank, he was rather contemptuous of *Huckleberry Finn* and *Tom Sawyer* about which he shared Arnold Bennett's opinion that they are " episodically magnificent ", but " as complete works... of quite inferior quality [8] ".

He thus systematically underrated Mark Twain's accomplishments, the better to overrate his potentialities. He claimed that there was in him the makings of a great satirist :

" It was satire that he had in mind when he wrote these lines [a passage in *The Mysterious Stranger*], the great purifying force with which nature had endowed him, but of the use of which his life deprived him [9]. "

---

1. Cf. nº *224*, p. 25.
2. *Ibid.*, p. 86.
3. *Ibid.*, p. 209.
4. *Ibid.*, p. 186.
5. Cf. nº *224*, p. 244.
6. *Ibid.*, p. 103.
7. *Ibid.*, p. 15.
8. *Ibid.*, pp. 15-16.
9. Cf. nº *224* p. 219.

" If anything is certain... it is that Mark Twain was intended to be a sort of American Rabelais who would have done, as regards the puritanical commercialism of the Gilded Age, very much what the author of *Pantagruel* did as regards the obsolescent medievalism of sixteenth-century France [1]. "

He could have been a Voltaire, a Swift or a Cervantes if he had wanted to and been able to resist the demands of his environment. The paradox of the book is that Brooks devotes more space to what Mark Twain might have been than to what he actually was. He pities the tragic fate of that " swan born among geese " which obliged him to behave like a goose.

The reason why Brooks turned Mark Twain into a swan was that he wanted the others to look more like geese by comparison. His criticism was not aimed so much at Mark Twain as at America through Mark Twain. Mark Twain was a mere pretext ; his real target was the United States [2]. For " if any country ever needed satire it is, and was, America [3] ".

" How can we compare the fertile human soil of any spot in Europe with that dry, old, barren, horizonless Middle West of ours ? [4] "
" Less than ever... after the Civil War, can America be said to have offered ' a career open to all talents '. It offered only one career, that of sharing in the material development of the continent. Into this one channel passed all the religious fervor of the race [5]. "

When Brooks wrote " America ", he was not thinking only of the America of the Gilded Age but also of the America of his own time whose materialism and intolerance he hated. His conclusion was an appeal to his " confrères " not to betray their vocation like Mark Twain :

" Read, writers of America, the driven, disenchanted, anxious faces of your sensitive countrymen ; remember the splendid parts your confrères have played in the human drama of other times and other peoples, and ask yourselves whether the hour has not come to put away childish things and walk the stage as poets do [6]. "

Thus, strangely enough, the revolt of the Younger Generation against the puritan ideal of their elders brought about the " debun-

1. *Ibid.*, p. 223.
2. Cf. C. E. Bechhofer in *The Literary Renaissance in America* (n° *294*), p. 2 : " ... any one acquainted at first hand with American conditions must at once realize that Mr. Brooks is attempting through the example of Mark Twain, to set out the conflict between the America of the last century and of the present day, and, as it were, to analyse not only the mind of his hero, but that of the nation as a whole. "
3. Cf. n° *224*, p. 232.
4. *Ibid.*, p. 37.
5. *Ibid.*, p. 55.
6. *Ibid.*, p. 267.

king " of Mark Twain. Paine's hero, the idol of the pre-war, the great American humorist, shrank under their vitriol into a pathetic failure and a pitiable victim of America, and they revealed at the same time that that harmless conformist was at heart a rebel and a heretic, an " enemy of order " like themselves.

This interpretation of Mark Twain was so novel and provocative that it created a sensation in the literary world. All the reviews and magazines were full of articles which either praised it, or tried to refute it, and the controversy raged for several years and was revived in 1923, when Brooks published a second edition of his book [1].

Among his more moderate followers was Carl Van Doren who in *The Roving Critic*, in 1923, approved of the general drift of his thesis but made reservations as regards his method :

" That it is an arraignment... and exhibits instances of special pleading and definite animus must be admitted even by those who, like myself, agree that the picture here drawn of our great humorist is substantially accurate as well as brilliant [2]. "

" One thing that makes me suspect at times the general drift of Mr. Brook's argument is that a good many of the details of his psycho-analyzing look suspicious... I still think he has reduced Mark Twain too neatly to the dualistic formula [3]... "

This was also the standpoint of Blankenship in his *American Literature* eight years later :

" If Twain had been allowed to follow his natural bent and become a satirist of society, it is probable that he might not have looked back upon his life as a record of utter futility. The Gilded Age had worked its will upon him... In spite of a harrowing lack of humour, Mr. Brooks made an impressive case for his contention. But he made one very great mistake in laying all the sins of the Gilded Age upon the head of Mr. Clemens... [4] "

But others accepted Brooks's conclusions uncritically — O'Higgins and Reede for instance in their book on *The American Mind in Action* (1924) :

" Outside of his art, he [Mark Twain[was as profound a biological failure as America has produced [5]. "

---

1. Cf. n° *567*.
2. Cf. n° *302*. pp. 49, 50.
3. *Ibid*.
4. Cf. n° *512*, pp. 457, 470.
5. Cf. n° *329*, p. 47.

As to Frank Harris, he took pleasure in reviling Mark Twain in his *Contemporary Portraits* and based his attack on Brooks's thesis :

" Mark Twain made a Puritan maiden of the great Frenchwoman. It is to me a dreadful book... I do not think *Huckleberry Finn* among the best boy's books. *Treasure Island* of Stevenson seems to me infinitely better than anything Mark Twain has done in this way... speaking for myself, I simply cannot read him with any patience ; his humour seems to me, forced and unnatural ; and his most recent biographer [Van Wyck Brooks], I really believe, has explained correctly his extraordinary shallowness of soul [1]. "

Of course, *The Ordeal of Mark Twain* brought grist to the mill of the social and socialist writers. Upton Sinclair adopted it enthusiastically in *Mammonart* :

" There were only two possible ways for him [the artist] to survive ; one was to flee to New York and be lost in the crowd ; the other was to turn into a clown and join in laughing at himself and at everything he knew to be serious and beautiful in life. This latter course was adopted by a man of truly great talent, who might have become one of the world's satiric masters if he had not been overpowered by the spirit of America. His tragic story has been told in a remarkable study, *The Ordeal of Mark Twain*, by Van Wyck Brooks [3]. "

He had sent a copy of *The Jungle* to Mark Twain and the latter had written him that he had put the book down in the middle " because he could not endure the anguish it caused him ". This angered Sinclair : " What right has a man to refuse to endure the anguish of knowing what other human beings are suffering ? " he exclaimed. But Brooks had revealed the reason for this cowardice :

" Mark Twain lived a double life ; he, the uncrowned king of America, was the most repressed personality, the most completely cowed, shamed, and tormented great man in the history of letters [3]. "

Dreiser was more indulgent :

" He was too warm-hearted — among the tenderest of the humanists — and, as such, almost refuting his own charges [4]. "

Like Brooks however, he thought that Mark Twain was a thwarted genius :

1. Cf. n° *296*, pp. 165, 169-170, 173.
2. Cf. n° *369*, p. 327.
3. *Ibid.*, pp. 328-329.
4. Cf. n° *680*, p. 621.

" Ah, the twisted sociologic, as well as psychologic, forces playing upon a nature at once sensitive, kindly, and at the same time exaggeratedly humorous !... Why from his grave he fairly yells : ' I was restrained. I was defeated. I hate, the lying, cowardly world that circumvented me '... [4] "

But, projecting his own personality on that of the humorist he believed that Mark Twain was " a realist at heart " rather than a potential satirist :

" For most certainly in addition to, and in spite of, his humorous bent, he was a realist at heart, and a most extraordinary one. One need only thumb through the *Innocents Abroad*, or *Roughing It*, or *Tom Sawyer*, or *Huckleberry Finn*, or *The Gilded Age*, to find page after page, character after character, scene after scene, drawn movingly as well as brilliantly enough [2]. "

Newton Arvin, represented a more strictly Marxist point of view and tried to go farther than Brooks in his arraignment of American society :

" In 1935, it is easy to see that Brooks, diving into waters that his predecessors were incapable of imagining, was himself unable to touch bottom. With a few more coils of cable, he would have been there. What are those coils ? Briefly, a genuinely dialectical mastery of the development of American society [3]. "

According to Arvin Mark Twain failed because he was unable to understand the point of view of the proletariat and had never read Marx's *Capital* :

" Mark Twain could have become the destructive satirist of the American middle-class of his time only by adopting, no matter how intuitively, the point of view of another class... [Van Wyck Brooks] does not observe that Mark Twain could have seen through H. H. Rogers [the Standard Oil magnate] only by understanding the dialectics of American capitalism [4]. "

However, in spite of his dogmatism, Arvin was unable to resist the charm of Mark Twain's writings and towards the end of one of his articles he relented and admitted that

" despite the vast wastage of his career, Mark Twain may well survive as a writer in the affections of later generations and of a class to which he did not directly address himself [5]. "

1. *Ibid.*, pp. 623, 626.
2. Cf. n° *680*, p. 622.
3. Cf. n° *587*, p. 191.
4. *Ibid.*
5. Cf. n° *671*, p. 126.

V. F. Calverton had also proposed a Marxist explanation for Mark Twain's failure in *The Liberation of American Literature* (1932). He explained Mark Twain's pessimism by the changing social conditions that prevailed in his lifetime and by his inability to understand them and find a solution for them [1] :

" It was the change in the American scene, signified by the closing of the frontier and the disappearance of the freedom and autonomy of the West, resulting in the exploitation of the farmers by the forces of finance, that altered the character of Western literature and destroyed the optimism inspired by the early frontier force. The pessimism that followed wrote itself into the spirit of the nation. It was reflected in the changed philosophy of Mark Twain... Once that democracy had been destroyed... and the nation had fallen into the hands of the bankers and industrialists, his petty bourgeois enthusiasm turned into bitterness... [2] "

His pessimism could thus be accounted for by purely economic causes :

" It was pessimism... of an individual who deplored the growth of large capital at the expense of small capital [3]. "

Another Marxist, Granville Hicks, in *The Great Tradition* reproached Mark Twain with taking refuge in the past instead of boldly facing the problems of industrialism :

" Except *The Gilded Age*... not one of his major fictions concerns itself with the movements and events of American life in the latter half of the xixth century... In his principal satire he struck out against the evil of feudalism, evils that had disappeared or were far less important than the sins of American industrialism... [4] "

He explained the pessimism of Mark Twain's old age in exactly the same manner as Calverton :

" By a different process Mark Twain learned the lesson that hunger and homelessness were teaching so many settlers in the West : the era of pioneer self-reliance had ended [5]. "

Somewhat belatedly, in 1938, Edgar Lee Masters joined the socialist supporters of Van Wyck Brooks. In his *Mark Twain*

---

1. Walter Fuller Taylor in " Mark Twain and the Machine Age " (n° *831*) has tried to explain and justify Mark Twain's position : " ... as a pioneer democrat, inheritor of American liberalism, he joined his contemporaries in insisting on a wide diffusion of wealth [in *A Connecticut Yankee at King Arthur's Court*, for instance], and on the protection of the average man from economic, no less than political or religious tyranny " (p. 396). But, of course, for Marxists, this was no solution, but, at best, a palliative.
2. Cf. n° *545*, p. 337.
3. Cf. n° *545*, p. 338.
4. Cf. n° *573*, p. 45.
5. *Ibid.*, p. 48.

— *A Portrait*, he tried to do with a bludgeon what Brooks had done with a scalpel. His book was essentially a crude restatement of Brooks's thesis. Brooks's Mark Twain, though distorted, was still a portrait, but Masters's was a caricature. He evaluated Mark Twain's literary activity from a strictly proletarian point of view, blamed him for embracing bourgeois ethics and politics, and deplored that he refused to become a satirist at a time when American society needed one so badly [1].

However popular in some " advanced " circles, Brooks's thesis was far from universally accepted. Its excesses provoked violent reactions and a good many critics pointed out its weaknesses and errors.

The most obvious failing of Brooks was his lack of humour. As Alvin Johnson observed in the *New Republic*,

" ... it is a treacherous business for a critic devoid of a sense of humor to hold an incorrigible humorist too strictly to account [3]. "

Not only did Brooks fail to sense the humour of certain passages, but he did not even grasp the essence of humour. He seems to have been unable to understand that humour can express the tragic incongruities of life just as fitly as any other medium — and that anyway Mark Twain could not express himself otherwise. C. Hartley Grattan was the only critic who realized it :

" It is wrong to try to split him into two fragments — part humorist, part pessimist. He was both because of an ambivalent emotional equipment... [3] "

But, besides this fault, there were also some serious bones of contention in Brooks's book — his representation of American institutions as hopelessly corrupt in particular, and his conception of Mark Twain as a potential satirist. Against these Johnson also protested :

" There are two questions here : one whether American institutions are in fact so hopelessly corrupt as Van Wyck Brooks assumes ; the other, whether Mark Twain was by temperament fitted to perceive institutional corruption, and perceiving it, to undertake the work of exposure [4]. "

And he answered :

1. Cf. n⁰ *797*.
2. Cf. n⁰ *235*, p. 203. Cf. also n⁰ *721*, p. 373.
3. Cf. n⁰ *516*, p. 282.
4. Cf. n⁰ *235*, p. 202.

" ... he accepted American institutions as a tremendous improvement on the rest of the world... Mark Twain was not in revolt against American institutions ; therefore he could not have made himself a satirist according to Van Wyck Brooks's taste [1]. "

An anonymous reviewer in the *Weekly Review* saw the weak spot in Brooks's argumentation much more clearly and put his finger on the central sophism in the thesis when he wrote :

" Mr. Brooks... is reduced to the necessity of proving that Mark Twain fell short of a hypothetic, an inferential Mark Twain, whom he has thrust upon the world, thrust upon the real Mark Twain, for the express purpose of demonstrating his apostasy [2]. "

This is true, Brooks constantly condemns Mark Twain for not being an essential Mark Twain who never existed except in his imagination. For, as the anonymous reviewer pointed out : " Can Mr. Brooks name a time when the higher Mark Twain grasped the helm ? [3] " So, very sensibly, he concluded :

" Mr. Brooks seems to me to succeed far better with his lemmas than with his thesis... He does prove that Mark Twain was crossed and chafed by conventional restrictions on the freedom of speech. But discontent does not always mean essential maladjustment [4]. "

F. W. Duppee, later, made the same objection, but formulated it more brilliantly :

" ... the *Ordeal* is full of difficulties. It is one thing to muckrake a period, as Brooks here so effectively muckrakes the genteel era, pointing out its stultifying effects on a writer of genius, but it is another thing again to assume that in happier conditions your writer would have been a Tolstoy. That is more or less what Brooks does assume, with the result that the historical Mark Twain is everywhere dogged by the shadow of an ideal or potential or Unconscious Mark Twain, a kind of spectral elder brother whose brooding presence is an eternal reproof to the mere author of *Huckleberry Finn* [5]. "

Henry S. Canby very ingeniously made a distinction between suppressed and oppressed. In his opinion, Mark Twain was never suppressed, as Brooks claimed, but merely oppressed [6]. Besides, he argued, some sort of suppression is always necessary for artists and

1. *Ibid.*, p. 203.
2. Cf. n° *236*, p. 108.
3. Cf. n° *236*, p. 109.
4. *Ibid.*
5. Cf. F. W. Duppee, " The Americanism of Van Wyck Brooks " (in Robert W. Stallman, *Critiques and Essays in Criticism, 1920-1948* with a foreword by Cleanth Brooks. New York. The Ronald Press, xii + 571 pp.), p. 463.
6. Cf. n° *674*, p. 3.

" Clemens was the kind of spirit that needed a certain amount of suppression without which he would have fizzed his life through like an uncapped soda spring [1]. "

According to him, the critics of Brooks's school relied too much on psychology and should have studied the circumstances of Mark Twain's life more closely. They would have reached simpler and more sensible conclusions :

" They do not understand his boisterousness because it is not a literary boisterousness, nor his pessimism because it is not a literary pessimism, the first being a lecture habit by which he roused his own mind to humorous pitch and set his audience laughing, the second a direct expression of brooding thought which uses words in default of action [2]. "

Other critics tried to show that, contrary to Brooks's opinion, Mark Twain had never been repressed at all and had always freely expressed the boldest political views. This line of argument was chosen in particular by an anonymous contributor to the *Saturday Review of Literature* :

" Mark Twain was a radical nevertheless... His attack upon vested injustice, intolerance, and obscurantism in *A Yankee at King Arthur's Court* and *The Prince and the Pauper* is quite as indignant as Samuel Butler's *The Way of All Flesh*. Critics forget the social courage of his anti-imperialism and the commercial courage of his onslaught upon Christian Science [3]. "

He conceded however that " Mark Twain was a humanitarian and not a reformer... he found it increasingly difficult to be angry with individuals [4] ". And this enabled him to rehabilitate America and clear her from the accusations of the Younger Generation :

" Mark Twain knew much more of America than his more scornful successors. Perhaps that is why he liked his country in spite of the deeds of his countrymen. And he knew and liked too many successful men to believe that they were all oppressors and crooks [5]. "

But by far the most popular argument used against Brooks — because of its sentimental appeal, — was that neither Mark Twain's mother nor his wife were in any way guilty of suppressing the great humorist's genius. One of the first champions who

1. Cf. n° *325*, p. 158.
2. *Ibid.*, p. 164.
3. Cf. n° *359*, p. 241.
4. Cf. *Ibid.*
5. *Ibid.*

rushed to the rescue of Mrs. Olivia Clemens was Richard Burton who wrote in the *Bookman* :

" As for the idea that Mrs. Clemens... cramped the full expression of her husband's powers, it is, however plausible, not convincing, For one thing, it overlooks her unquestionable... service to him in the way of restraint from what would certainly have injured his reputation and in no way helped the revelation of his genius... to the present critic, the writings of Mark Twain amply prove his inability to be muzzled by his family... [1] "

Samuel J. Fisher, later, found a more convincing argument :

" ... the wife of Mark Twain can hardly be termed an ' arch-Puritan '... Mark Twain... openly avowed that he had destroyed his wife's religious convictions [2]. "

To this Fred Lewis Pattee added in 1928 :

" To say that Mark Twain was hamstrung by the East and that as a result he lived his later years a thwarted genius is to argue that ignorance which has in it a touch of genius should be quarantined from all contact with art and culture lest its originality be vitiated [3]. "

Finally, in 1931, Clara Clemens published *My Father, Mark Twain* [4], which, as De Voto pointed out, was intended as a " rebuttal of Mr. Van Wyck Brooks's arraignment of her mother, which few people, these days, take seriously [5] ".

As to Mark Twain's mother, her memory was vindicated by two great grandchildren of hers, Doris and Samuel Webster :

" Van Wyck Brooks's conception of her as a Puritan is based on the fact that she made her son promise not to drink or play cards while he was on the river ; but the exaction of such a promise was by no means unreasonable in a day when the Mississippi was full of tragedies largely caused by gambling or drink... As far as her religious convictions are concerned, Jane Clemens seems to have been unusually liberal for her day [6]. "

Thus all the villains in Brooks's story were one by one rehabilitated. There was one left however : the West. But it was soon to find defenders in its turn. A fiery polemist, Bernard De Voto, was about to enter the stage.

1. Cf. nº *258*, p. 335.
2. Cf. nº *313*, p. 922.
3. Cf. nº *443*, p. 187.
4. Cf. nº *504*, especially pp. 67-68 :
" How often did my father express his gratitude to the marvelous fate that had given him such a companion, one who was as deeply absorbed in his work as he was himself! One who had a pure instinct for the correct values in literature as well as in life, and one whose adverse criticism proved invariably to be a just criticism because her intuition — born of a large heart and mind — hit the target plumb in the center. " Cf. also p. 209.
5. Cf. nº *553*, p. 170.
6. Cf. nº *388*, pp. 531-532.

CHAPTER IV

Mr. DE VOTO IN ERUPTION or
MARK TWAIN AS A WESTERNER

Van Wyck Brooks and his followers were more interested in what Mark Twain might have been than in what he was, and more in what America should be in the XXth century than in what she really was in Mark Twain's time [1]. A more positive approach had been long overdue when *Mark Twain's America* [2] by Bernard De Voto at last appeared in 1932.

The author was a pugnacious young writer and scholar who in order to clear the ground for his own critical interpretation began by smashing Brooks's thesis to pieces. He pitilessly ridiculed its exaggerations :

" ... it is Mr. Brooks's strange thesis that Clemens really wanted to be Shelley [3]. "

" Between his assertion that the thwarted artist in Mark Twain avenged his betrayal by inducing Mark Twain to murder his son [4], for instance, and the parlor entertainer's notion that the American Radiator Tower is a phallic symbol, or his host's parrot a partial sublimation of the Œdipus complex or a master-slave constellation, or a symptom of the inferiority complex. — I can perceive no important difference [5]. "

Above all, he successfully proved that some of Brooks's most impressive psycho-analytical conclusions were based on shaky or even imaginary foundations. Thus the famous scene of the oath Mark Twain was supposed to have taken in front of his

---

1. Cf. De Voto (n° 537, p. 224) : " ... a similar necessity results from the decision of New Jerusalem [i.e. those who believe in a mythical America] to study an eidolon, ' Mark Twain ', in its relation to another phantom, ' America '. "
2. Cf. n° 537.
3. Cf. n° 537, p. 101.
4. A rather extravagant inference which Brooks omitted in the second edition of his book ; cf. below n. 2, p. 53.
5. *Ibid.*, p. 228.

father's coffin, which Brooks held to be the moment of supreme betrayal, probably never occurred at all according to De Voto [1]. Brooks's error was to apply his psycho-analytical methods to Paine's biography rather than to Mark Twain himself, and Paine's account of the humorist's childhood is wholly unreliable. He had to depend on Mark Twain for his information and the latter very often confused fact and fiction and attributed to Sam Clemens adventures which could have happened only to Tom Sawyer. So De Voto could point out a certain number of factual mistakes in Brooks's book which greatly impaired its value [2].

But the most original contribution of De Voto was, as the title of his volume announced, his study of Mark Twain's America, his vindication of XIXth century frontier life [3]. He had a first-hand knowledge of frontier society himself, since he was born and brought up in Utah :

" My claim to some measure of authority in these pages derives from the fact that I have lived in a frontier community and known frontiersmen, as none of the literary folk who now exhibit ideas about frontier life have done... [4] "

This circumstance helped him to understand an aspect of Mark Twain's personality and art which had wholly escaped Brooks's attention. So, to Brooks's thesis that Mark Twain was a thwarted satirist, he opposed his own that Mark Twain was above all a frontier humorist and nothing else :

" It is not only that Mark Twain never became anything but a humorist, realist, and satirist of the frontier ; he never desired to be anything else [5]. "

And De Voto very skilfully showed that newspaper humour, a typical product of the frontier, taught Mark Twain a style, provided him with forms and themes, in short, was the " matrix " of his humour [6]. His art was rooted in the folk-lore of the frontier and owed nothing to European culture :

1. *Ibid.*, p. 230.
2. *Ibid.*, pp. 78-99.
3. Parrington, though a champion of the West, can hardly be considered a forerunner of De Voto. He adopted Brooks's conclusions, and was more interested in Mark Twain as a victim of the Gilded Age than as a Westerner. The posthumous edition of his *Main Currents in American Thought* (1930) contained a well-balanced account of the Western origins of Mark Twain's art (vol. 3, pp. 86, 91-92).
4. Cf. n° *537*, p. xii.
5. *Ibid.*, p. 99.
6. Cf. n° *526*.

" Of the folk arts developed by the frontier, perhaps the richest was its stories... from his earliest days he read books which were a continent away from the damned shadow of Europe, and a continent away from the shadow, he lifted the *genre* into immortality [1]. "

Carried away by his local patriotism and his enthusiasm for Mark Twain's humour, De Voto painted the West in glowing colours and grew lyrical to sing its praises. Brooks had described it as a land of squalor and a cultural vacuum where prevailed " a spirit inflexibly opposed... to the development of individuality [2] ". This conception De Voto rejected :

" On evidence not submitted the frontier folks are now held to have been Puritans given to a rigid suppression of emotion, particularly of sexual emotion... [3] "

On the contrary, according to De Voto, " the Puritan is nowhere discoverable on the frontier, if the Puritan be a man who hates loveliness, fears passions, represses his instincts and abstains from joy [4] ". For the settlers led an idyllic life, surrounded with lovely and grandiose scenery. In spite of the Calvinistic gloom with which they have been credited, they had a jolly time. All bucolic activites were pretexts for festivities, from cornshucking to roof-raising. They attended horse-races, enjoyed cock-fights, bear-baiting and shooting-matches. The Mississippi and its tributaries were the itinerary of countless show-boats. True, the camp-meeting was a harrowing experience, but only to about one fifth of those who attented it. To the others, it was a commercial bazaar and " a focus of dynamic joy [5] ". The sexual customs of the frontier were freer than those of the sea-board and the settlers were not in the least sexually repressed, as the presence among them of so many half-breeds testified.

Besides, the West had a culture of its own. People were incurably musical and extremely fond of ballad-singing and story-telling. There were lots of folk-tales, often combining white, Negro and Indian folk-lore. So life in Missouri in Mark Twain's childhood far from being squalid and starved was full of colour, charm and romance. He was born in the right place. The West alone could shape his genius.

" Then he came East and accepted tuition [6] ". But De Voto

1. Cf. n° *537*, p. 99.
2. Cf. n° *224*, p. 75.
3. Cf. n° *537*, p. 28.
4. *Ibid.*, p. 42.
5. Cf. n° *537*, p. 43.
6. *Ibid.*, p. 207.

claims that he did not appreciably change. " He accepted, to the small extent of which he was capable, with no awareness of any surrender, the dominant criteria of his age [1]. " But those Eastern criteria altered very little what he was and had only little influence on his books. His Western buoyancy was not to be repressed or oppressed by the East.

So, on this point too, De Voto had to take the opposite view to Van Wyck Brooks. In his opinion, when Mrs. Clemens and Howells went over his manuscripts, they only deleted a few slang words and softened some expressions of statements likely to offend [2]. But there is no evidence that Mark Twain's censors had many such horrid words to contend with :

" Mark's vocabulary on the Pacific Coast is just what it was in the East. The convention seemed to him quite sane and he had not violated it [3]. "

As Ferguson and Dixon Wecter will show later [4], the damage was purely verbal and practically negligible. In spite of his concessions to the East, Mark Twain remained a Western humorist.

Though reviews often deplored the violent controversial tone of the volume and wished that De Voto " had thrown his stones in a pamphlet and written his book afterward [5] ", *Mark Twain's America* was in general considered a major contribution to Mark Twain criticism. Canby, for one, endorsed his conclusions as regards the West :

" Clemens was essentially a Western democratic man... [6] "

Others dissented — like Newton Arvin in particular who exclaimed :

" ... a shallow and romantic theory... It is impossible to accept his views of Mark Twain as merely a humorist [7]. "

As to Lewis Mumford, he maintained that the Western society described by De Voto was infantile and concluded :

" About the facts of pioneer life Mr. De Voto and Mr. Brooks are, then, in substantial agreement ; the slight discrepancy in their points

1. *Ibid.*
2. " Literature is thus poorer in that Tom Sawyer must say that the Pain Killer griped Peter's bowels, rather than his guts ; in that Huck Finn must be combed all to thunder instead of all to hell ; and in that feminine oaths are elsewhere substituted for the profanity of the frontier. " *Ibid.*, p. 209.
3. *Ibid.*, p. 209.
4. Cf. below Chapter V, n. 3, p. 57.
5. Cf. n° *558*, p. 202 ; cf. also n° *580*.
6. Cf. n° *558*, p. 202.
7. Cf. n° *557*, p. 212.

of view comes from the fact that what Mr. Brooks calls Hell, Mr. De Voto patriotically calls Heaven [1]. "

Yet, in spite of these detractors, the representation of Mark Twain as essentially a Westerner was quite fashionable for a few years. In 1934, Minnie M. Brashear, a Missourian herself, sought in her turn to prove in *Mark Twain — Son of Missouri* [2] that " he really came into his own in the West [3] ". But instead of depicting the West like De Voto as the domain of folk art, under the influence of F. Schönemann [4], she attempted to show that Missouri in the 1840's and 1850's was far from culturally barren and that Mark Twain had ample opportunities to read the best literature of Europe [5], a conclusion which did not prevent Edgar Lee Masters from proclaiming in 1935 that " his best books came out of the frontier, out of the uncontaminated American soil of the West, owing their quality to nothing foreign whatever [6]."

A few years later, in 1938, the birth-place of Mark Twain's genius moved farther West. Miss Brashear had insisted on the determinative influence of the Midwestern years, but Ivan Benson in *Mark Twain's Western Years* [7] tried to show that the time Mark Twain spent on the Western Coast was still more important — and the appearance of his book coincided with the publication of *The Washoe Giant in San Francisco* [8] and *Mark Twain's Letters from the Sandwich Islands* [9].

Mark Twain had thus become a coveted hero whom the different sections of the country were endeavouring to appropriate. After California came Nevada's turn. In 1947, in *Mark Twain in Nevada*, E. M. Mack laid claim to him in the name of his state :

" It was in this territory that he incubated ; it was in Virginia City that he became a full-fledged writer... During these years his personality took on definite characteristics. These attributes were reflected in his writings. They were carefree, unrestrained, vigorous, and dynamic... [10] "

1. Cf. n⁰ *583*, p. 575.
2. Cf. n⁰ *601*.
3. Cf. *ibid.*, p. XII.
4. Cf. n⁰ *362*.
5. But, as H. H. Waggoner pointed out (n⁰ *792*, pp. 368-369) : " As for Miss Brashear's theory that Mark Twain's philosophy springs directly from the XVIIIth century and was untouched by the intellectual development of his own times, it seems to me that the weight of the evidence makes some other explanation more probable. If Mark Twain's philosophy has points in common with those of Hobbes and Hume, that is not strange : Hobbes and Hume influenced the whole course of modern thought. "
6. Cf. n⁰ *694*, p. 67.
7. Cf. n⁰ *796*.
8. Cf. n⁰ *801*.
9. Cf. n⁰ *800*.
10. Cf. n⁰ *1095*, pp. VII-VIII.

In the meantime, the East refused to surrender its old favourite. After all, De Voto himself had had to concede that its influence had not been harmful to Mark Twain. So in 1935 Pattee felt justified in advancing the theory that the East instead of thwarting Mark Twain's genius had matured it and made him a " universal classic " [1]. Three years later, Max Eastman demonstrated that Elmira, the birthplace of Olivia Langdon, far from being one of those " up-State towns... without traditions of moral freedom and intellectual culture ", as Brooks had asserted, was one of the most progressive communities in the country and went so far as to proclaim that :

" Olivia's gospel, in so far as she learned it from the church in which her mother and father were the central social and financial force, was one of self-reliant revolt against forms and conventions as such... [2] "

In 1950, Kenneth R. Andrews attempted a similar demonstration for Hartford in *Nook Farm — Mark Twain's Hartford Circle* [3], developing the thesis that Mark Twain's Hartford friends had exerted a beneficial and not a repressive influence on his work.

" It has often been said that the gentility of Hartford, supposedly hostile, to the burgeoning of Mark Twain's satiric power, helped warp him as a satirist of his own time and imposed upon him a mediocre conventionality that emasculated his work and frustrated his spirit. The obvious untruth of such a judgment does not mean that Mark Twain was unaffected by the standards of taste operative in Hartford and in Elmira... The gentility of Hartford... was more flexible, amiable and genial than sinister. The narrowness, complacence, sterility, and Grundyism sometimes thought to have vitiated the literature of the post-War decades and to have prevented Mark Twain from attaining his full greatness do not appear decisive in Nook Farm [4]. "

This tug-of-war between the different sections and states raised so much dust that gradually the main issues became obscured and the two principal champions, though still unreconciled, became less and less sure of what they stood for. Brooks was the first to make concessions. The second edition of his *Ordeal of Mark Twain* [5] came out about the same time as *Mark Twain's America*, but as his opponent had published several chapters

1. Cf. n° *658*.
2. Cf. n° *816*, p. 627. Dixon Wecter qualified Eastman's conclusions in his introduction to *The Love Letters of Mark Twain* ; cf. n° *1205*, pp. 8-9.
3. Cf. n° *1230*.
4. *Ibid.*, pp. 188, 198.
5. Cf. n° *567*.

of his book in *Harper's Monthly* and the *Bookman* [1], he knew his theses and arguments in advance ; so, without warning, surreptitiously, he corrected some of the errors which De Voto had pointed out and toned down a few of his more extravagant statements [2]. As to De Voto, as years elapsed, his point of view, though he refused to admit it, became closer and closer to that of Brooks, until in the conclusion of his *Mark Twain at Work* (1942) [3] he practically recognized the existence of an " ordeal of Mark Twain " [4]. Gladys C. Bellamy has been able in her book on Mark Twain to devote several pages to a list of the points on which De Voto and Brooks are agreed [5].

So all this controversy was to a certain extent vain. Yet, it was an important phase of Mark Twain criticism. First of all, it prevented what might have been the apotheosis of Mark Twain as a superhuman figure. It brought him back to earth and cleared away a certain number of hypocrisies and misconceptions. It caused a re-examination of everything that pertained to him and stimulated the study of his sources. Besides, the debate drew attention to his posthumous works which, according to Mark Van Doren, perhaps appeared more important then they really were — but at least supplied " the undertones which without them might never have been detected at all " in his other works [6].

1. Cf. nos *525* & *526*, and also *527*.
2. Stanley Edgar Hyman in *The Armed Vision* (no *1153*) has given a list of the main corrections. Here are a few others which he has overlooked :
On p. 207 (of the 1933 ed. — p. 167 of the 1st ed.), Brooks omitted a paragraph commenting on the marginal note which, according to Paine (*Biography*, p. 1), Twain once wrote in an old volume of Suetonius. He was right ; this paragraph betrayed a sad lack of humour.
On page 222 (of the 1933 ed., p. 181 of the 1st ed.) a major correction : Brooks omitted a long passage in which he practically accused Mark Twain of having unconsciously wanted to kill two of his children. It was a rather bold inference.
On p. 228 (of the 1933 ed., p. 186 of the 1st ed.), the psycho-analytical dogmatism is somewhat toned down by the suppression of " perfectly " in the sentence : " For is it not perfectly plain that Mark Twain's books are shot through with all sorts of unconscious revelations cf this inner conflict. "
Brooks also made a few additions. For instance, on p. 151, he inserted a reminiscence of Mrs. James T. Fields tending to show that Mark Twain suffered from having to restrain himself in front of his wife.
On p. 120 (of the 1933 ed., p. 91 of the 1st ed.) he made a significant alteration in order to hide the fact that " humorist " was a pejorative word in his vocabulary — which was rather regrettable in a book on Mark Twain, — he changed it to " funny man ". But this shows that originally, a humorist, to his mind, was nothing more than a " funny-man ".
3. Cf. no *933*.
4. Cf. W. Blair (no *968*, p. 448) : " This essay [on the genesis of the *Mysterious Stranger*] in a sense the De Voto version of *The Ordeal of Mark Twain*, has at least two advantages over the Brooks psychological interpretation : it is based on much more detailed and less manipulated evidence, and it is interpreted on the basis of what appears to be more complex and rather sounder psychological methods. "
5. Cf. no *1231*, pp. 29-34.
6. Cf. no *492*, p. 198.

CHAPTER V

THE REHABILITATION OF MARK TWAIN
or MARK TWAIN AS A LITERARY ARTIST

In spite of its stimulating value, the controversy between Brooks and De Voto was not an unmixed blessing. It diverted attention from Mark Twain's works to his personality and so it contributed to postpone a final estimate of his literary quality. Too much time was spent in analysing — and even psycho-analysing — the man and too little in reading and studying his books. He was of course a favourite of the general public, but too many critics during the controversial phase thought only of denigrating his taste and questioning his spiritual integrity or his morality [1]. As late as 1932, Grant C. Knight could still write in his *American Literature and Culture* :

" Criticism which emphasizes the esthetic value of literature will spend little time on Samuel L. Clemens [2]. "

In his opinion, *Huckleberry Finn* compared unfavourably with *The Scarlet Letter* :

" There are those who elevate *Huckleberry Finn* to a place beside *The Scarlet Letter* in the roll of the great American novels. Perhaps careful reflection will convince us that this judgment may rely too much upon the liking which we had for Clemens's books from the time of our own childhood. The book does not strike the bottom of human experience. All its events are seen through immature eyes [3]. "

In the early twenties, however, a few scholars began to protest against Howells's dictum that Mark Twain was an unliterary

---

1. For instance, William J. Long who in his *American Literature* (1913) (n⁰ *144*) complained that Mark Twain's heroes were liars ; G. Bradford, who in 1922 in *American Portraits* (n⁰ *272*) accused him of destroying reverence ; James M. Gillis, who, in *False Prophets* (1925) (n⁰ *367*), maintained that Mark Twain's despondency in his old age was condign punishment for his attacks on religion.
2. Cf. n⁰ *547*, p. 358.
3. Cf. n⁰ *547*, p. 365. Cf. also Pattee, " On the Rating of Mark Twain ", n⁰ *443*, p. 11.

artist, an uncultured genius [1]. O. H. Moore in particular attempted to prove in a very learned article that Mark Twain who had read Cervantes (he quoted him in *Life on the Mississippi*), imitated Don Quixote in *Tom Sawyer*, *Huckleberry Finn* and *A Connecticut Yankee at King Arthur's Court* [2]. In 1925 a German professor, F. Schönemann ironically entitled one of the chapters of his thesis " Der unliterarische Mark Twain ", and attempted to show that Mark Twain was a close student of literature [3]. Though his book was not translated, it was discussed in the United States [4], and, in 1934, Minnie M. Brashear followed his lead in her *Mark Twain, Son of Missouri*, especially in her chapter on " Sam Clemens's Reading " [5].

These claims were much exaggerated, but, at least, they evinced a new respect for Mark Twain as an artist which was a pleasant change from the patronizing attitude generally adopted by highbrow critics. Besides, they were a healthy reaction against the chauvinism and isolationism of so many readers. They tended to destroy the myth of Mark Twain as a self-made writer and a home-made product owing nothing whatever to European culture. As Moore wrote :

" It will... come as a rude shock to many readers who have habitually fled to Mark Twain as a refuge from Europeanism to know that their favorite drew much of his inspiration from European models ; that he was in earnest when he declared in a heated controversy, that ' there is not a single human characteristic which can be safely labeled as American ' [6]. "

In *Mark Twain's America* De Voto had also well served Mark Twain's cause by extolling his masterpieces lyrically and giving him higher praise than he customarily received. Unlike Paine, De Voto discriminated between Mark Twain's books and frankly acknowledged that " except for *Mardi* " American fiction has nothing so " chaotic " as *A Connecticut Yankee at King Arthur's Court* [7] and that *Joan of Arc* is " mediocre or worse " [8]. But these qualifications gave more authority to his praises of *Tom Sawyer* and, above all, of *Huckleberry Finn*. Unfortunately he

1. Cf. n⁰ 33, p. 17 : " Of all the literary men I have known he was the most unliterary in his make and manner. "
2. Cf. n⁰ *287*.
3. Cf. n⁰ *362*.
4. Cf. nᵒˢ *376, 377, 379, 407*.
5. Cf. n⁰ *601*. Cf. also n⁰ *1046*.
6. Cf. n⁰ *287*, p. 325.
7. Cf. n⁰ *537*, p. 279.
8. Cf. n⁰ *537*, p. 280.

had emphasized the American at the expense of the artist and had been more frequently lyrical than critical, considering it his duty to describe rather than to compare [1], which is a somewhat unexpected principle of criticism.

So, gradually [2], under the combined influence of the Brooks-De Voto controversy, of a few scholarly studies and De Voto's infectious enthusiasm for Mark Twain's masterpieces, readers and critics became more and more aware of the great humorist's artistry. In 1935, a hundred years after Mark Twain's birth, Mark Van Doren could assert :

" ... he has grown into an object of thought, a stimulus to abstraction. For better or for worse, he has become the author he never quite dared to hope he would have to be [3]. "

The appearance in the centennial year of Edward Wagenknecht's *Mark Twain — The Man and His Work* immediately justified this assertion. Though the book was essentially a study of Mark Twain's personality, it also contained several chapters on his art. It was more topical than biographical. The author was clearly not interested in taking sides in the Brooks-De Voto dispute. On the contrary, he tried to mediate between the two parties and minimize the problem which obsessed them. He concentrated on the works, taking it for granted that Mark Twain was a literary artist of the first rank, an assumption which he probably would not have dared to make in the twenties. However, as the title of one of his chapters indicates, " The Divine Amateur " [4], he laid emphasis on the spontaneity and natural power of Mark Twain's genius and did not bother to analyse his technique. For him Mark Twain was above all an " improvisator ", a " raconteur ", an extraordinary talker rather than a writer [5], a folk and not a conscious artist. When it came to the writing of fiction, he was quite incapable of calculating his effects [6]. But, on the other hand, Wagenknecht underlined his insistence on style and the exceptional quality of his English [7], a point which was also stressed by Otto Heller in an article on Mark Twain's seriousness :

---

1. *Ibid.*, p. 312 : " ... I regard comparisons as worthless in aesthetics... "
2. It was not an " about face of criticism " as De Voto asserted in n° *739*, p. 337.
3. Cf. n° *709*, p. 472.
4. Cf. n° *639*, pp. 50-80.
5. *Ibid.*, p. 55.
6. *Ibid.*, p. 57.
7. *Ibid.*, pp. 73-76.

" Without endorsing Mr. H. L. Mencken's extreme idea of an independent American language, few will disagree with his statement that
' Mark Twain's language is as American as the point of view under-
lying it '. But although pronouncedly vernacular, his diction springs
from the best wells of English undefiled [1]. "

This kind of homage, though, did not do full justice to Mark
Twain's art in the opinion of some of his admirers. De Lancey
Ferguson in 1938 protested that " Mark Twain was not a folk
humorist but a highly skilled man of letters [2] ". He had reached
this conclusion after a minute study of the original manuscripts
of Mark Twain's novels. When he understook this task, he merely
wanted to refute Brooks's theory by showing that the corrections
which Mark Twain had made to please his wife and Howells
were insignificant concessions to the ruling taste, but he found
out as well that :

" the Mark Twain who emerges from this study is a man of letters
practising his art, a humorist who knows what he is doing and making
the most of his materials [3]. "

And a few years later he added in his book on *Mark Twain,
Man and Legend* :

" But whatever their date, nature or extent, all the revisions are of
the same sort. They are not the dilution of grim realism to make it
meat for babes ; they are the work of a skilled craftsman removing
the unessential, adding vividness to dialogue and description, and
smoothing out incongruities [4]. "

The example set by Ferguson was soon followed by Walter
Blair [5] who in 1939 engaged in a very attentive study of the
structure of *Tom Sawyer*. Earlier critics, like Pattee and Carl
Van Doren, had maintained that the book showed " little skill
in construction " [6] and was " occasionally loaded with matters
brought in at moments when no necessity in the narrative calls
for them [7] ". Blair brilliantly succeeded in proving that they
were mistaken and that :

1. Cf. n⁰ *635*, p. 7.
2. Cf. review of Blair's *Native American Humor* (1937) in *AL*, 1938, p. 483.
3. Cf. *817*. This article was the starting point of a minor controversy. Cf. *867, 870,
871*. Dixon Wecter supported Ferguson's conclusions in his edition of *The Love Letters
of Mark Twain* (cf. n⁰ *1205*, pp. 11-15). However, Dickinson reviewing his book thought
the evidence inconclusive (cf. n⁰ *1240*).
4. Cf. n⁰ *963*, p. 219.
5. Cf. n⁰ *863*.
6. Cf. n⁰ *168*, pp. 59-60.
7. Quoted by Blair ; cf. n⁰ *863*, p. 80.

" If *Tom Sawyer* is regarded as the working out in fictional form
of [the] notion of a boy's maturing, the book will reveal... a structure
quite well adapted to its purpose... [1] "

And he demonstrated that this was the unifying theme of the
story by a careful consideration of the " units of narrative "
and the lines of action in the novel.

This attempt at introducing logic and order into a book which
had been rather desultorily composed was interesting, but not
fully convincing. Such *a posteriori* conclusions, however tempt-
ing, smacked of artificiality and could contain only a measure
of truth. De Voto's approach in *Mark Twain at Work* (1942)
was much more satisfactory. Renouncing the study of Mark
Twain's environment, he now undertook in his turn the study
of " the actual writing of *Tom Sawyer* and the actual writing of
Huckleberry Finn [2] ", together with an examination of the genesis
of *The Mysterious Stranger*. But he frankly confessed that :

" Most of [Mark Twain's] books show signs of having been... sporadic-
ally composed. It is the way of inspiration if you like, but it is not
the way of a conscious literary workman [3]. "

He faced the facts and acknowledged that Mark Twain was an
uneven writer whose method

" resulted in some of the most brilliant improvisations in American
literature — and in some of the most painful disharmonies [4]. "
" He lacked the discipline of revision and the discipline that makes
a writer uneasy until his material has been completely thought through
into form [5]. "
" ... there is the central limitation of Mark Twain's genius. He felt
no difference in value between the highest truths of fiction and merely
literary burlesque — if in fact he could at all discriminate between
them [6] ".

A few years later, John W. Hollenbach tried to clear Mark
Twain from these charges of improvisation and carelessness.
Taking up a notion already used by Wagenknecht, be asserted
that as a " raconteur " in his humorous stories Mark Twain was
" a painstaking artist " [7], as his essay on " How to tell a story "
shows. Comparing the successive versions of " Grandfather

1. *Ibid.*, p. 84.
2. Cf. n⁰ 933, p. VIII.
3. *Ibid.*, p. 3.
4. *Ibid.*
5. *Ibid.*, p. 10.
6. Cf. n⁰ 933, p. 91.
7. Cf. n⁰ 1078, p. 304.

Ram's Story " as given in *Roughing It* and in *Mark Twain in Eruption* [1], Hollenbach claimed that " it illustrates that he was capable of the discipline of revision, constant revision at that ", which suggests the conscious artist at least " in the smaller unit of the tale or the lecture [2] ". He could not of course make the same claims for Mark Twain's technique as a novelist.

About the same time George Feinstein was giving a different answer to the same problem [3]. He also attempted to discover the reason for Mark Twain's success as a " raconteur ", but, instead of attributing it to hard work, he simply saw in it the working of genius. According to him, Mark Twain systematically rejected the Aristotelian theory of strict story structure and, convinced that " execution transcends design ", preferred discursiveness to logical development — a dangerous method which might lead to incoherence, but which succeeded brilliantly in his case because of the unifying power of his strong personality :

" ... his own best essays and stories of the nineties are animated by an identical and idiosyncratic method — a method apparently of methodlessness [4]... "

This was a return to De Voto's views and the latter probably felt justified in sticking to his guns and concluding in his introduction to *The Portable Mark Twain* in 1946 :

" ... he had no conscious esthetic. He stood at the opposite pole from Henry James... he was not a fully conscious artist [5]. "

Dixon Wecter expressed the same opinion more picturesquely in the *Literary History of the United States* :

" ... Mark Twain the artist had always been a kind of pocket miner, stumbling like fortune's darling upon native ore of incredible richness and exploiting it with effortless skill — but often gleefully mistaking fool's gold for the genuine article, or lavishing his strength upon historical diggings long since played out [6]. "

Yet, there remains one element in Mark Twain's books to which all the critics paid little attention, though it is probably what G. Feinstein had in mind when he pedantically spoke of Mark Twain's " identical and idiosyncratic method " — and that is his style. It is there however that the magic lies. George May-

1. Cf. n° *888*, pp. 217-224.
2. Cf. n° *1078*, p. 311.
3. Cf. n° *1074*, pp. 162-163.
4. *Ibid.*
5. Cf. n° *1058*, p. 20.
6. Cf. n° *1155*, p. 939.

berry was perfectly aware of it when, commenting on the description of the circus in *Huckleberry Finn*, he wrote in *Reading and Writing* (1944) :

" It is prose that superbly fulfills its function here of rendering the color, pageantry and above all the movement of a circus performance as it works upon a boy's imagination... there are elements in the rest of the passage that lead directly to O. Henry and Penrod. But the clean-limbed functional quality of the prose, its exciting exploitation of language, its rightness in inherent details... are the chief, if not the only, virtues of our best writing in the last twenty-five years. They are to be found in Sherwood Anderson and Ernest Hemingway, whose debt to Twain is obvious and acknowledged, in Lardner, Fitzgerald, Dos Passos, Faulkner and Caldwell [1]. "

He was right. Hemingway had acknowledged his debt to Mark Twain in *Green Hills of Africa* in 1935 :

" All modern American literature comes from one book by Mark Twain called *Huckleberry Finn*... it's the best book we've had. All American writing comes from that. There was nothing before. There has been nothing as good since [2]. "

And Lionel Trilling in his introduction to *Huckleberry Finn* has very clearly explained the reason why Mark Twain's style was so much admired and exerted such strong influence on modern writers :

" In form and style *Huckleberry Finn* is an almost perfect work... The prose of *Huckleberry Finn* established for written prose the virtues of American colloquial speech...   Forget the misspellings and the faults of grammar, and the prose will be seen to move with the greatest simplicity, directness, lucidity and grace. These qualities are by no means accidental. Mark Twain who read widely, was passionately interested in the problems of style ; the mark of the strictest literary sensibility is everywhere to be found in the prose of *Huckleberry Finn* [3]. "

Even such a fastidious writer as T.S. Eliot whose parents forbade him to read *Huckleberry Finn*, because they considered it unsuitable reading for boys, has recently paid homage to Mark Twain's masterpiece :

" Repeated readings of the book only confirm and deepen one's admiration of the consistency and perfect adaptation of the writing.

---

1. Cf. n° *1009*, p. 608.
2. Cf. Ernest Hemingway, *Green Hills of Africa*, New York, Scribner's, 1935, p. 22. Cf. Also the chapter entitled " Adventures of Huckleberry Finn " in Philip Young, *Ernest Hemingway*, New York, Rinehart, 1952, pp. 181-212.
3. Cf. n° *1239*, p. 117.

This is a style which at the period, whether in America or in England, was an innovation, a new discovery in the English language [1]. "

This is a consecration which Mark Twain would have appreciated, for he prided himself on the quality of his English [2], but he would have been still prouder if he could have read two books which came out in 1950, *The Literary Apprenticeship of Mark Twain* by Edgar M. Branch [3] and especially *Mark Twain as a Literary Artist* by Gladys Ċ. Bellamy [4].

In the foreword, Gladys Bellamy very frankly states that the starting-point of her book was her " conviction that Mark Twain was much more the conscious craftsman than is generally believed [5] ". And to prove her point she quotes very striking passages from some of his letters (published by De Voto in *Mark Twain in Eruption*). She can thus show that he had a keen sense of form (« There is only one right form for a story [6] ") and that contrary to the beliefs of those who consider him a mere " raconteur " he could make " delicate distinctions and fine-drawn shadings between spoken and written art ". So he was not the " careless writer who simply wrote as he talked [7] ". On the contrary he was a very careful and conscientious craftsman. He thus wrote " The Recent Carnival of Crime in Connecticut " in two days, but spent four more days " trimming, altering and working at it [8] ". Hence the perfection of his style :

" To sum up the style of Mark Twain, his stylistic excellence arises from simplicity, long rhythms, idiomatic phrasing, colloquial ease, vivid vocabulary, and an imagery in intimate accord with the senses... Mark Twain's artistic conscience is reflected in his intense care for the exact word and in his ability, usually, to give an effect of perfect naturalness and unself-consciousness — the art that seems no art — although in the travel books there is sometimes a mannered rhythm which lets the careful craftsmanship show through [9]. "

And she devotes a whole chapter to a minute study of his stylistic excellence. She is the first critic ever to have done so. Yet, in spite of her enthusiasm, she is not blind to Mark Twain's faults :

1. Cf. nº *1234*, p. x.
2. Cf. a passage quoted by Wagenknecht, nº *633*, p. 76.
3. Cf. nº *1232*.
4. Cf. nº *1231*.
5. Cf. nº *1231*, p. vii.
6. *Ibid.*, p. 34.
7. *Ibid.*, p. 37.
8. *Ibid.*, p. 135.
9. Cf. nº *1231*, pp. 264-265.

" His stylistic weaknesses appear to arise from carelessness or indifference, but sometimes from the larger structural failure contingent upon a clash of unreconciled ideas and sometimes from the smaller but more immediate obstacle of his indignation [1]. "

This clash she attributes, not as Brooks does, to a thwarting of his genius by a hostile environment, but to

" ... a violent conflict, a logical dilemma, which forced much of his work into distorted patterns of both thought and structure, frequently making it impossible for him to achieve unity of any sort.

On the one hand, he was a rabid reformer, eager to uplift and purify mankind. On the other, he was the dogmatic determinist, preaching as the text of his ' Gospel ' that the inborn disposition of mankind " is a thing which is permanent as rock, and never undergoes any actual or genuine change between cradle and grave ' — a doctrine which in effect renders useless all attempts to uplift, instruct, or purify mankind [2]. "

It is only in his best fiction that

" he is finally able to combine the aesthetic inclination which leads him to create and the ethical inclination which leads him to teach — or, as he put it, to " preach ". It is only when the two are fused that his imagination can work with the freedom necessary to the artist [3]. "

According to Gladys Bellamy, through years of practice, Mark Twain evolved methods by which he managed to attain that freedom : either by speaking through the lips of Huck Finn or some other child, or by placing satirical scenes far off in time or space (as in *A Connecticut Yankee at King Arthur's Court*), or by diminishing the human race to microscopic proportions so that its wrongs could be treated with detachment (as in " The Great Dark " published by De Voto in *Mark Twain at Work*), or by reducing life to a drama in which the greatest wrongs became tolerable because they seemed unreal (as in *The Mysterious Stranger*). When one of these four conditions was fulfilled, Gladys Bellamy claims, the " rabid reformer " and the " dogmatic determinist ", instead of arguing, put their heads together and wrote masterpieces under one pen-name.

With this thorough and well-balanced study, Gladys Bellamy has certainly set " the appropriate keystone on the arch of Mark Twain criticism ", as George Whicher put it [4]. After four decades

---

1. *Ibid.*, p. 265.
2. *Ibid.*, p. 56.
3. Cf. n° *1231*, p. 155.
4. Cf. n° *1245*, p. 6.

of discussions about Mark Twain's personality — real or hypo-
thetical, — his books have at last obtained the critical attention
which they deserved, they have finally been regarded as the work
of a literary artist. The wheel has come full circle since the
time when his best friend and staunchest supporter considered
him an unliterary artist.

CONCLUSION

The forty years of Mark Twain criticism which we have surveyed in this essay, thus make a coherent whole. In these four decades, Mark Twain has passed from the hands of the hagiographers into those of the critics, after some rough handling by the debunkers and psycho-analysts of the twenties. He began by being worshipped as a great American hero and an admirable personality, but the next generation — after the First World War — called him a hen-pecked husband and a coward and accused him of truckling to bourgeois conventions and to capitalism. This ordeal did not last, however. People grew tired of discussing Mark Twain the man, to no purpose. They started reading his books with greater care and, to their delight, discovered that he was a clever writer and an artist in prose. 1950 was a decisive year in this respect since within a few months T. S. Eliot rendered homage to *Huckleberry Finn* and a distinguished academic critic officially dubbed Mark Twain " a literary artist ".

Whether worshipped or vilified, Mark Twain has held the stage since 1910. He has managed to retain the attention of the successive generations and, being a typical American, has been treated as a contemporary by all. His books have always provoked violent reactions now of admiration, now of anger or contempt. The fluctuations of his reputation can be explained by changes in the American spiritual climate. The pre-war public worshipped his personality because it had known him personally and laughed at his jokes as they fell from his lips — and also because it was gay and care-free. The Lost Generation " debunked " him in a spirit of adolescent perversion because their fathers had considered him a great man and because they hated the America that had fêted him. Later this bitterness dissipated, the public became more and more interested in art — especially American art — as an escape from the drabness of the Depression years. Universities created degrees in American literature and offered courses on American authors. American classics were needed, and Mark Twain, among others, was found.

His *Huckleberry Finn* was proclaimed a masterpiece and an American Odyssey. After missing his apotheosis as a hero, Mark Twain is now being apotheosized as an artist.

These changes in the attitude of the public and critics have in turn lit up the different aspects of his works. He was at first acclaimed as a jester and a wonderful " raconteur " of humorous stories. Then the Lost Generation revelled in the pessimism of his posthumous books. As to the latter-day connoisseurs, they above all like his personalized fiction and his travel books, and they laud *Huckleberry Finn* to the skies. These vacillations have resulted in a deeper understanding and more searching analysis of his works. Like T. S. Eliot, America had to go through the Waste Land of the post-war fully to appreciate his genius. The pre-war generation saw in him only the celebrant of expanding democracy. The bitterness of the post-war years were necessary to open the eyes of the public to the fact that he was also a prophet of frustration. And his potential readers of the last twenty years had to be educated by more sophisticated writers before they could find out that, like *Gulliver's Travels*, *Huckleberry Finn* can be enjoyed by adults as well as by children and has several levels of significance [1].

This gradual discovery of the merits of Mark Twain's works, this constantly deeper and better-motivated appreciation of his books is the best guarantee that his literary reputation will suffer no eclipse in the coming years. His present apotheosis — after a stay in the Purgatory of psychoanalysis — seems well deserved. Henry S. Canby has just placed him side by side with Henry James in the American literary Pantheon [2] and it is improbable that he should ever be dislodged from there [3].

1. A European might be tempted to accuse American readers of a sentimental and unreasonable attachment for a book which they loved as children. But who would dare to do so after such an unsentimental author as T. S. Eliot — who did not read it as child, — has made common cause with them.

2. Cf. n° *1271*.

3. This does not mean, however, that Mark Twain is going to be blindly worshipped. In the eyes of many young Americans, it is not enough to be a supreme artist. A writer must commit himself and not stop half-way in his denunciation of shams and social evils. In their opinion, Mark Twain was guilty of having only " half escaped the genteel tradition ". As an example of these new trends in Mark Twain criticism. cf. Leo Marx, " Mr. Eliot, Mr. Trilling and *Huckleberry Finn* ", *American Scholar*, vol. 22, 423-440, Autumn 1953. Leo Marx writes in his conclusion : " ... the faint-hearted ending of *Huckleberry Finn* remains an important datum in the record of American thought and imagination... To minimize the seriousness of what must be accounted a major flaw in so great a work is, in a sense, to repeat Clemens' failure of nerve... Today we particularly need a criticism alert to lapses of moral vision. A measured appraisal of the failures and successes of our writers, past and present, can show us a great deal about literature and about ourselves. That is the critic's function. But he cannot perform that function if he substitutes considerations of technique for considerations of truth. " (pp. 439-440).

BIBLIOGRAPHY

(1910-1952)

ABREVIATIONS USED IN THIS BIBLIOGRAPHY

AL	American Literature.
Am.	American
Am. Mag.	American Magazine.
Am. Merc.	American Mercury.
Am. Rev.	American Review.
Angl. Bbl.	Beiblatt zur Anglia.
AS	American Speech.
Bull.	Bulletin.
Current Lit.	Current Literature.
EA	Études Anglaises.
Eng. Jour.	English Journal.
Harper's M.	Harper's Monthly Magazine.
Harper's W.	Harper's Weekly.
Hist.	Historical.
Ibid.	*Ibidem.*
JEGP	Journal of English & German Philology.
Jour.	Journal.
Lit. Digest	Literary Digest.
Lit. Review	Literary Review.
M.	Monthly.
Mag.	Magazine.
Merc. de France	Mercure de France.
Michigan Hist. Mag.	Michigan History Magazine.
Missouri Hist. Rev.	Missouri Historical Review.
MLN	Modern Language Notes.
MLQ	Modern Language Quarterly.
MP	Modern Philology.
NEQ	New England Quarterly.
North Am.	North American Review.
NR	New Republic.
N. & Q.	Notes and Queries.
Overland M.	Overland Monthly.
p.	page.
Pacific M.	Pacific Monthly.
PMLA	Publications of the Modern Language Association of America.
pp.	pages.
PQ	Philological Quarterly.
Pub. W.	Publishers' Weekly.
Quar.	Quarterly.
RAA	Revue Anglo-Américaine.
Rev.	Review.
Rev. of Rev.	Review of Reviews.
Sat. Evg. Post	Saturday Evening Post.
South Atlantic Quar.	South Atlantic Quarterly.
SRL	Saturday Review of Literature.
TLS	London Times Literary Supplement.
Va. Quar. Rev.	Virginia Quarterly Review.
YR	Yale Review.

N. B. — Such references as " Cf. n° *271* " refer to the entries in the Bibliography.

BEFORE 1910

(A Selection in Chronological Order)

1870   *1* MARK TWAIN. *The Innocents Abroad,* A Book of Travel in Pursuit of Pleasure with an introduction by Edward P. Hingston. London, J. C. Hotten, 1870, 256 pp.

1872   *2* BENTZON, Thérèse (Mme Marie-Thérèse Blanc). " Les Humoristes Américains : I. Mark Twain. " *Revue des Deux-Mondes,* 42e année, 2e période, vol. 100, 313-335, 15 juillet 1875.

1875   *3* — " L'Age Doré en Amérique ". *Ibid.,* 45e année, 3e période, vol. 8, 319-343, 15 mars 1875.

        A discussion of *The Gilded Age.*

1882   *4* — *Littérature et Mœurs Étrangères : Etudes.* Paris, G. Lévy, 2 vols., 1882.

        On Mark Twain, vol. 2, pp. 1-38, 231-271 ; these essays are mere reprints of the articles she had published in the *Revue des Deux-Mondes,* in 1872 and 1875.

1884   *5* GAUTHIER-VILLARS, Henry (Willy). *Mark Twain.* Paris, Gauthier-Villars, 1884, VI + 111 pp.

1886   *6* FORGUES, Eugène. " Les Caravanes d'un Humoriste : Mark Twain ". *Revue des Deux-Mondes,* 56e année, 3e période, vol. 73, 879-918, 15 février 1886.

        A review of *Life on the Mississippi.* According to the author, all efforts to import American humor into France were a failure, with the exception of *Tom Sawyer,* an " exquisite idyll ". Otherwise, to French taste, Mark Twain's pleasantry appears " macabre " and his wit brutal. Some have even regarded his exaggerations as " symptoms of mental alienation ".

1887   *7* MARK TWAIN. *The Innocents Abroad,* with an Introduction by the Rev. Hugh Reginald Haweis, (abridged ed.). London, Routledge's World Library, 1887, 160 pp.

1890 *8* KIPLING, Rudyard. " An Interview with Mark Twain. "
The Pioneer (Allahabad), March 18, 1890 ; *The Pioneer
Mail*, March 19, 1890.
An interview with Mark Twain at Elmira in 1889 ; cf.
n⁰ *19.*

1891 *9* LANG, Andrew. " Mr. Lang on the Art of Mark Twain. "
The Critic, vol. 16, n. s., 45-46, July 25, 1891.
" If you praise [Mark Twain] among persons of culture,
they cannot believe that you are serious. They call him a
Barbarian... Now I do not mean to assert that Mark Twain
is ' an impeccable artist ', but he is just as far from
being a mere coarse buffoon. " Lang considers *Huckleberry
Finn* a great " Historical novel ", superior to *Uncle Tom's
Cabin* and comparable to the *Odyssey.*

1892 *10* CLEMENS, Will M. *Mark Twain, His Life and Work*, A Bio-
graphical Sketch. San Francisco, The Clemens Publishing
Co., 1892 (New York, 1894), 211 pp.
A garrulous and unreliable book.

1895 *11* O'REILL, Max (Paul Blouet). " Mark Twain and Paul Bour-
get. " *North Am. Rev.*, vol. 160, 302-310, March 1895.

1896 *12* TRENT, W. P. " Mark Twain as an Historical Novelist. "
Bookman, vol. 3, 207-210, May 1896.
On *Joan of Arc.*

13 TWICHELL, Joseph H. " Mark Twain. " *Harper's M.*, vol. 92,
817-827, 1896.

1897 *14* MATTHEWS, Brander. " Mark Twain — His Work. " *Book-
Buyer*, vol. 13, 977-979, Jan. 1897.

15 THOMPSON, C. M. " Mark Twain as an Interpreter of American
Character. " *Atlantic Monthly*, vol. 79, 443-450, April 1897.

1898 *16* BROOKS, Noah. " Mark Twain in California. " *Century Magazine*, vol. 57, 97-99, 1898.

1899 *17* DOUMIC, René. " Nos Humoristes. " *Revue des Deux-Mondes*,
69ᵐᵉ Année, 924-935, 15 octobre 1899.
Cf. n⁰ *22.*

18 KEELING, Anne E. " American Humour : Mark Twain. "
London Quar. Rev., n. s., vol. 2, 147-162, 1899.

19 KIPLING, Rudyard. *From Sea to Sea*, New York, Doubleday
and McClure, 1899, 2 vols.
A collection of articles published between 1887 and 1890 ;
contains " An Interview with Mark Twain. " Cf. n⁰ *8.*

1900 *20* MARK TWAIN. *Contes Choisis*, traduits par G. de Lautrec
et précédés d'une étude sur l'humour. Paris, Mercure de
France, 2ᵉ éd., 1900, 263 pp.

First dated edition of Twain's *Sketches* in French translation, preceded only by a selection published by Nelson.

21 BELLEZZA, Paolo. *Humour*, Strenna a beneficio del Pio
Istituto dei Rachitici. Milan, P. Agnelli, 1900, 315 pp.
This book was reviewed by Howells : " An Italian's
Views of Mark Twain. " *North Am. Rev.*, Nov. 1901 —
(reprinted in Howells's *My Mark Twain*, 1910, pp. 157-165).

1901 *22* DOUMIC, René. *Études sur la Littérature Française.* Paris,
Perrin & Co., 4e série, 1901.
P. 257, in the chapter entitled " Nos Humoristes "
Doumic mentioned " Le vol de l'éléphant blanc " and
declared : " Cela est puéril et long. "

23 PHILLIPS, R. E. " More than Humorist. " *Book-Buyer*, vol. 23,
196-201, April 1901.

24 POND, James Burton. *Eccentricities of Genius.* Memories of
famous men and women of the platform and stage. London,
Chatto and Windus, xxvi + 564 pp., 1901.

25 FRANCE, Clemens J. " Mark Twain as an Educator. " *Education*, vol. 21, 265-274, 1901.

1904 *26* SIMBOLI, Raffaele. " Mark Twain from an Italian Point of
view. " *The Critic*, vol. 44, 518-524, July 1904.

1905 *27* BRUNI, Livia. " L'Umorismo americano, Mark Twain. "
Nuova Antologia, ser. 4, vol. 115 (vol. 199), 697-709, 1905.
A translation of this article was published in *Rev. of
Rev.*, vol. 31, 743-744, June 1905, under the title of " An
Italian Estimate of Mark Twain. "

1907 *28* MATTHEWS, Brander. *Inquiries and Opinions.* New York,
C. Scribner's Sons, vii + 305 pp., 1907.
A chapter on Mark Twain, pp. 137-166. Cf. his 1897
article (no *14*).

1910

BIBLIOGRAPHIES :

29 Johnson, Merle. *A Bibliography of the Works of Mark Twain.*
New York and London, Harper & Brothers, xv + 203 pp.

30 Livingston, Luther S. *The Works of Mark Twain.* The description
of a set of the first editions of his books in the library of a
New York collector [R. F. Pick]. With Facsimiles. vii + 91 pp.,
only 75 copies were printed according to Wilfred Partington
(cf. *Bookman*, March 1933).

31 Anon. " Mark Twain. — First Editions of His Books. " *Nation*,
vol. 91, 260, Sept. 22.

32 — " Bibliography of the Works of Mark Twain ." *Ibid.*, 601,
Dec. 22.

BIOGRAPHIES AND BOOKS OF CRITICISM :

33 Howells, William Dean. *My Mark Twain : Reminiscences and
Criticism.* New York & London, Harper & Brothers, 186 pp.
This book contains recollections of Mark Twain, his friend
and " protégé ", together with early reviews of Twain's works
by the author, reprinted " with no sort of correction ".

34 Hyatt, Edward. (Superintendent of Public Instruction). *A Calaveras Evening with Mark Twain and Bret Harte*, a diversion
for the English class. Sacramento, W. W. Shannon, Supt.
State Printing, 8 pp.

INTRODUCTIONS AND PREFACES :

35 Mark Twain. *Speeches*, with an introduction by W. D. Howells.
New York & London, Harper & Brothers, v + 433 pp.

36 — *The Adventures of Tom Sawyer*, illustrated by Worth Brehm.
New York and London, Harper & Brothers, vii + 319 pp.

37 — Travels at Home and Abroad, selected from the works of Mark Twain by Percival Chubb and arranged for home and supplementary reading in the 6th, 7th and 8th grades. New York & London, Harper & Brothers, xi + 142 pp.

38 MARK TWAIN. *Travels in History*, selected from the works of Mark Twain by C. N. Kendall and arranged for home and supplementary reading in the 6th, 7th and 8th grades. New York & London, Harper & Brothers, viii + 170 pp.

Extracts from *The Prince and the Pauper*, *A Connecticut Yankee*, and *Joan of Arc*.

39 DAWSON, W. J. & DAWSON, C. W. (ed.). *The Great English Short-Story Writers*, with introductory essays. New York & London, Harper & Brothers, 2·vols.

In vol. I, " A Dog's Tale " by Mark Twain.

40 EPUY, Michel. *Anthologie des humoristes anglais et américains.* Paris, Delagrave, 486 pp.

On Mark Twain, pp. 422-423 ; extracts pp. 423-481.

41 — Le legs de 30.000 Dollars et autres contes, traduits et préfacés d'une étude sur l'auteur par Michel Epuy. Paris, Mercure de France, 319 pp.

OTHER BOOKS DEALING WITH MARK TWAIN :

42 DICKIE, James F. *In the Kaiser's Capital.* New York, Dodd, Mead and Co., 315 pp.

A chapter on Mark Twain's stay in Berlin : chap. xvii, pp. 182-190.

43 EGGLESTON, George Cary. *Recollections of a Varied Life.* New York, Henry Bolt & Co., viii + 354 pp.

Scattered allusions to Mark Twain.

44 PEARSON, Edmund Lester. *The Library and the Librarian.* Woodstock, Vt, The Elm Tree Press, 87 pp.

A chapter entitled " The children's librarian versus Huckleberry Finn " (pp. 26-32) takes the defence of Mark Twain's boys' books.

45 PHELPS, William Lyon. *Essays on Modern Novelists.* New York, Macmillan, ix + 293 pp.

On Mark Twain, pp. 99-114. Considers him as " our foremost living American writer. "

46 STEDMAN, Lucy & GOULD, George M. *Life and Letters of Edmund Clarence Stedman.* New York, Moffat, Yard & Co., 2 vols.

PERIODICAL LITERATURE :

47 ADE, George. " Mark Twain and the old time subscription book. "
   Rev. of Rev., vol. 41, 703-704, June.

48 — " Mark Twain as Our Emissary. " *Century*, vol. 81, 204-206, Dec.
   Mark Twain explained America to Europe.

49 ALDEN, H. M. " Mark Twain — An Appreciation. " *Bookman*,
   vol. 31, 366-369, June.

50 — " Mark Twain ; Personal Impressions. " *Book News Monthly*,
   vol. 28, 579-582.

51 BEARD, Dan. " Mark Twain as a Neighbor. " *Rev. of Rev.*, vol. 41,
   705-709, June.

52 " BRITANNICUS " (BROOKS, Sidney). " England and Mark Twain. "
   North Am., vol. 191, 822-826, June.

53 CARMAN, Bliss. " Last Day at Stormfield. Poem. " *Collier's*, vol. 45,
   10-11, May 7.

54 COLBY, F. M. " Mark Twain's Illuminating Blunder ." *Bookman*,
   vol. 32, 354-358, Dec.
      On Mark Twain's speech at the dinner given by the *Atlantic
   Monthly* to Whittier in 1877 for his seventieth birthday.

55 EPUY, Michel. " Mark Twain. " *Grande Revue*, vol. 61, 66-76,
   10 mai.

56 GAINES, C. N. " Mark Twain *the* Humorist. " *Books News Monthly*,
   vol. 28, 583-588.

57 HENDERSON, Archibald. " The International Fame of Mark Twain. "
   North Am., vol. 192, 805-815, Dec.
      On Mark Twain's reception in France and Germany.

58 HERON, H. " Mark Twain ; Poem. " *Harper's W.*, vol. 54, 24,
   June 11.

59 HOWELLS, W. D. " Critical Comment on Mark Twain's Work. "
   Harper's W., vol. 54, 10, 57, April 30.
      Excerpts from an article already published in the *North Am.*
   in Feb. 1901.

60 HOWELLS, W. D. " Mark Twain ; An Inquiry. " *North Am.*, vol. 191,
   836-850, June.
      Ditto.

61 — " My Memories of Mark Twain. " *Harper's M.*, vol. 121, 165-178,
   340-348, 512-529 (July-Sept.), also in *Current Lit.*, vol. 49,
   445-447, Oct.

62 JAMES, George, Wharton. " Mark Twain and the Pacific Coast. "
   Pacific M., vol. 24, 115-132, Aug.
      On Mark Twain in Nevada and California.

63 JERROLD, Walter. " Mark Twain, the Man and the Jester. " *Bookman* (London), vol. 38, 111-116, June.

64 KING, F. A. " Story of Mark Twain's Debts. " *Bookman*, vol. 31, 394-396, June.

65 MAURICE, A. B. " Mark Twain's ' The Innocents Abroad '. " *Bookman*, vol. 31, 374-379, June.

65* MICHAUD, Régis. " L'Envers d'un Humoriste — Mark Twain. " *Revue du Mois*, vol. 9, 430-444 (April 10).

66 MILLARD, B. " Mark Twain in San Francisco. " *Bookman*, vol. 31, 369-373, June.

67 MURRAY, A. F. " To Mark Twain : Poem. " *Harper's W.*, vol. 54, 27, May 7.

68 NESBIT, W. D. " Samuel L. Clemens : Poem. " *Harper's W.*, vol. 54, 30, May 7 (reprinted from *Chicago Evening Post*).

69 PAIN, Barry. " The Humour of Mark Twain. " *Bookman* (London), vol. 38, 107-111, June.
    Mark Twain as a successful fun-maker but a bad artist.

70 PAINE, A. B. " Biographical Summary. " *Harper's W.*, vol. 54, 6-10, April 30.

71 PECK, Harry Thurston. " Mark Twain a Century Hence. " *Bookman*, vol. 31, 382-393, June.
    His works will live.

72 PHELPS, W. L. " Notes on Mark Twain. " *Independent*, vol. 68, 956-960, May 5.

73 — " Mark Twain Artist. " *Rev. of Rev.*, vol. 41, 702-703, June.
    " Mark Twain was a greater artist than he was humorist. "

74 RIDEING, W. H. " Mark Twain in Clubland. " *Bookman*, vol. 31, 379-382, June.

75 SHERMAN, S. P. " Mark Twain. " *Nation*, vol. 90, 477-480, May 12.

76 STERN, C. " Mark Twain ; Poem. " *Harper's W.*, vol. 54, 32, July 2.

77 STODDART, A-Mc. " Twainiana. " *Independent*, vol. 68, 960-963, May 5.

78 THOMPSON, J. W. " Mark Twain ; Poem. " *Harper's W.*, vol. 54, 34, May 14.

79 VALE, C. " Mark Twain as an Orator. " *Forum*, vol. 44, 1-13, July.

80 WATTERSON, H. " Mark Twain — An Intimate Memory. " *Am. Mag.*, vol. 70, 372-375, July.
    Personal recollections of a distant cousin of Mark Twain. Some information on the original of Col. Sellers.

81 WHITE, F. M. " Mark Twain as a newspaper reporter. " *Outlook*, vol. 96, 961-967, Dec. 24.

Recollections of the time when Mark Twain covered the Jubilee procession in London in 1897.

82 WILLIAMS, C. " Mark Twain ; Poem. " *Sunset* (San Francisco), vol. 25, 58, July — also in *Harper's W.*, vol. 54, 21, Aug. 20.

83 WOOLF, S. J. " Painting the Portrait of Mark Twain. " *Collier's*, vol. 45, 42-44, May 14.

84 " Tributes to Mark Twain ", *North Am.*, vol. 191, 827-835, June.
Tributes by Andrew Carnegie, A. B. Paine, Booker T. Washington, Booth Tarkington, S. Gompers, Wilbur D. Nesbit, G. Ade, H. Garland, J. K. Bangs, B. Matthews.

85 " Mark Twain — Some Personal Recollections and opinions " by Jerome K. Jerome, E. V. Lucas, Walter Emmanuel, J. J. Bell, Leonard Henslowe, A. Bennett, Owen Seaman, W. Pett Ridge, and F. Anstey Guthrie ", *Bookman* (London), vol. 38, 116-119, June.

86 Anon. " Mark Twain. " *Missouri Republican*, April 22.
Horace E. Bixby, the Mississippi pilot, discusses Mark Twain's war experiences.

87 — " Mark Twain and his Works. " *Independent*, vol. 68, 934-935, April 28.

88 — " Two Frontiersmen. " *Nation*, vol. 90, 422-423, April 28.

89 — " Mark Twain. " *Collier's*, vol. 45, 10-11, April 30.

90 — " Mark Twain as an Author. " *Outlook*, vol. 94, 971-972, April 30.

91 — " Mark Twain. " *Spectator* (London), vol. 104, 720-721, April 30.

92 — " Mark Twain. " *Dial*, vol. 48, 305-307, May 10.

93 — " Mark Twain. " *Living Age*, vol. 265, 564-567, May 28.
Reprinted from *The Times*.

94 — " Great Career. " *Chautauquan*, vol. 59, 9-10 June.

95 — " Mark Twain's Pessimistic Philosophy. " *Current Lit.*, vol. 48, 643-647, June.
On *What is Man ?*

96 — " Mark Twain as a Serious Force in Literature. " *Current Lit.*, vol. 48, 663-667, June.

97 — " Serious Humorists. " *Nation*, vol. 90, 645-646, June 30.

98 — " Great Individual. " *Am. Mag.*, vol. 70, 428-432. July.

99 — " Originals of Some of Mark Twain's Characters. " *Rev. of Rev.*, vol. 42, 228-230, Aug.

100 — " Mark Twain's Investments. " *Collier's*, vol. 46, 32, Nov. 12.

101 — " Mark Twain Commemorated. " *Outlook*, vol. 96, 801-802, Dec. 10.

102 — " Mark Twain in Memoriam ; Memorial Meeting in Carnegie Hall, New York ", *Harper's M.*, vol. 54, 8-10, Dec. 17.

1911

BIBLIOGRAPHIES

103 Mark Twain; Autograph Manuscripts and First Editions Offered by Dodd & Livingston. New York, 14 pp.

104 Anderson Auction Co. *Catalogue of the Library and Manuscripts of Samuel L. Clemens...* to be sold Feb. 7 & 8, 1911. New York, The Anderson Auction Co., 73 pp.

These two catalogues are chiefly of value to bibliographical specialists and book-collectors. They can be of help in tracing the whereabouts of certain of Twain's original manuscripts.

BIOGRAPHIES AND BOOKS OF CRITICISM :

105 HENDERSON, Archibald, *Mark Twain.* London, Duckworth & Co., XIII + 230 pp.

Mark Twain as a great creative genius and even as a great artist.

OTHER BOOKS CONTAINING MATERIAL ABOUT MARK TWAIN

106 HERTS, Alice Minnie. *The Children's Educational Theatre*, with an introduction by Charles W. Eliot. New York & London, Harper & Brothers, x + 150 pp.

Contains a few pages on *The Prince and the Pauper.*

PERIODICAL LITERATURE :

107 CAMPBELL, K. " From Aesop to Mark Twain. " *Sewanee Rev.*, vol. 19, 43-49, Jan.

108 HENDERSON, A. " Mark Twain als Philosoph, Moralist and Soziol-
oge. " *Deutsche Revue* (Stuttgart), Jahrg. 36, part I, 189-205.

109 JAMES, George Wharton. " How Mark Twain Was Made. " *National
Mag.*, vol. 33, 525-537, Feb.

110 MBC. " Mark Twain as a Reader. " *Harper's W.*, vol. 55, 6,
Jan. 7.

111 Anon. " Twain's European Fame. " *Bookman*, vol. 33, 347-348,
June.

112 — " Mark Twain as the Embodiment of American Romance. "
Current Lit., vol. 51, 566-568, Nov.

A review of A. Henderson's *Mark Twain.*

1912

BIOGRAPHIES AND BOOKS OF CRITICISM :

113 Paine, Albert Bigelow. *Mark Twain; A Biography*, The Personal
and Literary Life of Samuel Langhorne Clemens. New York &
London, Harper and Brothers, 3 vols., xv + 1719 pp. (Part
of this biography was published serially in *Harper's M.* from
Nov. 1911 to Nov. 1912).
   Paine was Mark Twain's Secretary and had been commissioned
to write his life. His study is ardently appreciative and wholly
uncritical.

INTRODUCTIONS AND PREFACES :

114 Mark Twain. *Cuentos Escogidos;* traducción directa y esmerada
de A. Barrado, precedidos de un prólogo de Angel Guerra. Madrid,
Noticiero-guía de Madrid, 107 pp.

OTHER BOOKS DEALING WITH MARK TWAIN :

115 Cairns, William B. *A History of American Literature.* New York,
Oxford University Press, vii + 502 pp.
   On Mark Twain, pp. 444-450. Considers him as overrated.

116 Perry, Bliss. *The American Mind* (E. T. Earle Lectures, 1912).
Boston and New York, Houghton, Mifflin Co., 249 pp.
   On Mark Twain, pp. 197-202. Perry sees in this " versatile
and richly endowed humorist " a great American idealist and
" one of the most representative of American writers ".

117 Rideing, William H. *Many Celebrities and a Few Others.* Garden
City, Doubleday, Page & Co., 335 pp.
   Contains a chapter on Mark Twain and E. C. Stedman.

118 Smith, Alphonso. *Die amerikanische Literatur*, Verlesungen, geh.
am. d. Kgl. Friedrich-Wilhelms-Universität zu Berlin. Berlin,

Weidmannsche Buchh. (Bibliothek der amerikanischen Kultur-
geschichte), vii + 388 pp.

Chap. xv, pp. 312-337 : " Mark Twain und die amerikanische
Humor ."

119 Trent, William Peterfield & Erskine, John. *Great Writers of
America* (Home University of Modern Knowledge). New York,
Henry Holt & Co., 256 pp.

On Mark Twain, pp. 244-250. He will live as a novelist rather
than a humorist.

PERIODICAL LITERATURE :

Reviews of A. B. Paine's *Mark Twain* :

120 Bacheller, I. in *Lit. Digest*, vol. 45, 909, Nov. 16.

Sees Mark Twain essentially as an antipuritan. " Lincoln
freed the Negro, Mark Twain freed the white man. "

121 Bicknell, Percy F. in *Dial*, vol. 53, 290-292, Oct. 16.

Paine's book vies in interest with Mark Twain's own works.

122 Anon. in *Spectator*, vol. 109, 557-558, Oct. 12.

123 — in *Nation*, vol. 95, 457-459, Nov. 14.

" ... the prose Odyssey of the American people... it will continue to be read when half of Mark Twain's writings are forgotten... "

124 — in *Hearst's Mag.*, vol. 22, 135-138, Dec.

*
* *

125 Bodine, T. V. " A Journey to the Home of Mark Twain. " *Kansas
City Star Mag.*, May 19.

126 Kyne, P. B. " Great Mono Miracle ; An Echo of Mark Twain. "
Sunset, vol. 29, 37-49, July.

A joke supposed to have been played by Twain on the popu-
lation of a mining camp in Nevada.

127 Anon. " Mark Twain's Private Girls' Club. " *Ladies' Home Journal*,
vol. 29, 23, 54, Feb.

His friendships with little girls in his old age.

128 — " Cub Days with Mark Twain. " *Lit. Digest*, vol. 44, 305-307,
Feb. 10.

When Mark Twain was on the staff of *The Entreprise*.

129 — " Mark Twain's Lucky Failure. " *Lit. Digest*, vol. 45, 391-
392, Feb. 24.

On his failure as a gold-miner.

130 — " Mark Twain's Failures. " *Lit. Digest*, vol. 45, 150, July 27.
On the books he never finished.

131 — " Story of Grant's Memoirs. " *Lit. Digest*, vol. 45, 373-375,
Sept. 7.

132 — " How ' The Players' was formed. " *Lit. Digest*, vol. 45, 621,
Oct. 12.
On a New York Club of which Mark Twain was a member.

133 — " Origin of Pudd'nhead Wilson. " *Lit. Digest*, vol. 45, 740,
Oct. 26.

134 — " Napoleon III in America. " *Bookman*, vol. 36, 238, Nov.
This deals with Mark Twain's consultation of Cheiro, a famous
chiromancer (cf. nº *513*).

135 — " Punch Brothers. " *Bookman*, vol. 36, 236-237, Nov.
An extract from Paine's *Mark Twain*.

136 — " Spiritual Tragedy of Mark Twain. " *Current Lit.*, vol. 53,
582-584, Nov.
He wanted to be more than a mere humourist but his vast
and merry public refused to take him seriously.   Hence his
sense of failure.

137 — " Mark Twain's Portrait. " *Outlook*, vol. 102, 528-529, Nov. 9.

138 — " One Who Didn't Like Mark Twain. " *Lit. Digest*, vol. 45,
909, Nov. 16.
Sir Robertson Nicoll, in his capacity as editor of the *Bookman*
(London) and more especially the *British Weekly*, did not like
Mark Twain because of the latter's hostility to Christianity.

1913

BIOGRAPHIES AND BOOKS OF CRITICISM :

139 WALLACE, Elizabeth. *Mark Twain and the Happy Island*, Chicago, A. C. McClury, 139 pp.

Memories of Mark Twain's stays in Bermuda. On his friendships with little girls.

OTHER BOOKS DEALING WITH MARK TWAIN :

140 CARUS, Paul. *The Mechanistic Principle and the Non-Mechanical.* An inquiry into Fundamentals with Extracts from Representatives of Either Side. Chicago, The Open Court Publishing Co., IV + 125 pp.

Contains a chapter on " Mark Twain's Philosophy " (pp. 54-97) made up largely of quotations from *What is Man?* A reprint of his article in *The Monist;* cf. vol. 23 ; pp. 181-223, April.

141 GOODWIN, C. C. *As I remember Them.* Salt Lake City, Utah, published by a special committee of the Salt Lake Commercial Club, 360 pp.

Charles Carroll Goodwin was a friend of Mark Twain's during the latter's stay in Nevada. Cf. De Voto's *Mark Twain's America*, p. 135, n. 2.

142 KELLNER, Leon. *Geschichte der Nordamerikanischen Literatur.* Berlin, G. J. Göschen, 2 vols. (116 & 94 pp.). Cf. below n° *167.*

143 LEWIS, Dudley Payne (ed.). *History of the Class of 1903*, Yale College, New Haven, Conn.

Contains " Mark Twain " by Joseph H. Twichell.

144 LONG, William J. *American Literature.* A Study of the Men and the Books that in the Earlier and the Later Times Reflect the American Spirit. Boston and New York, Ginn & Co., XXI + 481 pp.

Considers Mark Twain a creator of vital characters, but prefers *The Prince and the Pauper* to *Huckleberry Finn.*

145 MACY, John Albert. *The Spirit of American Literature.* New York, Doubleday, Page & Co., 347 pp.

Chapter XIII (pp. 248-277) on Mark Twain whom the author considers " a powerful, original thinker ", " greater than his reputation ".

146 PERRY, Bliss. *The American Mind* (The E. T. Earle Lectures, 1912). London, Constable & Co., 248 pp.

A reprint of the American edition. Cf. above nᵒ *116*.

147 *Proceedings of the American Academy of Arts and Letters and the National Institute of Arts and Letters.* Vol. I : 1909-1913. New York.

Contains " In Memory of Mark Twain " ; cf. nᵒ *266*.

PERIODICAL LITERATURE :

Reviews of A. B. Paine's *Mark Twain* (1912) :

148 HOWELLS, W. D. " Editor's Easy Chair. " *Harper's M.*, vol. 126, 310-312, Jan.

Very favourable.

149 PHELPS, W. L. in *Independent*, vol. 74, 531-533, March 6.

Very enthusiastic.

150 RICHARDSON, Charles F. in *Yale Rev.*, vol. 2, 563-567, April.

A dissenting voice. Prefers Poe and Hawthorne to the crudeness of Mark Twain.

151 Anon. in *North Am.*, vol. 197, 136-138, Jan.

* *
*

152 ABBOTT, K. " Tom Sawyer's Town ", *Harper's W.*, vol. 57, 16-17, Aug. 9.

153 CARUS, Paul. " Mark Twain's Philosophy. " *Monist*, vol. 23, 181-223, April (Cf. nᵒ *140*).

154 MILLARD, Bailey. " When They Were Twenty-One. " *Bookman*, vol. 37, 298-299, May.

155 WIER, Jeanne Elizabeth. " Mark Twain's Relations to Nevada and to the West. " *Nevada Historical Society Papers*, vol. I, 99-104.

156 Anon. " Mark Twain as Publisher. " *Bookman*, vol. 36, 489-494, Jan.

1914

BIOGRAPHIES AND BOOKS OF CRITICISM :

None.

INTRODUCTIONS AND PREFACES :

157 RICHARDS, P. *Mark Twain Anekdoten*, gesammelt und mit einem Vorwort von P. Richards, mit neun Bild-beigaben. Berlin, Reflektor-Verlag, VIII + 222 pp.

OTHER BOOKS DEALING WITH MARK TWAIN :

158 BURTON, Richard. *Little Essays in Literature and Life.* New York, The Century Co., 356 pp.

A chapter on Twain, insists on his seriousness and even sadness, pp. 201-208.

159 MURET, Maurice. *Les Contemporains étrangers.* Lausanne, Payot, 2 vols.

On Mark Twain, vol. 2, pp. 133-189.

160 PHELPS, W. L. *Essays on Books.* New York, Macmillan, VII + 319 pp.

Contains " Notes on Mark Twain. "

161 UNDERWOOD, John C. *Literature and Insurgency.* New York, Mitchell Kennerley, 480 pp.

Contains " Democracy and Mark Twain " (pp. 1-40) which represents Twain as a democratic hero akin to Lincoln and Grant.

PERIODICAL LITERATURE :

162 HAWTHORNE, H. " Mark Twain and the Immortal Tom. " *St. Nicholas* (a children's magazine), vol. 42, 164-166, Dec.

163 Howe, J. Olin. " Twichell, Chum of Mark Twain. " *Boston Evening Transcript*, April 4.

164 Street, J. " In Mizzoura. " *Collier's*, vol. 53, 18-19, 31, Aug. 29.

165 Ticknor, C. " Mark Twain's Missing Chapter. " *Bookman*, vol. 39, 298-309, May.

Gives the text of a chapter of *Life on the Mississippi* in which the South was unfavourably compared to the North. Mark Twain suppressed it before publishing the book.

1915

BIOGRAPHIES AND BOOKS OF CRITICISM :

None.

OTHER BOOKS DEALING WITH MARK TWAIN :

166 JAMES, George Wharton. *The Lake of the Sky, Lake Tahoe*. Pasadena, Calif., G. W. James, XIII + 395 pp.

Two appendices on Mark Twain : " Mark Twain at Lake Tahoe ", pp. 359-362, and " Mark Twain and the Forest Rangers ", pp. 363-365.

167 KELLNER, Leon. *American Literature*, translated from the German by Julia Franklin, with a preface by Gustav Pollak, Garden City, Doubleday, Page and Co., XIV + 254 pp.

On Mark Twain, pp. 200-211 — full of inaccuracies, insists too much on the humour of " The Jumping Frog ". Cf. above n⁰ *142*.

168 PATTEE, F. L. *A History of American Literature since 1870*. New York, The Century Co., 449 pp.

On Mark Twain, Chapter III, pp. 45-62.

169 POLLAK, Gustav. (ed.). *Fifty Years of American Idealism* (Extracts from the New York *Nation*). Boston.

Reprints " Mark Twain " by Stuart P. Sherman ; (pp. 388-400) ; cf. 1910, n⁰ 75.

170 WHITE, Ida Belle. *Spirits Do Return*. Kansas City, Mo., The White Publishing Co., 251 pp.

" This book was written through the inspirational spirit of the well-known writer, Samuel L. Clemens, Mark Twain. "

171 YOUNG, John Philip. *Journalism in California*, San Francisco, Chronicle Publishing Co., x + 362 pp.

Contains a few pages on " Mark Twain's Contribution to the *San Francisco Chronicle* ".

PERIODICAL LITERATURE :

172 Corey, W. A. " Memories of Mark Twain. " *Overland M.*, n. s.,
vol. 66, 263-265, Sept.
>On Mark Twain in the West.

173 Anon. " Captain Horace E. Bixby ; who taught Mark Twain
how to pilot. " *New England Mag.*, n. s., vol. 52, 281-283, April.

174 — " Mark Twain's War Map. " *North Am.*, vol. 201, 827-829,
June.
>On Mark Twain's humorous map of Paris in 1870.

1916

BIOGRAPHIES AND BOOKS OF CRITICISM :

175 PAINE, Albert Bigelow. *The Boy's Life of Mark Twain;* The Story of a Man who made the world laugh and love him, with many anecdotes, letters, illustrations, etc... New York and London, Harper & Brothers, 354 pp. (had appeared serially in vol. 43 of *St. Nicholas*, a juvenile magazine).

OTHER BOOKS DEALING WITH MARK TWAIN :

176 FITCH, George Hamlin. *Great Spiritual Writers of America.* San Francisco, P. Elder & Co., XIX + 163 pp.
Insists most unspiritually on the success story in a chapter entitled " Mark Twain — Our Finest Humorist ", pp. 111-118.

PERIODICAL LITERATURE :

177 BOWEN, Edwin W. " Mark Twain. " *South Atlantic Quar.*, vol. 15, 250-268, July.

178 McCLELLAND, Clarence Paul. " Mark Twain and Bret Harte. " *Methodist Rev.*, series 5, vol. 32 (vol. 98), 75-85, Jan.
" The greater is undoubtedly Mark Twain, the most characteristically American of all writers. " (p. 75).

179 ROSEWATER, V. " How a Boy Secured a Unique Autograph of Mark Twain. " *St. Nicholas* (a juvenile magazine), vol. 43, 515, March.

180 Anon. " Capitalizing Mark Twain. " *Lit. Digest*, vol. 53, 959-960, Oct. 14.
On the exploitation of Mark Twain's reputation by Hannibal, his home-town.

181 — " Grant and Mark Twain were in neighboring towns at first of Civil War. " *Daily Chronicle-Herald* (Macon, Mo.), Dec. 11.

1917

BIOGRAPHIES AND BOOKS OF CRITICISM :

None.

INTRODUCTIONS AND PREFACES :

182 MARK TWAIN. *Letters*, arranged with comment by A. B. Paine.
New York & London, Harper & Brothers, 2 vols., 855 pp.
Some of these letters were previously published in *Harper's M.*,
vol. 134, 135.

OTHER BOOKS DEALING WITH MARK TWAIN :

183 BARRIE, Sir James M. *Who Was Sarah Findlay ? by Mark Twain
with a suggested solution of the mystery* by J. M. Barrie, London,
privately printed by Clement Shorter, 11 pp.

184 HERRON, Jap. *A Novel Written from the Ouija Board*, with an
introduction entitled " The Coming of Jap Herron. " New York.
Supposed to have been communicated from the " other side "
by Mark Twain.

185 LINDSAY, Vachel. *The Chinese Nightingale and Other Poems.*
New York, Macmillan, x + 127 pp.
Contains a poem entitled " Mark Twain and Joan of Arc ",
p. 47.

186 SHERMAN, Stuart P. *On Contemporary Literature.* New York, Henry
Holt & Co., 312 pp.
Pp. 18-49, " The Democracy of Mark Twain ". The author
sees in Twain predominantly the champion of American optimism
and ignores the undoubted pessimism of later works such as
The Mysterious Stranger.

PERIODICAL LITERATURE :

187 CLEMENS, Mildred Leo. " Tracking Mark Twain through Hawai. " *Sunset*, vol. 38, 7-9 + 95-98, May.

188 SHUSTER, G. N. " The Tragedy of Mark Twain. " *Catholic World*, vol. 104, 731-737, March.
Mark Twain's pessimism came from his lack of religious faith.

189 WHITE, Edgar. " Mark Twain's Printer Days. " *Overland M.*, n. s., vol. 70, 573-576, Dec.

190 WOODBRIDGE, H. E. " Mark Twain's Fatalism. " *Nation*, vol. 105, 399, Oct. 11.

191 WYATT, Edith. " Inspired Critic. " *North Am.*, vol. 205, 603-615, April.
On Mark Twain as a critic of American Democracy and Christian theology.

192 Anon. " Editing Mark Twain. " *Lit. Digest*, vol. 54, 127-128, Jan. 20.
On R. W. Gilder, the editor of *The Century Mag.*, who edited the text of *Huckleberry Finn* before publishing it in his magazine.

193 — " Mark Twain's Pen Picture of his all-too-human Brother. " *Current Opinion*, vol. 62, 351-352, May.
On Orion Clemens.

194 — " When Twain Conquered Grant. " *Lit. Digest*, vol. 55, 57, July 21.

195 — " Saving of Mark Twain. " *Lit. Digest*, vol. 55, 54-59, Nov. 24.
On H. H. Rogers who saved Mark Twain's " financial life ".

196 — " Mark Twain's Relation to Nevada and the West. " *Nevada Historical Society Papers*, 1913-1916, Carson City, Nevada.

UNPUBLISHED THESES :

197 SCOTT, Harold Philip. " *Mark Twain's Theory of Humor : An Analysis of the Laughable in Literature.* " An unpublished thesis for the University of Michigan, published in part as " The Laughable in Literature " in *The Fred Newton Scott Papers*, University of Chicago Press, 1929, pp. 241-262.
Contains frequent references to Mark Twain.

1918

BIOGRAPHIES AND BOOKS OF CRITICISM :

None.

INTRODUCTIONS AND PREFACES :

198 Mark Twain. *The Adventures of Huckleberry Finn*, with an introduction by Brander Matthews. New York & London, Harper & Brothers, xx + 404 pp.

OTHER BOOKS DEALING WITH MARK TWAIN :

199 Castellanos Jesús. *Los Optimistas*. Madrid, Editorial America, Biblioteca Andrés Bello, 219 pp.
>On Mark Twain, pp. 115-120. Ranks Twain with Cervantes and Molière.

200 Michaud, Régis. *Mystiques et Réalistes Anglo-Saxons, d'Emerson à Bernard Shaw*, Paris, A. Colin, 294 pp.
>Chap. v : " L'épopée humoristique de Mark Twain ", pp. 133-166. Good second-hand criticism.

201 Perry, Bliss. *The American Spirit in Literature*. New Haven, Yale University Press, x + 281 pp.
>On Twain, pp. 237-240, 265. The public seems now to prefer the writer of romance to the humorist.

202 Shoemaker, Floyd Calvin. *Missouri's Hall of Fame; Lives of Eminent Missourians*. Columbia, Mo., The Missouri Book Co., viii + 269 pp.
>Pp. 3-18 : " Samuel L. Clemens, Mark Twain, America's Greatest Humorist. "

PERIODICAL LITERATURE :

Reviews of Paine's edition of Mark Twain's *Letters* (1917).

203 HENDERSON, A. in *Bookman*, " A Laughing Philosopher. " Vol. 46, 583-584, Jan.

> Protests against Paine's lack of humour.

204 HOWELLS, W. D. in *Harper's M.*, " Editor's Easy Chair ", vol. 136, 602-604, March.

> Lays stress on Twain's wholesomeness, on his " good average American make ".

205 Anon. in *Current Opinion*, " Literature and Life Mirrored in Mark Twain's Letters ", vol. 64, 50-51, Jan.

> Wholesome literature at last !

*
* *

206 HYSLOP, James H. " The Return of Mark Twain. " *American Society of Psychical Research Journal*, vol. 12, 4-38, Jan.

207 S. D. " Democracy of Mark Twain. " *Public* (New York), vol. 21, 242-243, Feb. 23.

> Comments on *A Connecticut Yankee*.

208 Anon. " Mark Twain's Childhood Sweetheart Recalls their Romance. " *Lit. Digest*, vol. 56, 70-75. March 23.

> Mrs. Laura Frazer, the original of Becky Thatcher.

209 — " Mark Twain's Unedited and Unpublished Satire ; 3,000 years among the Microbes. " *Current Opinion*, vol. 65, 48-49, July.

1919

BIOGRAPHIES AND BOOKS OF CRITICISM :

None.

OTHER BOOKS DEALING WITH MARK TWAIN :

210 BOYNTON, Percy H. *A History of American Literature*. Boston, Ginn & Co., v + 513 pp.

Chapter xxv, " The West and Mark Twain " (pp. 380-395) discusses only *Innocents Abroad* and *Joan of Arc*.

211 ELLSWORTH, William Webster. *A Golden Age of Authors*. Boston, Houghton, Mifflin Co., xiii + 304 pp.

Cf. pp. 221-242, a chapter on Mark Twain chiefly made up of personal recollections.

212 FRANK, Waldo. *Our America*. New York, Boni and Liveright, xi + 232 pp.

On Mark Twain, pp. 38-44. According to the author, he was a victim of his environment, " a defeated soul ". First appearance of a thesis later to be developed by Van Wyck Brooks. Cf. Introduction, pp. 34-35.

213 HYSLOP, James Hervey (formerly professor of logic and ethics in Columbia University). *Contact with the Other World ;* the latest evidence as to communication with the dead. New York, The Century Co., 493 pp.

Contains a chapter on Mark Twain : Chap. xvi, pp. 249-281. The spirit of Twain claimed that he hever had to suppress anything he wanted to say in his lifetime.

214 WATTERSON, Henry. *Marse Henry — An Autobiography*. New York, George H. Doran Co., 2 vols.

A chapter on " Mark Twain — The Original of Col. Mulberry Sellers — The ' Earl of Durham ' ", pp. 119-133.

PERIODICAL LITERATURE :

215 Bosc, R. " Mark Twain et l'humour américain ". *Revue de Synthèse Historique*, vol. 29 (n. s., vol. 3), 181-187.

A discussion of Régis Michaud's chapter on Twain in *Les Mystiques et Réalistes Anglo-Saxons*.

216 Hyslop, J. H. " Mark Twain Returns ? " *Unpartizan Rev.*, vol. 12, 397-409, Oct.

Psychic experiments.

217 James, G. W. " Mark Twain ; An appreciation of his Pioneer Writing on Fasting and Health ", *Physical Culture*, May.

218 Milbank, E. P. " In Mark Twain Land. " *St. Nicholas*, vol. 46, 934, Aug.

219 Schoenemann, F. " Mark Twain and Adolf Wilbrandt. " *MLN*, vol. 34, 373-374, June.

Mark Twain saw the *Meister von Palmyra* in Vienna and was deeply impressed. Wilbrandt's philosophy was in harmony with his own pessimism and may have had some influence on *The Mysterious Stranger* and *What is Man?*

220 Woodbridge, H. E. " Mark Twain and the *Gesta Romanorum.* " *Nation*, vol. 108, 424-425, March 22.

On a possible source of *The Mysterious Stranger*.

221 Anon. " When Mark Twain Petrified the Brahmans. " *Lit. Digest*, vol. 62, 28-29, July 12.

About an article by E. B. Osborn in the (London) *Morning Post* on the speech which Twain delivered at the dinner given by the staff of the *Atlantic Monthly* to Whittier for his 70th birthday in 1877.

222 — " Belaboring the Brahmans again. " *Lit. Digest*, vol. 62, 31, Oct. 4.

1920

BIOGRAPHIES AND BOOKS OF CRITICISM :

223 PAINE, Albert Bigelow. *A Short Life of Mark Twain.* New York &
London, Harper & Brothers, 343 pp.

224 BROOKS, Van Wyck. *The Ordeal of Mark Twain.* New York,
E. P. Dutton & Co., VII + 267 pp.
> Presents Mark Twain as a thwarted genius. Cf. Introduction,
pp. 35-39.

INTRODUCTIONS AND PREFACES :

225 MARK TWAIN. *Letters,* with a biographical sketch and a commentary
by A. B. Paine. London, Chatto & Windus, XV + 433 pp.
> An abridged edition of the two volume collection of Mark
Twain *Letters* which had appeared in America in 1917. —
Cf. above n⁰ *182.*

226 — *Moments with Mark Twain,* selected by Albert Bigelow Paine.
New York and London, Harper & Brothers, 296 pp.
> Extracts from Mark Twain's works arranged in chronological
order.

227 — *The Prince and the Pauper* (with an introduction by Arthur
Hobson Quinn). New York and London, Harper & Brothers
(Harper's Modern Classics, ed. for educational use by Prof.
W. T. Brewster), XXX + 280 pp.

228 MARK TWAIN. *The Adventures of Tom Sawyer,* with an introduction
by Dr. Percy Boynton. New York & London, Harper & Broth
ers (Harper's Modern Classics ; cf. above n⁰ *227*), XXIV + 290 pp.

229 HOWELLS, W. D. *The Great Modern American Stories.* New York,
Boni & Liveright, XX + 432 pp.
> Contains " The Jumping Frog ".

230 JESSUP, Alexander, (ed.). *Best American Humorous Short Stories,*
New York, Boni & Liveright, 276 pp.
> Contains The " Jumping Frog " too.

OTHER BOOKS DEALING WITH MARK TWAIN :

231 ALDRICH, Mrs. Thomas Bailey. *Crowding Memories.* Boston,
Houghton Mifflin Co., VIII + 295 pp.
Contains some personal recollections of Mark Twain ; *passim.*

232 FARRAN I MAYORAL, J. *Llettres a un amiga estrangera.* Barcelona,
84 pp.

233 JAMES, William. *The Letters of William James,* ed. by his Son,
Henry James. Boston, The Atlantic Monthly Press, 2 vols.
Contains a few references to Twain whom W. James met
several times in Italy.

234 RICHEPIN, Jean. *L'Ame Américaine.* Paris, Flammarion, 317 pp.
On Mark Twain, chap. VII (pp. 155-174) : " Les Humoristes
— Marck (*sic*) Twain. " Rather poorly documented : " Je ne
sais si Marck (*sic*) Twain vit encore, je l'ignore ; en tout cas,
il doit être assez âgé... " (p. 173). Consists chiefly of quotations.

PERIODICAL LITERATURE :

1) Reviews of Van Wyck Brooks's *The Ordeal of Mark Twain* :

235 JOHNSON, Alvin. in *NR*, " The tragedy of Mark Twain. " vol. 23,
201-204, July 14.
Qualifies Brooks's thesis.

236 Anon. in *Weekly Rev.*, vol. 3, 108-109, Aug. 4.
Brooks has failed to prove his thesis.

*
* *

2) Reviews of A. B. Paine's new edition of Mark Twain's
Letters :

237 Anon. in *TLS*, Sept. 23, 615.
The letters reveal the conscientious craftsmanship of Twain.

238 — in *New Statesman*, vol. 15, 707-710, Oct. 2. (extracts from this
review were published in the *Lit. Digest*, vol. 67, 34-35, Nov. 13,
under the title of " Taming Mark Twain ").

239 Anon. in *Living Age*, vol. 307, 555-557, Nov. 27.

*
* *

240 BRADFORD, Gamaliel. " Mark Twain. " *Atlantic M.*, vol. 125,
462-473, April.

Follows Paine's interpretation (cf. above n⁰ *113*) but insists on the melancholy and lack of religious faith of Mark Twain.

241 Brooks, Van Wyck. " Mark Twain's Humour. " *Dial*, vol. 68, 275-291, March.

An abridged version of Chap. viii of his book. Cf. above n⁰ *224*.

242 — " The Genesis of *Huckleberry Finn.* " *The Freeman*, I, March 31.

243 — " Mark Twain's Satire. " *Dial*, vol. 68, 424-443, April.

An abridged version of chapter x of his book ; cf. above n⁰ *224*.

244 Eyck, A. Ten. " Uncle Sam's Tin Halo ; Something about Mark Twain, Europe and the Poor American Diplomat. " *Outlook*, vol. 126, 724-727. Dec. 22.

Almost nothing on Twain contrary to what the title would lead one to expect.

245 Matthews, Brander. Memories of Mark Twain. *Sat. Evg. Post*, vol. 192, 14-15, March 6.

246 — " Mark Twain and the Art of Writing. " *Harper's M.*, vol. 141, 635-643, Oct.

On Mark Twain mastery of style.

247 O'Day, E. Clarence. " Stories from the Files. " *Overland M.*, n. s., vol. 75, 326-328, 407-409, 517-519, April-June.

Stories sent by Twain to the *Overland M.*, during his stay in Europe in 1868.

248 Peckham, H. Houston. " The Literary Status of Mark Twain, 1877-1890. " *South Atlantic Quar.*, vol. 19, 332-340.

A superficial study.

249 Phillips, M. J. " Mark Twain's Partner. " *Sat. Evg. Post*, vol. 193, 22-23, 69-73, Sept. 11.

On Calvin H. Highbie who is mentioned in *Roughing It.*

250 Schoenemann, Friedrich. " Amerikanischer Humor. " *Germanistisch-Romanistische Monatsschrift*, vol. 8, 152-154, 216-227.

1921

BIBLIOGRAPHIES :

251 RINAKER, Clarissa. Bibliography of Mark Twain in the *Cambridge History of American Literature*, vol. 4, pp. 635-639.

BIOGRAPHIES AND BOOKS OF CRITICISM :

None.

INTRODUCTIONS AND PREFACES :

252 RAMSAY, Robert L. *Short Stories of America*, edited with an introductory essay, course outline and reading lists. New York, Boston, Houghton, Mifflin Co., xi + 348 pp.
Pp. 5, 15-16 devoted to Mark Twain.

253 VAN VECHTEN, Carl. *Lords of the Housetops*, Thirteen cat tales, with a preface. New York, A. A. Knopf, xiii + 238 pp.
Pp. 144-148, " Dick Baker's Cat. "

OTHER BOOKS DEALING WITH MARK TWAIN :

254 HAM, George H. *Reminiscences of a Raconteur, between the forties and the twenties*. Toronto, The Masson Book Co., xvi + 330 pp.
A chapter on " Mark Twain, The Great Humorist ", pp. 142-147.

255 MATTHEWS, Brander. *Essays on English*. New York, Charles Scribner's Sons, 284 pp.
A chapter on " Mark Twain and the Art of Writing ",
pp. 243-268 ; an article published in *Harper's M.* in 1920.

256 SHERMAN, Stuart P. " Mark Twain " in *Cambridge History of American Literature*, vol. 3, pp. 1-20.

A severe critical survey laying stress on the unevenness of Mark Twain's works whether travel books or fiction.

257 VAN DOREN, Carl. *The American Novel.* New York, Macmillan, IX + 295 pp.

On Mark Twain, pp. 157-187. He is given as much space as Howells and Henry James.

PERIODICAL LITERATURE :

Review of Van Wyck Brooks's *The Ordeal of Mark Twain* :

258 BURTON, Richard, in *Bookman,* " The Mystery of Personality. " vol. 52, 333-337, Jan.

The author who was a friend and neighbour of Mark Twain at Hartford accuses Brooks of subduing the data to buttress his *a priori* thesis.

*
* *

259 HEWLETT, Maurice. " Mark Twain and Sir Walter Scott. " *Sewanee Rev.,* vol. 29, 130-133, April-June.

260 MORISSEY, F. R. " The Ancestor of the Jumping Frog. " *Bookman,* vol. 53, 143-145, April.

A true story about grasshoppers in Virginia, which, according to the author, may have been the source of Mark Twain's tale.

261 SCHOENEMANN, Friedrich. " Mark Twains Weltanschauung ". *Englische Studien,* vol. 55, 53-84.

262 Anon. " A Scotch Tilt against Mark Twain. " *Lit. Digest,* vol. 68, 35, Jan.8.

On Robert Blatchford who had attacked Mark Twain in the *Clarion* because of his condemnation of Walter Scott.

263 — " Tom, Mark and Huck. " *Eng. Journ.,* vol. 10, 403-404. Sept.

1922

BIOGRAPHIES AND BOOKS OF CRITICISM :

264 Brooks, Van Wyck. *The Ordeal of Mark Twain*. London, W. Heinemann, vii + 267 pp.
This is the English edition of nº *224*.

265 Fisher, Henry, W. *Abroad with Mark Twain and Eugene Field*.
— Tales they told to a fellow-correspondent. New York,
N. L. Brown, xxi + 246 pp.
Anecdotes about Mark Twain (pp. xv-xvi, 25-219).

*266 Public Meeting under the Auspices of the American Academy and
the National Institute of Arts and Letters Held at Carnegie Hall,
New York, Nov. 30, 1910 in Memory of Samuel Langhorne
Clemens (Mark Twain)*. New York, American Academy of
Arts and Letters, 103 pp.
Addresses by W. D. Howells, Joseph H. Coate, Joseph H. Twi-
chell, Joseph G. Cannon, Champ Clark, George W. Cable, Col.
Henry Watterson + a poem by Henry Van Dyke.
Personal recollections.

INTRODUCTIONS AND PREFACES :

267 Mark Twain. *Die Abenteuer Tom Sawyers und Huckleberry Finns*.
Berlin, Mitteldeutsche Verlangstalt, Lehmann and Fink,
iv + 236 pp.
An introduction signed by Dr. Franz Kwest.

268 Mark Twain. *Contes Choisis*, traduits par Gabriel de Lautrec
et précédés d'une étude sur l'humour. Paris, Nelson, 283 pp.

269 Masson, Thomas Lansing. *Our American Humorists*. New York,
Moffat, Yard & Co., 448 pp.
A few anecdotes on Mark Twain in the introduction, but he
is not represented in the selection.

OTHER BOOKS DEALING WITH MARK TWAIN :

270 ADE, George. *Single Blessedness and Other Observations.* New York, Doubleday, Page & Co., VIII + 224 pp.
A chapter entitled " Mark Twain — Emissary ", pp. 203-210, containing a few remarks on his popularity.

271 AYERS, Col. James. *Gold and Sunshine,* Reminiscences of Early California, Boston, R. G. Badger, XIV + 359 pp.
Contains a chapter on " Mark Twain in Honolulu ", pp. 223-227.

272 BRADFORD, Gamaliel. *American Portraits.* Boston and New York, Houghton, Mifflin Co., XII + 248 pp.
A chapter on " Mark Twain, the Giver of Mirth " (pp. 1-28), in which he is accused of being more iconoclastic and irreligious than Voltaire.

273 " A BURGLAR ". *In the Clutch of Circumstances. — My Own Story.* New York, London, D. Appleton Co., 272 pp.
Contains a chapter on " The Mark Twain Burglary ", pp. 168-182, an incident told by A. B. Paine in his *Biography,* vol. 3, pp. 1462-1463.

274 HOWE, M. A. De Wolfe. *Memories of a Hostess,* A Chronicle of Eminent Friendships, Boston, The Atlantic Monthly Press, 312 pp.
Pp. 244-256, on Mark Twain's life at Hartford in 1876.

275 MATTHEWS, Brander. *The Tocsin of Revolt, and Other Essays.* New York, Charles Scribner's Sons, 295 pp.
Pp. 253-294, " Memories of Mark Twain ".

276 WADE, Mrs. May Hazleton Blanchard. *Real Americans.* Boston, Little, Brown & Co., VIII + 277 pp.
A chapter on " Mark Twain, the Giver of Mirth ", (pp. 192-241) which is merely a sentimental biographical sketch.

PERIODICAL LITERATURE :

1) Review of Brooks's *The Ordeal of Mark Twain* :
277 Anon. in *TLS,* Oct. 26, p. 678.
A mere summary of Brooks's thesis.

*
* *

2) Reviews of Fisher's *Abroad with Mark Twain and E. Field* :
278 L. B. in *Freeman* (New York), vol. 5, 429, p. 10.

279 Pearson, E. L. in *Independent*, vol. 108, 353, April 8.
     Unfavourable.

280 Anon. in *Lit. Rev.*, April 1, 550.

281 — in *Boston Transcript*, April 8, p. 10.

282 — in *Dial.*, vol. 73, 235, Aug.

* *
*

3) Review of *Bummel durch Europe (A Tramp Abroad)* :

283 Schoenemann, Friedrich. in *Das literarische Echo*, vol. 25, p. 177,
     Nov. 1.

* *
*

284 Holmes, Ralph. " Mark Twain and Music. " *Century*, vol. 104,
     844-850, Oct. (also in *Etude*, vol. 41, 295-296, May).

285 Howe, M. A. DeWolfe. " Bret Harte and Mark Twain in the
     seventies, passages from the diaries of Mrs. James T. Fields. "
     Atlantic Monthly, vol. 130, 341-348, Sept.
     James T. Fields had been editor of the *Atlantic Monthly*.

286 McCutcheon, George Barr. " When Mark Twain Was a ' New '
     Writer. " *The Lit. Digest International Book Rev.*, vol. I, 16-17,
     Dec.
     A review of *The Writings of Mark Twain*.

287 Moore, O. H. " Mark Twain and *Don Quixote*.'" *PMLA*, vol. 37,
     324-346, June.
     Mark Twain, a well-read writer, was influenced by *Don
     Quixote* when he composed *Huckleberry Finn*. Cf. nᵒ *1319* and
     Introduction p. LXVI.

288 Schoenemann, F. " Amerikanisch Mark Twain-Literatur. "
     Englische Studien, vol. 56, 148-153.

289 Anon. " Tells of Mark Twain's Brief Soldiery in 1861. " *Courier-
     Post* (Hannibal, Mo.), Sept. 2.

1923

BIOGRAPHIES AND BOOKS OF CRITICISM :

None.

INTRODUCTIONS AND PREFACES :

290 MARK TWAIN. *Europe and Elsewhere*, with an appreciation by Brander Matthews and an introduction by A. B. Paine. New York and London, Harper & Brothers, xxxv + 406 pp.

291 — *Life on the Mississippi*, with an introduction by J. W. Rankin. New York and London, Harper & Brothers, xvii + 526 pp. (Modern Classics). (Another issue : xxiv + 173 pp.).

292 — *Speeches*, with an introduction by A. B. Paine and an appreciation by W. D. Howells, New York & London, Harper & Brothers, xv + 396 pp.

293 JESSUP, Alexander. *Representative American Short Stories*. Boston, New York, Allyn & Bacon, xxviii + 974 pp.
    Pp. 343-347, " The Jumping Frog ".

OTHER BOOKS DEALING WITH MARK TWAIN :

294 BECHHOFER, C. E. *The Literary Renaissance in America*. London, William Heinemann, Ltd., xi + 138 pp.
    Pp. 2-7, a discussion of Brooks's thesis which Bechhofer thinks is the best way of accounting for Mark Twain's pessimism.

295 BRIDGES, Horace James. *As I Was Saying — A Sheaf of Essays and Discourses*. Boston, Marshall Jones Co., xiii + 268 pp.
    Contains a chapter (pp. 35-51) on " The Pessimism of Mark Twain ". According to him, satire inevitably leads to pessimism.

296 HARRIS, Frank. *Contemporary Portraits*, 4th series. New York, Brentano's, 318 pp.

Contains a savage attack on Mark Twain : " Memories of Mark Twain ", pp. 162-173.

297 HOLT,Henry. *Garrulities of an Octogenarian Editor.* Boston, Houghton, Mifflin Co., viii + 460 pp.

298 JOHNSON, Robert Underwood. *Remembered Yesterdays.* Boston, Little, Brown & Co., xxi + 624 pp.

A chapter of personal recollections on Mark Twain, pp. 319-325.

299 MATTHEWS, Brander. *Playwrights on Playmaking.* New York, London, Charles Scribner's Sons, xiii + 315 pp.

A chapter on " Mark Twain and the Theatre ", pp. 159-184.

300 O'BRIEN, Edward J. *The Advance of the American Short Story.* New York, Dodd, Mead & Co., 302 pp.

Devotes a chapter to " Bret Harte and Mark Twain " (98-116), but gives more space to the former and adopts Brooks's thesis.

301 PHELPS, W. L. *Some Makers of American Literature.* Boston, Marshall Jones Co., ix + 187 pp.

A chapter on " The American Humorist : Mark Twain ", (pp. 163-187).

302 VAN DOREN, Carl. *The Roving Critic.* New York, A. A. Knopf, 262 pp.

In a chapter entitled " The Lion and the Uniform " (pp. 45-55), the author discusses Brooks's thesis which he thinks " substantially accurate as well as brilliant ", but too systematic and exhibiting instances of special pleading.

PERIODICAL LITERATURE :

1) Review of Mark Twain's *Tolle Geschichten* :

303 SCHOENEMANN, F. in *Die Literatur*, vol. 26, p. 179, Dec.

* *

2) Reviews of *Europe and Elsewhere* :

304 BERGENGREN, Ralph. in *Boston Transcript*, Oct. 13, p. 2.

305 Anon. in *Springfield Republican*, Oct. 26, p. 16.

* *

3) Reviews of Mark Twain's *Speeches* :

306 COOK, S. L. in *Boston Transcript*, June 16, p. 3.

307 HUTCHISON, Percy A. in *New York Times Book Rev.*, June 10, p. 8.

These speeches show that Twain was not a pessimist.

308 MATTHEWS, Brander. " Mark Twain stands and delivers " in *Lit. Digest International Book Rev.*, vol. I, 9, 23-24, 57.
Insists on the careful preparation of Mark Twain's speeches, a proof of his artistry.

309 Anon. in *New Yort World*, May 27, p. 7.

310 — in *Springfield Republican*, June 22, p. 16.

311 — in *Outlook*, vol. 134, 287-288, June 27.
A good deal of the original humour is lost in the printed text.

*
* *

4) Reviews of Brooks's *The Ordeal of Mark Twain* :

312 KREYMBORG, Alfred. *in Spectator*, vol. 130, 701, April 28.
Praises Brooks's " passion for intellectual honesty ". Sees in Twain " America's last buffoon ".

313 FISHER, Samuel J. " Mark Twain ", *Spectator*, vol. 130, 922, June 2.
Answers Kreymborg and tries to refute Brook's thesis.

*
* *

313* CANBY, Henry S. " Mark Twain. " *Lit. Review*, vol. 4, 201-202, Nov. 3.

314 LINDSAY, Vachel, " Mark Twain ". *NR*, Dec. 5.
Reviewing the Inner Santum Edition of *The Prince and the Pauper*, he devotes a paragraph to Twain's worship of Woman.

315 PHELPS, W. H. " Mark Twain, the American Humorist. " *Ladie's Home Journal*, vol. 40, 18, March.
Cf. his book.

316 SCHOENEMANN, F. " Mr. Samuel L. Clemens. " *Archiv für das Studium der neueren Sprachen und Literaturen*, Band 144, 184-213.
A biographical sketch based on Twain's *Letters*.

317 UNDERHILL, Irving S. " Diamonds in the Rough ; Being the Story of Another Book that Mark Twain Never Wrote. " *Colophon*, Pt XIII.

318 Anon. " Missouri Honors the Prince of Humorists. " *Lit. Digest*, vol. 78, 30, Aug. 11.

UNPUBLISHED THESES :

319 DURRIGL, Karl. *Die Abweichungen vom Standard English in ' The Adventures of Tom Sawyer' von Mark Twain.* University of Vienna. (Cf. *AL*, vol. 21, 351, Nov. 1949).

1924

BIOGRAPHIES AND BOOKS OF CRITICISM :

320 FINGER, Charles J. *Mark Twain, The Philosopher Who Laughed at the World.* Girard, Kansas, Haldeman-Julius Co., 64 pp.
Pays homage to Mark Twain's condemnation of mob-rule and anti-semitism.

321 GILLIS, William R. *Memories of Mark Twain and Steve Gillis,* a record of mining experiences, Sonora, Calif., Printed by *The Banner,* 96 pp.

INTRODUCTIONS AND PREFACES :

322 MARK TWAIN. *Autobiography,* with an introduction by A. B. Paine. New York and London, Harper & Brothers, 2 vols., XVI + 368 + 365.
" Chapters from My Autobiography " were published in the *North Am.* from Sept. 1906 to Dec. 1907. They had been passed for publication by Mark Twain himself. A. B. Paine revised and expurgated the text for publication in book form.

323 FRENCH, Joseph Lewis (ed.). *Sixty Years of American Humor — A Prose Anthology.* Boston, Little, Brown & Co., x + 401 pp.
Contains a notice on Twain and " The Jumping Frog " (original version, French translation and Mark Twain's retranslation from the French), pp. 57-74.

OTHER BOOKS DEALING WITH MARK TWAIN :

324 BOYNTON, Percy H. *Some Contemporary Americans — The Personal Equation in Literature.* Chicago, The University of Chicago Press, IX + 289 pp.
A chapter on " Biography and Personal Equation " (pp. 242-264) discusses Paine's, Howells's and Brooks's books on Mark

Twain, disapproves of Brooks's systematic dissent from accepted opinion. Also some comments on Bradford's portrait of Twain.

325 CANBY, H. S. *Definitions : 2nd series.* New York, Harcourt, Brace & Co., x + 308 pp.

On Mark Twain, pp. 157-165 ; an article published in 1923 in the *Lit. Rev.* (cf. *313**).

326 JORDAN-SMITH, Paul. *On Strange Altars — A Book of Enthusiasms.* New York, A. & C. Boni, 293 pp.

Claims that Mark Twain's pessimism is not synonymous with despair.

327 LEISY, Ernest E. *American Literature, An Interpretative Survey.* New York, Thomas Y. Crowell Co., x + 299 pp.

" The irreverence of *Innocents Abroad* was not directed so much at old world institutions... as at the romantic tourist with his sentimental conception of art and travel " (pp. 171-172). " Mark Twain's pessimism, ironical as it may seem, is at bottom sentimental... " (p. 178).

328 MITCHELL, Edward Page. *Memoirs of an Editor.* New York, Charles Scribner's Sons, xii + 458 pp.

Contains scattered references to Twain.

329 O'HIGGINS, Harvey & REEDE, Edward H. *The American Mind in Action.* New York & London, Harper & Brothers, 336 pp.

A chapter on Twain, pp. 26-49, takes up again Brooks's thesis : Mark Twain " was as profound a biological failure as America has produced. "

330 ROBINSON, Kenneth Allan, and Others (compilers). *Essays Towards Truth.* New York, Henry Holt & Co., VII + 395.

Contains Stuart P. Sherman's essay on " The Democracy of Mark Twain " (pp. 368-395), reprinted from *On Contemporary Literature*, 1917.

331 SHAW, G. B. *Saint Joan.* London, Constable & Co., LXIV + 114 pp.

Several references to Twain's *Joan of Arc* in the preface (" The Maid in Literature ", " Protestant Misunderstanding of the Middle Ages ").

PERIODICAL LITERATURE :

Reviews of Mark Twain's *Autobiography* :

332 LITTELL, Robert. in *NR*, vol. 40, 230, Oct. 29.

A disappointing book.

333 MATTHEWS, Brander. in *International Book Rev.*, " The Truth about Mark Twain ", vol. 2, 845-848, Nov.

Favourable.

334 Pearson, E. L. in *Outlook*, " Huckleberry and Sherlock, vol. 138, 256-257, Oct. 15.

" ... here is one reader of Mark Twain... who regrets that the book has been published. "

335 Rogers, Cameron. in *World's Work*, " In Which Mark Twain Reveals Himself ", vol. 48, 679-681, Oct.

Enthusiastic.

336 Seitz Don C. in *Bookman*, vol. 60, 446-448, Dec.

337 Van Doren, Carl. " Posthumous Thunder ", in *SRL*, vol. 1, 225, Oct. 25.

Twain's relative failure was caused by his own lack of discipline rather than by some hidden neurosis.

338 Van Doren, Mark. in *Nation*, vol. 119, 524, Nov. 12.

A shapeless book, but a great one.

339 Anon. in *TLS*, Nov. 6, p. 701.

340 — " Self-Revelation of our Greatest Humorist. " in *Current Opinion*, vol. 77, 578-580, Nov.

*
* *

341 Clemens, Clara. " My Father. " *Mentor*, vol. 12, pp. 21-23, May.

342 Larom, W. H. " Mark Twain in the Adirondacks. " *Bookman*, vol. 58, 536-538, Jan.

343 Marshall, Archibald. " Huckleberry Finn. " *International Book Rev.*, vol. 2, 104, 106, Jan.

344 Matthews, Brander. " Mark Twain as Speech-Maker and Story-Teller. " *Mentor*, vol. 12, 24-28, May.

345 Mierow, H. E. " Cicero and Mark Twain. " *Classical Jour.*, vol. 20, 167-169, Dec.

A parallel between Cicero and Mark Twain after each of them had lost a beloved daughter.

346 Nelson, W. H. " Mark Twain Out West. " *Methodist Quar. Rev.*, vol. 73, 65-83, Jan.

347 Paine, A. B. " Mark Twain, Boy and Man. " *Mentor*, vol. 12, 3-20, May.

348 Rice, C. " Mark Twain as his Physician Knew Him ". *Mentor*, vol. 12, 48-49, May.

349 Rodgers, Cleveland. " The Many Sided Mark Twain. " *Ibid.*, 29-44.

350 Seabright, J. M. " A Shrine to the Prince of Humorists. " *International Book Rev.*, vol. 2, 848-849, Nov.

On the Mark Twain Memorial Park at Florida, Mo.

351 STEINDORFF, Ulrich. " Mark Twain's Broad German Grin. " *New York Times*, July 13, III, 6A.

352 STRATE, J. B. " Mark Twain and Geography. " *Journal of Geography*, vol. 23, 81-92, March.
On the geographical descriptions in Twain's works.

353 WHITE, Edgar. " The Old Home Town. " *Mentor*, vol. 12, 51-53, May.

354 Anon. " Conrad pays tribute to Mark Twain. " *Mentor*, vol. 12, p. 45, May.

355 — " Mark Twain and General Grant. " *Mentor*, vol. 12, pp. 46-47.

356 — " One Love of a Lifetime. " *Ibid.*, p. 50.

357 — " Mark Twain Memorial Park. " *Ibid.*, pp. 54-55.

358 — " Gleams of Mark Twain's Humor. " *Ibid.*, pp. 56-58.

359 — " Mark Twain, Radical. " *SRL*, vol. I, 241, Nov. 1.
An attempt to refute Brooks's thesis. Mark Twain *was* a radical and not a cowardly conformist.

UNPUBLISHED THESES :

360 POCHMANN, Henry A. *The Mind of Mark Twain*, M. A. thesis, University of Texas.

1925

BIOGRAPHIES AND BOOKS OF CRITICISM :

361 LAWTON, Mary. *A Lifetime with Mark Twain : The Memoirs of Katy Leary, for Thirty Years His Faithful and Devoted Servant.* New York, Harcourt, Brace & Co., xviii + 352 pp. (parts of it appeared serially in the *Pictorial Rev.*, vol. 26, April-Sept. 1925 and in *Lit. Digest*, vol. 85, 36-40 & 86, 38-40).

362 SCHOENEMANN, Friedrich. *Mark Twain als Literarische Persönlichkeit.* Jena, Heft 8 der Jenaer germanistischen Forschungen, 119 pp.

Summed up in Hemminghaus, *Mark Twain in Germany*, 1939, pp. 97-122. An interesting study in sources and influences which shows that Twain was much better read than is commonly realized. Cf. Introduction, p. 15.

INTRODUCTIONS AND PREFACES :

363 MARK TWAIN, *1601, or Conversation at the Social Fireside As It Was in the Time of the Tudors*, introduction by Charles Erskine Wood, and other letters by Mark Twain. New York, Grabhorn Press.

364 CLARK, Barrett H. & LIEBER Maxim. *Great Short Stories of the World*, New York, R. M. McBride & Co., xv + 1072 pp.

Contains a biographical sketch and " Journalism in Tennessee ", pp. 950-955.

OTHER BOOKS DEALING WITH MARK TWAIN :

365 CATHER, Katherine, Dunlap. *Younger Days of Famous Writers.* New York & London, The Century Co., xiii + 326 pp.

The chapter entitled " The Boy That Went Back ", pp. 185-204, is about Mark Twain.

366 COLLINS, Joseph. *The Doctor Looks at Biography;* Psychological Studies of Life and Letters. New York, George H. Doran Co., x + 344 pp.

> Pp. 73-79, a chapter on " Mark Twain ".

367 GILLIS, James M. *False Prophets.* New York, Macmillan, 201 pp.

> Contains a chapter on Mark Twain, pp. 125-145, " the greatest cynic and infidel that America has produced ".

368 HOPPE, Willie. *Thirty Years of Billiards.* New York, G. P. Putnam's Sons, VIII + 255 pp.

> On Twain as a billiard-player.

369 SINCLAIR, Upton. *Mammon art; An Essay in Economic Interpretation.* Pasadena, Calif., The author, VI + 390 pp.

> " The Uncrowned King " (pp. 326-333) is Mark Twain ; but according to Sinclair, who adopted Brooks's interpretation, he sold his soul to the bourgeoisie of his time.

370 TANDY, Jennette Reid. *Crackerbox Philosophers in American Humor and Satire.* New York, Columbia University Press, XI + 181 pp.

> On Mark Twain, pp. 139-141.

371 WATKINS, Louise W. *Four Short Stories and a Play.* Los Angeles, Calif., privately printed, 78 pp.

> Contains a short essay on Twain.

PERIODICAL LITERATURE :

1) Reviews of Mark Twain's *Autobiography* (1924) :

372 BEERS, Henry A. in *YR*, vol. 15, 162-165, Oct.

373 BIRON, Charles. in *London Mercury*, vol. 11, 325-326, Jan.

> An incoherent book ; Twain was a lovable man with no artistic sense.

374 VAN DOREN Carl. in *Century*, vol. 109, 429-430, Jan.

> A fascinating collection of raw materials.

*

2) Reviews of Mary Lawton's *A Lifetime with Mark Twain* :

375 Anon. in *SRL*, vol. 2, 442, Dec. 26.

> Full of trivialities, but it shows that Twain could be a hero to his servant.

*
* *

3) Reviews of Schönemann's *Mark Twain als literarische Persönlichkeit* :

376 BRANDL, A. in *Die Literatur*, vol. 28, 627-628.

377 ELLINGER, J. in *Ang. Bbl*, vol. 36, 372-374, Dec.

378 LUEDEKE, H. in *Deutsche Literaturzeitung*, vol. 2, 1802-1813.

379 RANDALL, A. W. G. in *SRL*, vol. 2, 108, Sept. 5.
The first systematic attempt to show the literary side of Mark Twain's genius.

*
* *

4) Reviews of Mark Twain's *Complete Writings* (The Florida Edition, Chatto & Windus) :

380 HARWOOD, H. C. in *Spectator*, vol. 135, 1146-1148, Dec.

381 WOOLF, Leonard. in *Nation & Athenaeum*, vol. 37, 765, Sept. 26.

*
* *

382 BRAGMAN, Louis J. " The Medical Wisdom of Mark Twain. " *Annals of Medical History*, vol. 7, 425-439.
Made up of extracts from his works.

383 FEDERICO, P. J. " Mark Twain as an Inventor. " *Journal of Patent Office Society*, vol. 8, 75-79.

384 HIGGINS, A. C. " She Was Mark Twain's Sweetheart. " *Collier's*, vol. 75, 32, June 27.
On Mrs. Hawkins Frazer.

385 INGLIS, R. B. " A Lesson on Mark Twain. " *Eng. Jour.*, vol. 14, 221-232, March.
A model lesson on Mark Twain for secondary school teachers.

386 PAINE, A. B. " Innocents at Home ; How Mark Twain dictated his life story. " *Collier's*, vol. 75, 5-6, Jan. 3.

387 SCHOENEMANN, F. " Mark Twains Autobiographie. " *Hanoverscher Kurier*, Aug. 5 ; also in *Magdeburger Zeitung*, Oct. 4.

388 VAN DOREN, Carl. " Mark Twain and Bernard Shaw. " *Century*, vol. 109, pp. 705-710, March.

389 WEBSTER, Doris and Samuel. " Whitewashing Jane Clemens. " *Bookman*, vol. 61, 531-535.

A discussion of Brooks's thesis, but more gossipy than scholarly.

390 WHITE, E. " Tom Sawyer and Huckleberry Finn Memorial Statue. " *Mentor*, vol. 13, 54-55, Oct.

391 Anon. " Mark Twain as a billiard fan. " *Lit. Digest*, vol. 86, 55, July 25.

BIOGRAPHIES AND BOOKS OF CRITICISM :

392 MAYFIELD, John S. *Mark Twain vs. the Street Railway Co.* (New York), with an introduction by Charles J. Finger, n. p., privately printed, 25 pp.

INTRODUCTIONS AND PREFACES :

393 MARK TWAIN. *Rapporto della visita di Capitan Tempesta in Paradiso*, trad. di Laura Balini, prefazione di Conrado Alvaro. Aquila, Vecchioni ed., 113 pp.

394 CESTRE, Charles & GAGNOT, B. *Anthologie de la Littérature Américaine.* Paris, Delagrave, 402 pp.
On Mark Twain, p. 256 ; extracts, pp. 257-266.

OTHER BOOKS DEALING WITH MARK TWAIN :

395 HOWELL, John (ed.). *Sketches of the Sixties by Bret Harte and Mark Twain*, Being forgotten material now collected for the first time from *The Californian*. San Francisco, John Howell (author's edition).

396 BACHELLER, Irving. *Opinions of a Cheerful Yankee.* Indianapolis, The Bobbs-Merrill Co., 224 pp.
Interviews with Mark Twain, pp. 6-11.

397 GOURMONT, Rémy de. *Promenades Littéraires, 6e série.* Paris, Mercure de France, 240 pp.
On Mark Twain, pp. 126-138.

398 GRIMES, Absalom. *Confederate Mail Runner*, ed. from Captain's Grimes' Own Story by M. M. Quaife, New Haven, Yale University Press, XII + 216 pp.
Contains a chapter entitled " Campaigning with Mark Twain. "

399 HALDEMAN-JULIUS, Emmanuel. *Iconoclastic Literary Reactions.* Kansas City, Kansas, Big Blue Book, No B-16.
Contains three articles on Mark Twain.

400 MUMFORD, Lewis. *The Golden Day ; A Study in American Experience and Culture.* New York, Boni & Liveright, 283 pp.
On Mark Twain, pp. 170-179 ; a re-statement of Brooks's thesis.

401 NYE, Edgar Wilson. *Bill Nye, His Own Life Story,* continuity by Frank Wilson Nye. New York, The Century Co., xx + 412 pp.
On Bill Nye, cf. Paine's *Biography,* vol. 2, pp. 876-877.

402 PHELPS, W. L. *As I Like It, 3rd series.* New York, London, Scribner's Sons, xv + 309 pp.
Contains several short articles on Twain : " Autobiography ", pp. 99-100, " Statue of Huckleberry Finn and Tom Sawyer at Hannibal ", pp. 212-257.

403 SHERWOOD, Robert Edmund. *Here We Are Again — Recollections of an Old Circus Clown.* Indianapolis, The Bobbs-Merrill Co., 292 pp.
Pp. 213-218, " Regarding Tom Sawyer and Others. "

404 TURNER, Walter James. *Great Names ; Being an anthology of English and American literature from Chaucer to Francis Thompson.* New York, L. MacVeagh, The Dial Press, xi + 282 pp.
Contains " Mark Twain " by David Garnett.

PERIODICAL LITERATURE :

Reviews of Schönemann's *Mark Twain als literarische Persönlichkeit* (1925).

405 FISCHER, W. in *Englische Studien,* vol. 61, 135-139.

406 JANTZEN, H. in *Zeitschrift für französischen und englischen Unterricht,* vol. 25, 368-369.

407 JONES, Howard Mumford. in *JEGP,* vol. 25, 130-131, Jan.

* *

408 CHILDS, Marquis W. " The Home of Mark Twain. " *Am. Merc.,* vol. 9, 101-105, Sept.
A satirical description of Hannibal.

409 DONOVAN, M. M. " Custodian of a Famous Cabin : Mark Twain's Cabin on Jackass Hill. ' *Sunset,* vol. 57, 47, Sept.

410 Anon. " Sam Clemens in Sideburns to Dear Friend Annie. " *Lit. Digest*, vol. 89, 36-46, May 8.

Letters which Mark Twain sent from New Orleans to Annie Elizabeth Taylor, the 17 year-old daughter of a Mississippi pilot.

UNPUBLISHED THESES :

411 Roades, Sister Mary Teresa. *Cervantes and Mark Twain*, M. A. thesis for the Univ. of Kansas.

Cf. below nº *1329*.

1927

BIOGRAPHIES AND BOOKS OF CRITICISM :

None.

INTRODUCTIONS AND PREFACES :

412 MARK TWAIN. *The Innocents Abroad*, with an introduction by A. B. Paine. New York, Macmillan, XVI + 537 pp.
A mere biographical sketch.

413 HOWELL, John (ed.). *Sketches of the Sixties by Bret Harte and Mark Twain*. San Francisco, John Howell. (second ed. with new material and illustrations) (cf. 1926).

414 LIEBER, Maxim (ed.). *Great Stories of All Nations*. New York, Tudor Publishing Co., XII + 1132 pp.
On Mark Twain, pp. 613-614.

415 PATTEE, F. L. (ed.). *Century Readings in the American Short Story*. New York, London, The Century Co., IX + 562 pp.
Pp. 207-215, " The Facts Concerning the Recent Carnival of Crime. "

OTHER BOOKS DEALING WITH MARK TWAIN :

416 BENNETT, James O'Donnell. *Much Loved Books — Best Sellers of the Ages*. New York, Boni & Liveright, IX + 460 pp.
Pp. 210-216 : " Mark Twain's *Adventures of Huckleberry Finn* " & pp. 217-222 : " *How Huckleberry Finn Was Written*. "

417 BUSBEY, L. White. *Uncle Joe Cannon ; The Story of a Pioneer American as told to L. White Busbey, for 20 years his private secretary*. New York, Henry Holt & Co., LXIV + 362 pp.
Pp. 270-281, " A Distinguished Lobbyist — Mark Twain. "

418 HAZARD, Lucy Lockwood. *The Frontier in American Literature.*
New York, Thomas Y. Crowell Co., xx + 308 pp.
Pp. 220-230, " Mark Twain, Son and Satirist of the Gilded
Age. " According to her, Mark Twain was more of a rebel
than Brooks cares to admit.

419 LESSING, O. E. *Brücken Über den Atlantik — Beiträge zum amerikanischen und deutschen Geistesleben.* Stuttgart, Deutsche Ver-
lags-Anstalt, 171 pp.

420 NEVINS, Allan. *The Emergence of Modern America* (vol. 8 in
A History of American Life). New York, Macmillan, xix +
446 pp.
Cf. especially pp. 247-251 on Mark Twain as a representative
of the West.

421 SHERMAN, Stuart P. *The Main Stream.* New York, London,
Charles Scribner's Sons, xii + 239 pp.
Pp. 80-88, " Mark Twain's Last Phase " ; chiefly on the
Autobiography.

422 WOOD Charles Erskine Scott. *Heavenly Discourse.* New York,
Vanguard Press, xv + 325 pp.
Mark Twain takes part in some of these imaginary conver-
sations.

PERIODICAL LITERATURE :

423 BUXBAUM, Katherine. " Mark Twain and American Dialect. "
AS, vol. 2, 233-236, Feb.
Praises his " admirable usage of phonetic spelling " but
criticises his inconsistencies and concludes that in this as in
other domains Mark Twain was " a divine amateur ".

424 ERSKINE, John. " Huckleberry Finn. " *Delineator*, vol. 10, 10,
94-97, Feb.
" The first and best story of Main Street. "

425 ESPENSHADE, A. H. " Tom Sawyer's Fiftieth Birthday. " *St.
Nicholas*, vol. 54, 808-809, Aug.

426 GRIMES, Absalom. " Campaigning with Mark Twain. " *Missouri
Historical Rev.*, vol. 21, 188-201. (reprinted from the book he
had published the year before).

427 HARBECK, Hans. " Amerikanische Humor. " *Der Kreis, Zeitschrift
für künstliche Kultur*, vol. 4, 276-284.

428 MEYER Harold. " Mark Twain on the Comstock. " *Southwest
Rev.*, vol. 12, 197-207, April.
On Mark Twain in Nevada.

1928

BIOGRAPHIES AND BOOKS OF CRITICISM :

429 Paine, A. B. *A Short Life of Mark Twain*. Garden City, Doubleday, Doran & Co., vii + 319 pp.
(A second ed. ; cf. 1920, n⁰ *223*).

INTRODUCTIONS AND PREFACES :

430 Mark Twain. *The Adventures of Thomas Jefferson Snodgrass*,
ed. by Charles Honce, with a foreword by Vincent Starrett and
a note on " A Celebrated Village Idiot " by James O'Donnell
Bennett, Chicago, P. Covici Inc., xxxiii + 59 pp.
Mark Twain's earliest known writings as a newspaper correspondent. Letters sent to the *Keokuk Post* in 1856-57 from St.
Louis and Cincinnati.

431 Mark Twain. *Selections* with notes by Vincenzo Grasso. Palermo,
R. Gino, 62 pp.

OTHER BOOKS DEALING WITH MARK TWAIN :

432 Barton, Sir Dunbar Plunket. *Links Between Shakespeare and the
Law*. London, Faber & Gwyer Ltd., xxxix + 167 pp.
Contains some notes about Mark Twain's *Is Shakespeare
Dead ?*, pp. xvi-xxix.

433 Cowper, Frederick A. G. " The Hermit Story as used by Voltaire
and Mark Twain. " in *Papers... in Honor of... Charles Frederick
Johnson* (ed. by Odell Shepard and Arthur Adams). Hartford,
Conn., pp. 313-337.
Thinks that Chap. xx of Zadig (" L'hermite ") and the Faust
legend may be the sources of " The Manuscript ".

434 ERSKINE, John. *The Delight of Great Books.* Indianapolis, The Bobbs-Merrill Co., 365 pp.

> A chapter on *Huckleberry Finn*, pp. 263-274, first published as an article in 1927.

435 HOPE, Anthony. *Memories and Notes.* Garden City, Doubleday, Doran & Co., 247 pp.

> About an encounter with Twain and Lord Kelvin in London, pp. 172-173.

436 HOWELLS, William Dean. *Life in Letters of W. D. Howells,* ed. by Mildred Howells. Garden City, N. Y., Doubleday, Doran & Co., 2 vols.

437 MICHAUD, Régis. *Panorama de la Littérature Américaine Contemporaine.* Paris, Kra, 274 pp.

> On Mark Twain, pp. 78-79, 99-102.

438 ROURKE, Constance. *Troupers of the Gold Coast.* New York, Harcourt, Brace & Co., XIII + 262 pp.

PERIODICAL LITERATURE :

440 BECK, Warren. " Huckleberry Finn versus the Cash Boy. " *Education,* vol. 49, 1-13, Sept.

> A comparison between Huck and Horatio Alger Jr. to the disadvantage of the latter.

441 JAN, Eduard von. " Das literarische Bild der Jeanne d'Arc. " *Beihefte zur Zeitschrift für romanische Philologie.* Heft, 76.

> Pp. 139-143 on Mark Twain's *Joan of Arc.*

442 PAINE, A. B. " The Prince and the Pauper, " *Mentor,* vol. 16, 8-10, Dec.

443 PATTEE, Fred Lewis. " On the Rating of Mark Twain. " *Am. Merc.,* vol. 14, 183-191, June.

> Rates him as a thwarted creator and his works as a collection of glorious fragments.

444 ROSENBERGER, E. G. " Agnostic Hagiographer. " *Catholic World,* vol. 127, 717-723, Sept.

> On Twain's *Joan of Arc ;* praises his " reverential enthusiasm ".

445 Anon. " Mark Twain ", *Grand Lodge Bulletin,* Grand Lodge of Iowa, vol. 29, 575-576, May.

> On Mark Twain's masonic activities.

BIOGRAPHIES AND BOOKS OF CRITICISM :

446 PAINE, A. B. *The Boy's Life of Mark Twain*, ed. by Walter Barnes. New York and London, Harper & Brothers, xv + 368 pp. A new edition ; cf. 1916, nº *175*.

INTRODUCTIONS AND PREFACES :

447 MARK TWAIN. *The Innocents Abroad*, with an introduction by A. B. Paine. New York, Macmillan, xvi + 537 pp. (2nd ed. ; cf. 1927, nº *412*).

448 — *A Letter of Mark Twain to his Publishers, Chatto & Windus of London*, calling their attention to certain indiscretions of the proof-readers of Messrs. Spottiswoode & Co., printed for the first time from the letter in the collection of James Hart, with an introduction by Cyril Clemens and a portrait by Valenti Angelo. San Francisco, The Penguin Press, 4 pp.

449 HARPER, C. Armitage (ed.). *American Ghost Stories*. Boston & New York, Houghton, Mifflin Co., xiv + 287 pp.
Contains " A Ghost Story " by Mark Twain (from *Sketches New and Old*).

OTHER BOOKS DEALING WITH MARK TWAIN :

450 BAY, J. Christian. " Tom Sawyer Detective : The Origin of the Plot " in *Essays Offered to Herbert Putman*, ed. by William W. Bishop & Andrew Keogh. New Haven, Yale Univ. Press, pp. 80-88.
The source of Mark Twain's tale is a Danish novel, *The Minister of Veilby* by Steen Blicher.

451 CLEMENS, Cyril (ed.). *Mark Twain Anecdotes*, ed. by Cyril Clemens, tributes to Samuel L. Clemens by G. K. Chesterton & John

Galsworthy, members of the society. Webster Groves, Mo., Mark Twain Society, 31 pp.

Cf. below n⁰ *483* et n⁰ *572*.

One strongly suspects at times that Cyril Clemens, a remote cousin of Mark Twain, founded the Mark Twain Society (in 1923) merely to press into service important writers and politicians in the hope of increasing Mark Twain's fame and indirectly his own as " the greatest living authority " on S. L. Clemens. (Cf. below n⁰ *865* and *1216*). He later founded and edited the *Mark Twain Quarterly* (1936) which was at first mimeographed and then printed. The value of this review lies principally in the elucidation of difficult points in Twainiana — But examination of its contents yields little which can be esteemed of critical significance.

452 ESKEW, Garnett Laidlaw. *The Pageant of the Packets, A Book of American Steamboating.* New York, H. Holt & Co., XIV + 314 pp.

Contains a chapter entitled " Steamboats come back despite Mark Twain ", which deals more with the Mississippi than with Twain.

453 KELLER, Helen. *Midstream, My Later Life.* Garden City, The Sundial Press, XXIII + 362 pp.

Pp. 47-69, " Our Mark Twain ".

454 LEISY, Ernest Erwin. *American Literature, an Interpretative Survey.* New York, Thomas Y. Crowell Co., x + 299 pp.

Pp. 170-179 on Mark Twain — very superficial.

455 OVERTON, Grant. *An Hour of the American Novel.* Philadelphia & London, J. B. Lippincott Co., 155 pp.·

A chapter on " Howells : Twain ", pp. 37-43.

456 VAN DOREN, Mark (ed.). *An Autobiography of America.* New York, A. & C. Boni, XIV + 737 pp.

Several chapters devoted to Mark Twain : Mark Twain studies to be a pilot on the Mississipi ", pp. 353-367 ; " Mark Twain dreams of riches in Nevada ", pp. 432-445 ; " Mark Twain finds heroes and villains in the West ", 454-461.

457 WINTERICH, John T. *Books and the Man,* New York, Greenberg, XIV + 374 pp.

Contains " Mark Twain and *Innocents Abroad* ", pp. 170-192 — chiefly anecdotal.

PERIODICAL LITERATURE :

458 BRASHEAR, M. M. " Early Mark Twain Letter. " *MLN*, vol. 44, 256-259, April.
A Mark Twain letter reprinted from the *Hannibal Daily Journal* which Orion Clemens edited.

459 CLEMENS, Cyril. " Mark Twain : 1835-1910. " *Overland M.*, n. s., vol. 87, 103-104, April.

460 — " Visit to Mark Twain's Country. " *Ibid.*, n. s., vol. 87, 116-117, 145-146, April-May.

461 — " Becky Thatcher, Personal Reminiscences. " *Ibid.*, vol. 87 (n. s.), 142, 157, May.

462 — " The True Character of Mark Twain's Wife. " *Missouri Hist. Rev.*, vol. 24, 40-49, Oct.
A vindication of Olivia Clemens's character.

463 CLEMENS, J. R. " Some Reminiscences of Mark Twain. " *Overland M.*, n. s., vol. 87, 107-108, April.

464 GILLIS, William. " The Famous Jumping Frog Story. " *Ibid.*, 101-102.
William Gillis, one-time associate of Mark Twain, tells Fremont Older the true story of the Jumping Frog.

465 HAWTHORNE, E. J. " Mark Twain as I Knew Him. " *Ibid.*, 111-128.

466 JAMES, O. C. " Everlasting Author. " *Ibid.*, p. 106.

467 KELLER, H. " Mark Twain. " *Am. Mag.*, vol. 108, 50-51, July.

468 KENNEDY, K. " Mark Twain ; Poem. " *Overland M.*, n. s., vol..87, 111, April.

469 LORCH, F. W. " Orion Clemens. " *Palimpsest*, vol. 10, 353-386, Oct.

470 — " Mark Twain in Iowa. " *Iowa Journal of History and Politics*, vol. 27, 408-456 (July), 507-547 (Oct.).
On Mark Twain at Muscatine and Keokuk in his youth and his visits to Iowa as a lecturer.

471 McKAY, Donald. " On the Vanishing Trail of Tom Sawyer. " *New York Times Mag.*, Oct. 27, 8-9.
On Hannibal, Mo.

472 PHILLPOTS, E. " On Mark Twain's Visit to England ; Poem ". *Overland M.*, n.s., vol. 87, 106, April

473 RICHARDS. P. " Mark Twain als wildwest-Journalist. " *Westermanns Monatshefte*, vol 147, 158-160, Oct.

474 Sosey, Frank H. " Palmyra and Its Historical environment. "
Missouri Historical Rev. vol. 23, 361-379.

475 Van Dyke, H. " Mark Twain : Memorial Poem. " *Overland M.*,
104.

476 " Tributes to Mark Twain by members of the Mark Twain
Society. " *Overland M.*, n. s., vol. 87, 107-108, April.
Cf. below n° *483*.

477 Anon. " In School with Becky Thatcher and Tom Sawyer. "
Lit. Digest, vol. 100, 60-64, March 9.

478 — " Tom Sawyer and Huckleberry Finn : erronotts. " *World
Rev.*, vol. 8, pp. 201-203, May 6.

1930

BIBLIOGRAPHIES :

479 EDWARDS, Mrs. Frances M. *Twainiana Notes from the Annotations of Walter Bliss.* Hartford, The Hobby Shop, 24 pp.
   Annotations made by Bliss on his copy of Merle Johnson's bibliography.

BIOGRAPHIES AND BOOKS OF CRITICISM :

480 GILLIS, William R. *Gold Rush Days with Mark Twain.* New York, Boni, XIV + 264 pp. (with an introduction by Cyril Clemens).
   Gillis was Mark Twain's mining partner in Nevada.

481 MARTIN, Alma B. *A Vocabulary Study of the " Gilded Age ",* with an introduction by Robert L. Ramsay, a foreword by Hamlin Garland and a brief bibliography. Webster Groves, Mo., 55 pp.

482 WEST, Victor, Royce. *Folklore in the Works of Mark Twain.* Lincoln, Nebraska, University of Nebraska Studies in Language, Literature and Criticism, 81 pp. + Index.

483 *Tributes to Mark Twain by Members of the Society.* Paris, Printed for the Mark Twain Society by H. Clarke, 13 pp.
   Tributes by Galsworthy, Chesterton, Hamlin Garland, W. W. Jacobs, E. V. Lucas, Dunsany, Knut Hamsun, W. De La Mare, Pinero, G. M. Trevelyan, H. M. Tomlinson, E. A. Housman, etc. Conventional eulogies to be expected from fellow-writers on the passing of a great literary figure.

INTRODUCTIONS AND PREFACES :

484 MARK TWAIN. *A Connecticut Yankee in King Arthur's Court.* New York & London, Harper & Brothers, (Modern Classics), ed. by W. N. Otto, XVIII + 510 pp. (notes, pp. 451-510).

Insists on Twain's " intense Americanism " and " abiding faith in the ultimate triumph of democratic principles ".

485 — *The Million Pound Bank-Note* with notes by L. Riggio. Florence, Edizioni Riggio, 32 pp.

OTHER BOOKS DEALING WITH MARK TWAIN :

486 CAIRNS, William B. *A History of American Literature.* New York, Oxford University Press, ix + 569 pp.

Revised ed. of a book which had been published in 1912 for the first time. On Mark Twain, cf. pp. 444-452. Cf. above nᵒ *115*.

487 CHURCHILL, Winston. *A Roving Commission; My Early Life.* New York, Charles Scribner's Sons, xii + 377 pp.

On his meeting with Mark Twain in New York, cf. p. 375.

488 JOSEPHSON, Matthew. *Portrait of the Artist as American.* New York, Harcourt, Brace & Co., xxiii + 308 pp.

Passim on Mark Twain.

489 PARRINGTON, Vernon L. *Main Currents in American Thought.* New York, Harcourt, Brace & Co., 3 vols.

On Twain, vol. 3 *(The beginning of critical realism in America. 1860-1900)*, pp. 86-101. He is represented as faithfully reflecting the contradictions of the Gilded Age. The bitterness of his old age is explained partly by Brooks's thesis, partly by his sufferings under the blows of fate. Parrington praises his hatred of shams and his passionate republicanism. Cf. introduction, p. 48, n. 3.

490 PATTEE, Fred Lewis. *The New American Literature, 1890-1930 : A Survey.* New York & London, The Century Co., viii + 507 pp.

Scattered references to Mark Twain who has no chapter of his own.

491 READ, Opie. *I Remember.* New York, R. R. Smith, Inc., vi + 335 pp.

Contains a chapter entitled " Mark Twain and the Pilot " (pp. 155-165) in which the author tells how he met Mark Twain on a Mississippi steamboat.

492 VAN DOREN, " Mark. Mark Twain " in *Dictionary of American Biography*, vol. 4, pp. 192-198. New York, Charles Scribner's Sons.

His masterpieces are *Life on the Mississippi* and *Huckleberry Finn*, not the posthumous works which are interesting only in so far as they shed light on his personality and help find in his other works undertones which might never have been detected.

PERIODICAL LITERATURE :

493 ARMSTRONG, C. J. " Mark Twain's Early Writings Discovered ". *Missouri Historical Rev.*, vol. 24, 485-501.

494 BRASHEAR, Minnie M. " Mark Twain Juvenilia. " *AL*, vol. 2, 25-53, March.

Early pieces by Mark Twain published in the *Hannibal Journal*, by his brother Orion. " This early writing will not suggest the need of any new rating of Mark Twain. "

495 CLEMENS, Clara. " Recollections of Mark Twain. " *North Am.*, vol. 230, 522-529 (Nov.), 652-659 (Dec.).

496 CLEMENS Cyril. " Mark Twain's Favorite Book. " *Overland M.*, n. s., vol. 88, 157, May.

It was *Huckleberry Finn* and not *Joan of Arc* as the idea prevails — according to C. Clemens.

497 GARLAND, Hamlin. " Roadside Meetings of a Literary Nomad. " *Bookman*, vol. 71, 425-427, July.

On Twain's publication of Gen. Grant's *Memoirs* and his bankruptcy.

498 LORCH, Fred W. " A Mark Twain Letter. " *Iowa Journal of History and Politics*, vol. 28, 268-276.

499 MABBOTT, T. O. " Mark Twain's Artillery : A Mark Twain Legend. " *Missouri Historical Rev.*, vol. 25, 23-29, Oct.

Reprint of a Mark Twain article which had originally appeared in the *Carson City Appeal* early in 1880, " How He Defeated a Band of Redskins in the Days of '49 with Type as Grapeshots " with a foreword by T. O. Mabbott.

500 WINTERICH, John T. " The Life and Works of Bloodgood Haviland Cutter. " *Colophon*, I, Pt. 2, May.

On the " Poet Lariat " in *The Innocents Abroad*.

UNPUBLISHED THESES :

501 BRASHEAR, Minnie W. *Formative Influences in the Mind and Writings of Mark Twain*, Ph. D. Thesis, University of North Carolina.

502 BUXTON, Teresa. *A Study of the Relationship of William Dean Howells and Samuel L. Clemens*, Bucknell University.

503 DERRICK, L. E. *A Study in Mark Twain's Sources*, Univ. of Texas, M. A. thesis.

1931

BIOGRAPHIES AND BOOKS OF CRITICISM :

504 CLEMENS, Clara. *My Father, Mark Twain.* New York and London, Harper & Brothers, VII + 292 pp.
Many hitherto unpublished letters connected by biographical notes and personal reminiscences.

505 LEWIS, Oscar. *The Origin of the Celebrated Jumping Frog of Calaveras County.* San Francisco, The Book Club of California, 27 pp. + unpaged appendix.
Gives the different versions of the tale.

506 WALL, Bernhardt. *In Mark Twain's Missouri,* etched and published by Bernhardt Wall. Lime Rock, Conn., 4 pp.

INTRODUCTIONS AND PREFACES :

507 MARK TWAIN. *The Prince and the Pauper,* with an introduction by Emily F. Barry & Herbert F. Bruner. New York & London, Harper & Brothers, XXIII + 312 pp. (Modern Classics).
A school edition with " Some Teaching Suggestions ".

508 — *The Adventures of Huckleberry Finn,* edited by Emily F. Barry & Herbert B. Bruner. New York and London, Harper & Brothers, XVIII + 446 pp. (Harper's Modern Classics).

509 MARK TWAIN. *The Adventures of Tom Sawyer,* edited with an introduction by Bertha Evans Ward. Boston. New York, Ginn & Co., XXIV + 255 pp.

510 — *The Adventures of Tom Sawyer,* illustrated by Peter Hurd, with an introduction by Christopher Morley, Philadelphia, Chicago, The John C. Winston Co., XIV + 264 pp.
A children's edition.

511 — *Tom Sawyer. The 1.000.000 pound banknote,* with notes by V. Grasso (abridged). Palermo, R. Gino, 69 pp.

OTHER BOOKS DEALING WITH MARK TWAIN :

512 BLANKENSHIP, Russell. *American Literature as an Expression of the National Mind.* New York, Henry Holt & Co., and London, Routledge & Sons, xviii + 731 pp.

> A handbook for students. On Mark Twain, pp. 457-471 & 511-512 ; he is assigned unsurpassed rank among all American writers — except for the Transcendentalists.

513 CHEIRO (pseud. of HAMON, Louis). *Fate in the Making.* Revelations of a Lifetime. New York & London, Harper & Brothers, ix + 355 pp.

> This famous chiromancer once examined Mark Twain's hand ; cf. Paine's *Biography,* vol. 3, p. 1206.

514 GARLAND, Hamlin. *Companions on the Trail — A Literary Chronicle.* New York, Macmillan, vi + 539 pp.

> Contains a reprint of his 1930 article in the *Bookman.*

515 GILBERT, Ariadne. *Over Famous Thresholds.* New York, London, The Century Co., xix + 396 pp.

> On Mark Twain, a chapter entitled " Sam, Sinner and Saint ", pp. 233-262, a biographical sketch interspersed with anecdotes.

516 GRATTAN, C. Hartley. " Mark Twain ", pp. 274-284, in *American Writers on American Literature,* ed. by John Macy. New York, Horace Liveright, Inc., xxii + 539 pp.

> " Mark Twain was a man writing. Too many of his predecessors, fellows and successors have been writing men. " Rejects Brooks's thesis : " Mark Twain did not have the sort of temperament or mentality which would have allowed him to cut a narrow path personally surveyed through the jungle of the Gilded Age, even had he had the utmost freedom imaginable. "

517 MASSON, Thomas L. *Our American Humorists.* New York, Dodd, Mead & Co., 448 pp.

> A " new and enlarged edition " of a book first published in 1922, but unchanged as regards the earlier humorists and Mark Twain.

518 ROURKE, Constance. *American Humor : A Study of the National Character.* New York, Harcourt, Brace & Co., x + 324 pp.

> On Mark Twain, pp. 209-221. " It is a mistake to look for the social critic — even *manqué* — in Mark Twain... The talent of Mark Twain was consistently a pioneer talent. "

519 SHERMAN, Stuart. *On Contemporary Literature.* New York, P. Smith, 312 pp.

> A mere reprint of the 1917 edition.

PERIODICAL LITERATURE :

1) Reviews of West's *Folklore in the Works of Mark Twain* (1930) :

520 ASHTON, J. W. in *PQ*, vol. 10, 416, Oct.

521 DAVIS, A. K. in *MLN*, vol. 44, 350, May.

2) Review of Constance Rourke's *American Humor :*

522 BLAIR, Walter in *AL*, vol. 3, 340-343, Nov.

3) Review of A. B. Martin's *A Vocabulary of Mark Twain's The Gilded Age* (1930) :

522* CESTRE, Charles in *RAA*, vol. 8, 458-459, June.

*
* *

523 CLEMENS, Clara. " Recollections of Mark Twain — Last Years of the Humorist. " *North Am.*, vol. 231, 50-57, Jan.

Last of a series of articles whose publication began in 1930. Mere extracts from her book on her father.

524 BLAIR, Walter. " The Popularity of xix th Century American Humorists. " *AL*, vol. 3, 175-194, May.

Their tremendous success in a day of grandiloquence and pseudo-romantic writing paved the way for realism in thought and in fiction.

525 DE VOTO, Bernard. " The Real Frontier. " *Harper's M.*, vol. 163, 60-71, June.

" The Puritan is nowhere discoverable on the Frontier ", contrary to what Brooks may think. Cf. Introduction, Chap. iv.

526 — " The Matrix of Mark Twain's Humor. " *Bookman*, vol. 74, 172-178, Oct.

" Frontier humor passed from folklore to print by means of Frontier newspapers... [it] taught [Mark Twain] a style and provided him with forms and themes. It was the matrix of Mark Twain's humor. " Cf. Introduction, Chap. iv.

527 — " Mark Twain and the Genteel Tradition. " *Harvard Graduates' Mag*, vol. 40, 155-166, Dec.

Opposes Brooks's conclusions : " ... the books of Mark Twain suffered harm from the genteel tradition. This damage was purely verbal. The tradition may have wrought a greater damage by turning him from Pudd'nhead Wilsons and Huckleberry Finns to knights, kings and armored virgins. A doubt exists

that the blame can be so readily fixed... there is no assurance
that any decision can be reached outside the domain of sheer
conjecture. " Cf. Introduction, Chap. IV.

528 GOODPASTURE, A. V. " Mark Twain, Southerner. " *Tennessee
Hist. Mag.*, 2nd s., vol. 1, 253-260, July.
   " ... every drop of Mark Twain's blood was Southern... "

529 HUGHES, R. M. " A Deserter's Tale. " *Virginia's Mag. of History
and Biography*, vol. 39, 21-28, Jan.
   Accuses Twain of being a deserter from the Confederate
Army.

530 LORCH, Fred W. " A Source for Mark Twain's ' The Dandy
Frightening the Squatter '. " *AL*, vol. 3, 309-313, Nov.
   It probably was " A Scene on the Ohio ", in the *Bloomington
(now Muscatine, Iowa) Herald*, Feb. 13, 1849.

531 MASON, L. D. " Real People in Mark Twain's Stories. " *Overland M.*,
n. s., vol. 89, 12-13, Jan.
   Second hand information.

532 RAOUL, Margaret L. " Debunking a Famous Story. " *Bookman*,
vol. 73, 607-608, Aug.
   On the origin of the famous joke about the report of his
death being " an exaggeration. "

533 UNDERHILL, I. S. " An inquiry into *Huckleberry Finn.* " *Colophon*,
II, Pt 6, June.
   Bibliographical remarks on the 1st edition.

MISCELLANEOUS :

534 *The Story of the Paramount Picture " Huckleberry Finn "*, Lubin
Press, circa 1931.

535 *The Movie Story of Tom Sawyer.* Racine, Wisconsin, circa 1931.
   These two items listed in a typewritten bibliography of Mark
Twain kept in Widener Library (Harvard University) are
nowhere available. They were not deposited in the Library
of Congress.
   Tom Sawyer has been filmed twice, once as a silent picture
in 1930 and again as a talking picture in 1935. *Huckleberry
Finn* does not lend itself so easily to cinematographic treatment :
it does not afford a conventional heroine's part and touches
upon such controversial issues as the Negro problem. There has
been only one silen film on the subject.

1932

BIBLIOGRAPHIES :

536 POTTER, John Kelly. *Samuel Langhorne Clemens, First Editions and Values.* Chicago, The Black Archer Press. III + 80 pp.

BIOGRAPHIES AND BOOKS OF CRITICISM :

537 DE VOTO, Bernard. *Mark Twain's America.* Boston, Little, Brown & Co., XVI + 353 pp.

An aggressive book which takes Brooks to task for not knowing anything about Mark Twain's background, condemns his *a priori* methods and rejects all his conclusions.

538 LEACOCK, Stephen. *Mark Twain.* London, Peter Davies, 167 pp.

A sympathetic essay by a fellow-humorist who, as a Canadian, does not feel obliged to regard him as the literary champion of the American nation.

INTRODUCTIONS AND PREFACES :

539 MARK TWAIN. *The Adventures of Tom Sawyer*, ed. by Emily F. Barry & Herbert B. Bruner. New York and London, Harper & Brothers, XX + 326 pp. (Harper's Modern Classics ; cf. above n° *227.*)

540 — *The Notorious Jumping Frog of Calaveras County;* the original in English, the re-translation clawed back from the French into a civilized language once more by patient unremunerated toil. New York, P. C. Duschnes, v + 25 pp.

541 Mark Twain, *The Letter Writer*, ed. by Cyril Clemens, Boston, Meador Publishing Co., 181 pp.

Hitherto unpublished letters with a few comments by the editor.

542 MARSH, Susan Louise & VANNEST, Charles Garrett. *Missouri Anthology.* Boston, The Christopher Publishing House, VIII + 128 pp.

Pp. 91-96, " The Ancestry and Birth of Mark Twain " by Cyril Clemens.

543 RICE, Grantland. *The Omnibus of Sport.* New York & London, Harper & Brothers, XVII + 954 pp.

Pp. 514-519, " The Jumping Frog. "

OTHER BOOKS DEALING WITH MARK TWAIN :

544 BUCKBEE, Edna Bryan. *Pioneer Days of Angel's Camp,* published by *Calaveras Californian.* Angel's Camp, Calif., 80 pp.

Contains " Mark Twain's Treasure Pile ", pp. 21-35, on the origin of " The Jumping Frog. "

545 CALVERTON, V. F. *The Liberation of American Literature.* New York, Charles Scribner's Sons, XV + 500 pp.

On Mark Twain, pp. 319-328, 337-339. The author considers him " the first American prose writer of any importance " and praises him for serving well the cause of American liberalism though in thrall to petty bourgeois conventions especially as regards sex morality.

Cf. Introduction, p. 42.

546 KING, Grace. *Memories of a Southern Woman of Letters.* New York, Macmillan, 398 pp.

Personal memories on Twain, pp. 75-76, 168-179, 201-203.

547 KNIGHT, Grant C. *American Literature and Culture.* New York, Ray Long & Richards R. Smith, IX + 523 pp.

On Mark Twain, pp. 358-367 in chapter on " The Literature of Realism. " Considers Twain a mediocre artist and prefers *The Scarlet Letter* to *Huckleberry Finn;* qualifies Brooks's thesis.

548 LEWISOHN, Ludwig. *Expression in America.* New York & London, Harper & Brothers, XXXII + 624 pp.

On Twain, pp. 212-232. This book was later republished as *The Story of American Literature.*

549 RASCOE, Burton. *Titans of Literature from Homer to the Present.* New York & London, G. P. Putnam's Sons, XIII + 496 pp.

Pp. 421-429 ; " Mark Twain — The First American. " Accepts Brooks's thesis on the whole.

550 WARD, Alfred, Charles. *American Literature.* London, Methuen or New York, Lincoln MacVeagh, The Dial Press, X + 273 pp.

Scattered references to Twain — ranks him equal to Henry James, whose distinction lay in the opposed technique of conscious artistry.

PERIODICAL LITERATURE :

1) Reviews of Blankenship's *American Literature as an Expression of the National Mind* (1931) :

551 SMITH, Reed. in *AL*, vol. 4, 79-80, March.

2) Reviews of Clara Clemens's *My Father : Mark Twain* (1931) :

552 BOYNTON, P. H. in *NR.*, vol. 69, 302-303, Jan. 27.
" ... an obviously honest and candid piece of work... "

553 DE VOTO, B. in *NEQ*, vol. 5, 169-171, Jan.
" ... a dull book... " intended as " a rebuttal of Van Wyck Brooks's arraignment of her mother, which few people, these days, take seriously... "

554 PHELPS, W. L. in *Scribner's*, " As I Like It ; Mark Twain as a Man ", vol. 91, 54-55, Jan.

555 Anon. in *Quart. Jour. of the Univ. of North Dakota*, vol. 22, 277-278 Spring.

3) Review of Leacock's *Mark Twain :*

556 Anon. in *TLS*, Nov. 24, p. 886.
Favourable, but criticizes the author for considering *A Connecticut Yankee* one of Mark Twain's masterpieces : " ... it exhibited his insensitiveness to the ideal. "

4) Reviews of De Voto's *Mark Twain's America.*

557 ARVIN, N. in *NR*, vol. 72, 211-212, Oct. 5.
Accuses De Voto of unfairness and sides with Brooks.

558 CANBY, H. S. in *SRL*, " Mark Twain Himself ", vol. 9, 201-202, Oct. 29.
Accepts De Voto's thesis but condemns the violence of his attacks on Brooks.

559 SIEGEL, E. in *Scribner's*, " Literary Sign-Posts ", vol. 92, 5-6 Nov.
According to him, De Voto " goes critically wild and is unfair " to Brooks.

560 VAN DOREN, Mark, in *Nation*, vol. 135, 370-371, Oct. 19.
De Voto's views are just as theoretical and his interpretation just as subjective as those of Brooks ; but the former knows much more about the frontier than the latter.

*
* *

561 BROWNELL, G. H. " Mark Twain and the ' Hannibal Journal ' ".
Am. Book Collector, vol. 2, 173-176, 202-204.

562 CHAPMAN, J. W. " Germ of a Book. " *Atlantic M.*, vol. 150, 720-721,
Dec.

Letters sent by Mark Twain to Rev. Chapman who had been
present at the last moments of Jesse Leathers, the original of
Simon Lather, the " American Claimant ".

563 COOPER, Lane. " Mark Twain's Lilacs and Laburnums. " *MLN*,
vol. 47, 85-87, Feb.

The famous passage in *A Double-Barreled Detective Story*
was a parody of *The Seamy Side, a Story* by Walter Besant
& James Rice, 1880, p. 297.

564 DE VOTO, B. " Tom, Huck and America. " *SRL*, vol. 9, 37-39,
Aug. 13.

An extract from his book.

564* MARKOVITCH, M. " Servantes i Mark Tven. " *Venaz* (i.e. The
Crown, Belgrade), vol. 18, n° 1.

565 OLDS, N. S. " A Mark Twain Retort. " *SRL*, vol. 8, 722, May.

A letter Mark Twain sent to the author when he reviewed
and slated his *Double-Barreled-Detective Story*.

UNPUBLISHED THESES :

566 EMBERSON, Frances Guthrie. *The Vocabulary of Samuel L. Clemens
from 1852 to 1884*, University of Missouri.

1933

BIOGRAPHIES AND BOOKS OF CRITICISM :

567 Brooks, Van Wyck. *The Ordeal of Mark Twain*. New York, E. P. Dutton, 325 pp. (London, Dent, 1934).

A new and revised edition ; but few major changes. Cf. above n⁰ *224* and our introduction pp. 35-39.

568 Leacock, Stephen. *Mark Twain*. New York, Appleton, 161 pp.

American edition of a book published in England in 1932. Cf. above n⁰ *538*.

INTRODUCTIONS AND PREFACES :

569 Mark Twain. *The Adventures of Huckleberry Finn*, with a new introduction by Booth Tarkington. New York, The Limited Editions Club, 494 pp.

Attacks Brooks without naming him.

570 — *Tom Sawyer, Whitewasher*, with an introduction by A. B. Paine. New York & London, Harper & Brothers, vi + 16 pp.

OTHER BOOKS DEALING WITH MARK TWAIN :

571 Bradford, Gamaliel. *Portraits and Personalities*. Boston & New York, Houghton Mifflin Co., xx + 283 pp.

Contains a chapter on " Mark Twain ", pp. 213-235 + 265-266.

572 Clemens, Cyril. *The International Mark Twain Society. Its History and Members*. Webster Groves, Mo., International Mark Twain Society, 26 pp.

573 Hicks, Granville. *The Great Tradition*. New York, Macmillan, xv + 317 pp.

On Mark Twain, pp. 38-49, 68-72. Being a Marxist, the author condemns Mark Twain's acceptance of capitalism and adopts Brooks's thesis.

574 Loggins, Vernon. *Visual Outline of American Literature.* New York, Green & Co., 110 pp.

On Twain, pp. 76-78.

575 Morton, Henry & Partridge, D. C. *The Most Remarkable Echo in the World.* New York, privately printed, 160 pp.

A joke intended to make fun of the Baconian theory; claims to prove that Mark Twain wrote E. A. Poe's, Hawthorne's and Lewis Carroll's works as well as his own.

576 Van Doren, Carl. *American Literature, An Introduction.* Los Angeles, U. S. Library Association, 92 pp.

On Mark Twain, pp. 58-62.

PERIODICAL LITERATURE :

1) Reviews of Cyril Clemens's *Mark Twain, The Letter Writer* (1932) :

577 Blair, W. in *AL*, vol. 4, 399-404, Jan.

578 Anon. in *TLS*, Jan. 19, p. 38 D.

" ... the man who wrote the letters must indeed have been somebody, otherwise they would never have reached the printer. "

2) Reviews of De Voto's *Mark Twain's America* (1932) :

579 Blair, W. in *AL*, vol. 4, 399-404, Jan.

580 Boynton, P. H. in *NEQ*, vol. 6, 184-187, March.

Favourable but criticizes his arrogance.

581 Chase, M. E. in *Commonweal*, vol. 17, 303-304, Jan.

Favourable and superficial.

582 Matthiessen, F. O. in *YR*, vol. 22, 605-607, Spring.

Brooks's book was " too rigidly intellectualized ", but De Voto's is " the work of an enthusiast, praising Mark Twain rapturously, if in a somewhat turgid and heavy strain. "

583 Phelps, W. L. in *Scribner's M.*, vol. 93, 182-183, March, " The Real Mark Twain ".

" ... a weighty but lively contribution to knowledge. "

584 Russell, F. T. in *Univ. of Calif. Chronicle*, vol. 35, 157-161, Jan.

An uncritical summary of the book.

3) Reviews of Leacock's *Mark Twain* :

585 Arvin, N. in *NR*, vol. 74, 191, March 29.

586 Parks, E. W. in *Am. Rev.*, vol. 1, 363-367, June, " Mark Twain Misconstrued. "

Leacock should have read De Voto's book ; Mark Twain was " essentially a child of the frontier ".

4) Reviews of Brooks's *Ordeal of Mark Twain* :

587 Arvin, N. in *NR*, vol. 74, 191, March 29.

Brooks has shelved the shallow Mark Twain legend, but failed to realize that " Mark Twain could have seen through H. H. Rogers only by understanding the dialectics of American capitalism ".

588 Lorch, Fred W. in *AL*, vol. 5, 185-187, May.

Lists some of the concessions that Brooks has made to his critics since the first edition of his book, but does not accept his thesis : " ... why should one assume ... that a creative life is based upon freedom from restraint ? "

589 Mumford, Lewis. in *SRL*, vol. 9, 573-575, May, " Prophet, Pedant and Pioneer ".

" About the *facts* of pioneer life, Mr. De Voto and Mr. Brooks are... in substantial agreement ; the slight discrepancy in their points of view comes from the fact that what Mr. Brooks calls Hell, Mr. De Voto patriotically calls Heaven. " Frontier society was infantile. Cf. below n⁰ *593*.

* *
*

590 Brownell, G. H. " Mark Twainiana. " *Am. Book Collector*, vol. 3, 172-175, 207-212.

On the origin of Mark Twain's pseudonym.

591 — " Mark Twain First Published Effort. " *Ibid.*, 92-95.

592 Clemens, Cyril. " Mark Twain and Jane Austen. " *Overland M.*, vol. 91, 21, Jan.

An imaginary meeting on a transatlantic steamer.

593 De Voto, B. " Letter to the Editor. " *SRL*, vol. 10, 4, July 22.

An answer to Lewis Mumford's article on Brooks's book and his own.

594 Gary, L. M. " Mark Twain — Boy and Philosopher. " *Overland M.*, vol. 91, ser. 2, 154-155, Nov.

595 Partington, Wilfred. " Mark Twain — In Love, in Anger and in Bibliography. " *Bookman*, vol. 74, 313-314, March.

Bibliographical and anecdotal.

596 Richards, P. " Reminiscences of Mark Twain. " *Library Rev.*, n⁰ 25, 19-22.

Darwin was very fond of Mark Twain's books, met him several times between 1903 and 1910, and drew numerous caricatures and pendrawings of him.

597 UNDERHILL, I. S. " Diamonds in the Rough. " *Colophon*, IV, Pt 13, Feb.

Anecdotal ; contains unpublished letter to Riley, Dec. 2, 1870.

598 Anon. " Mark Twain biographer denies he had a shady side. " *Lit. Digest*, vol. 116, 23, July 29.

Mark Twain never wrote Rabelaisian stories, declares Paine indignantly.

599 — " Two Etymologies. " *Word-Study*, vol. 9, 5-6 Nov.

600 — " Mark Twain's New Deal : Connecticut Yankee at King Arthur's Court. " *SRL*, vol. 10, 352, Dec. 16.

F. D. Roosevelt borrowed the phrase from *A Connecticut Yankee*.

1934

BIOGRAPHIES AND BOOKS OF CRITICISM :

601 BRASHEAR, Minnie M. *Mark Twain : Son of Missouri.* Chapel Hill, N. C., Univ. of North Carolina Press, XVI + 294 pp.

A careful study of Mark Twain's formative years in Missouri, which, according to the author, was a center of gentility and intelligence. After an exhaustive investigation of his reading, she concludes he was much better read than is commonly realized and greatly indebted to XVIIIth century European writers.

602 BROOKS, Van Wyck, *The Ordeal of Mark Twain.* New and revised edition. London, J. M. Dent, 325 pp.

English edition of nº *567.*

603 DE CASSERES, Benjamin. *When Huck Finn Went Highbrow.* New York, Thomas F. Madigan, 8 unnumbered pp. + a facsimile reproduction.

On the Browning class which Mark Twain conducted at Hartford in 1887.

604 VYGODSKAYA, Emma Osipovna. *Marka Twena piedzivojumi.* Riga.

INTRODUCTIONS AND PREFACES

605 MARK TWAIN. *The Million Pound Bank-Note,* with notes by Vincenzo Grasso, Palermo, R. Gino, 125 pp.

606 McCALLUM, J. D. *The College Omnibus.* New York, Harcourt, Brace & Co., x + 982 pp.

Contains *The Man That Corrupted Hadleyburg.*

OTHER BOOKS DEALING WITH MARK TWAIN :

607 CLEMENS, Cyril. *Mark Twain and Mussolini.* Webster Groves, Mo., International Mark Twain Society, x + 56 pp.

The author recounts interviews with Mussolini, Shaw, Galsworthy, Maurois, Chesterton, Drinkwater and F. D. Roosevelt, on the subject of Mark Twain's importance.

608 COMPTON, Charles Herrick. *Who Reads What ?* Essays on the readers of Mark Twain, Hardy, Sandburg, Shaw, William James, and the Great Classics, with an introduction by Dorothy Canfield Fisher New York, The H. W. Wilson Co., 117 pp.

Pp. 11-34, " Who Reads Mark Twain ? " The records of the St. Louis Public Library show that Mark Twain is " the most widely read American author, living or dead ".

609 HARPER, Joseph Henry. *I Remember.* New York and London, Harper & Brothers, 281 pp.

Several pages of reminiscences about Mark Twain, pp. 134-149.

610 LYMAN, George D. *The Saga of the Comstock : Boon Days in Virginia City.* New York & London, Charles Scribner's Sons, III + 399 pp.

On Mark Twain, pp. 212-213 ; a very carefully documented book.

611 MILLER, James MacDonald. *An Outline of American Literature.* New York, Farrar & Rinehart, VIII + 386 pp.

Mark Twain had the defects of the America of his time, but " he was straightforward and passionately honest and altogether lovable " (pp. 234-237).

PERIODICAL LITERATURE :

1) Reviews of Brooks's *The Ordeal of Mark Twain* (1932) :

612 O'FAOLAIN, Sean. in *Spectator*, " The Slavery of Mark Twain ", vol. 153, 137, July 27.

Accepts Brooks's conclusions unreservedly.

613 Anon. in *TLS*, June 28, p. 456.

As favourable a review as that of 1920.

2) Reviews of Minnie M. Brashear's *Mark Twain, Son of Missouri :*

614 ARVIN, N., in *NR*, vol. 78, 194, March 28.

Genuinely interesting material, but her approach is condemned to a certain shallowness since she refuses to see any tragic complexity in Mark Twain. Besides she idealizes the Old South.

615 GRINSTEAD, F. in *Southwest Rev.*, vol. 19, 12-13, Jan.

615* LE BRETON, Maurice in *RAA*, vol. 12, 81-83, Oct.

616 Anon. in *Nation*, vol. 138, 395, April 4.

⁎

617 ADAMS, Sir John. " Mark Twain Psychologist. " *Dalhousie Rev.*, vol. 13, 417-426, Jan.

    The author claims that Mark Twain read his book *The Herbartian Psychology Applied to Education* in 1898 when he was writing *What is Man?*

618 ALTROCCHI, J. C. " Along the Mother Lode. " *YR*, vol. 24, 131-145, Sept.

    A trip in the gold fields of the Mother Lode.

619 BROWNELL, G. H. " Mark Twainiana. " *Am. Book Collector*, vol. 5, 124-126, April.

    History of the publication of " The Jumping Frog. "

620 CLEMENS, Cyril. " Mark Twain's Religion. " *Commonweal*, vol. 21, 254-255, Dec.

    Tries to prove that Mark Twain was not an atheist but a good christian.

621 COMPTON, Charles H. " Who Reads Mark Twain ? " *Am. Mer.*, vol. 31, 465-471, April.

    Published in book form the same year.

622 DOUGLAS, Gilbert. " Behind that Door. " *New York World Telegram*, Aug. 15, p. 21.

623 BOWELLS, W. D. " When Mark Twain Missed Fire. " *Golden Book*, vol. 20, 97-98, July.

    When he delivered his famous Whittier Birthday speech.

624 LEACOCK, S. " Two Humorists : Charles Dickens and Mark Twain. " *YR*, vol. 24, 118-129, Sept.

    Compares their techniques.

625 OLDER, Fremont. " Mark Twain and Jackass Hill. " *Overland M.*, vol. 92, 118, July.

626 PARTRIDGE, H. M. " Did Mark Twain Perpetrate Literary Hoaxes ? " *Am. Book Collector*, vol. 5, 351, 357, Dec.

627 PHELPS, W. L. " As I Like It. " *Scribner's M.*, vol. 95, 433-434, June.

    On a lecture Mark Twain once gave in Newark.

628 SMITH, Annella. " Mark Twain — Occultist. " *Rosicrucian Mag.*, vol. 26, 65-68.

628⁎ TINKER, E. L. " Cable and the Creoles. " *AL*, vol. 5, 313-326, Jan.

    Contains information on the reading tour of Cable and Mark Twain in 1884-1885 ; cf. pp. 321-322.

629 Warfel, H. R. " George W. Cable Amends a Mark Twain Plot — with text of a letter from Cable to R. W. Gilder. " *AL*, vol. 6, 328-331, Nov.

About a literary project Cable and Twain were to undertake together.

630 Weiss, H. B. " Mark Twain's Hidden Autograph. " *Am. Book Collector*, vol. 5, 289-293, Oct.

A summary of Morton and Partridge's *The Most Remarkable Echo in the World* (1933).

631 Anon. " Mark Twain Anticipates Roosevelt. " *Word Study*, vol. 9, 4, April.

On the origin of the phrase " New Deal ".

1935

BIBLIOGRAPHIES :

632 Johnson, Merle. *A Bibliography of the Works of Mark Twain, Samuel L. Clemens,* rev. & enlarged. New York & London, Harper & Brothers, xiii + 274 pp.

633 Anon. " Mark Twain Bibliography. " *Scholastic,* vol. 27, 17, Nov. 23.

BIOGRAPHIES AND BOOKS OF CRITICISM :

634 Clemens, Cyril. *Mark Twain's Religion,* with a foreword by Russell Wilbur. Webster Grove, Mo., International Mark Twain Society, 13 pp.

Published as an article in 1934. Cf. above nᵒ *620*.

635 Heller, Otto. *The Seriousness of Mark Twain.* Address at the Annual Dinner of the State Historical Society at Hannibal, Mo., May 9, 1935, published by the Hannibal Chamber of Commerce, 14 pp.

A protest against Brooks's thesis in the name of local patriotism.

636 Hueppy, A. *Mark Twain und die Schweiz,* Dem grossen Freund und Bewunderer unseres Landes zum 100 Geburtstag gewidmet. Zürich, Rütimann & Co., 99 pp.

Mark Twain's visits to Switzerland in 1878, 1891 and 1897.

637 Langdon, Jervis. *Mark Twain and Elmira,* Mark Twain Centennial Committee of New York, 6 l. (leaves).

The author was a nephew of Mark Twain.

638 Paine, A. B. *Mark Twain, A Biography ; the Personal and Literary Life of Samuel L. Clemens,* Centenary Ed., New York & London, Harper & Brothers, 2 vols.

639 WAGENKNECHT, Edward G. *Mark Twain : The Man and His Work*. New Haven, Yale Univ. Press, London, Oxford Univ. Press, x + 301 pp.

The author tries to make the synthesis of all the previous books on Twain, but feels more sympathy with Paine's angelic portrait than with Brooks's thwarted genius theory, though he is aware that " nobody can write about Mrs. Clemens in 1935 as he might have written in 1919. She is no longer an idyll, she is a problem ". Yet, he chooses to ignore this problem. He sees in Mark Twain essentially a product of the frontier, a folk and not a conscious artist.

INTRODUCTIONS AND PREFACES :

640 MARK TWAIN. *Life on the Mississippi*. Abridged and ed. by Edwin Van Knickerbocker. New York & London, Harper & Brothers, xxx + 298 pp,

Follows Paine, Howells, etc. ; no personal views.

641 MARK TWAIN. *Notebook* prepared for publication with comments by A. B. Paine. New York & London, Harper & Brothers, xi + 413 pp.

The editor feels nostalgic when he thinks of the purity of former days : " When restricted at all it was chiefly through his own expressed wish to observe the conventions and convictions of that more orthodox, more timid and delicate (possibly more immaculate), day. "

642 — *Tom Sawyer à travers le monde*. Préface de Rudyard Kipling, traduction d'Albert Savine. Paris, Albin Michel, 257 pp.

A translation of *Tom Sawyer Abroad*.

643 — *Slovenly Peter (Struwwelpeter)*; or Happy Tales and Funny Pictures, freely translated by Mark Twain, with Dr. Hoffmann's illustrations, adapted from the rare 1st 'ed. by Fritz Kredel, New York & London, Harper & Brothers, 31 pp.

644 — *Idem*, now printed for the first time for the members of the Limited Editions Club, New York, The Marchbanks Press, 34 pp.

645 *Mark Twain's Wit and Wisdom*, edited by Cyril Clemens, with a preface by Stephen Leacock. New York, Frederick A. Stokes Co., xi + 167 pp.

An anthology of Mark Twain's jokes.

646 *The Family Mark Twain*, with biographical summary by A. B. Paine and a foreword by Owen Wister. New York and London, Harper & Brothers, xxiv + 1462 pp.

647 *The Mark Twain Omnibus*, drawn from the works of Mark Twain, ed. by Max J. Herzberg. New York & London, Harper & Brothers, xxxvi + 441 pp.

648 MARK TWAIN. *Representative Selections*, ed. with an introduction and a bibliography by Fred L. Pattee. New York, American Book Co., LXIII + 459 pp.

A well informed introduction, but the selection includes nothing from *Huckleberry Finn*.

649 BECKER, May L. *Golden Tales of the Far West*, selected, with an introduction by May L. Becker. New York, Dodd, Mead & Co., XIII + 304 pp.

Contains " Millionnaires " by Mark Twain, and scattered references in the introduction.

650 TAYLOR Coley Banks. *Mark Twain's Margins on Thackeray's Swift*. New York, Gotham House, 55 pp.

OTHER BOOKS DEALING WITH MARK TWAIN :

651 *In Commemoration of the 100th Anniversary of the Birth of Samuel Langhorne Clemens, Famed as Mark Twain*, this book is affectionately dedicated, by the citizens of his boyhood home, Hannibal Mo., Hannibal, Mo., Lithographed by the Standard Printing Co., 24 pp.

652 CROSS, Wilbur L., Governor of Connecticut. *A Statement (regarding) The Centenary of Mark Twain*. A Proposal to designate Nov. 1st as Mark Twain Day, Broadside. Hartford.

653 DEANE, Anthony Charles. " Mark Twain " in *Transactions of the Royal Society of Literature of the U. K.*, Essays by divers hands, New (i.e. 3rd) Series, vol. 14, pp. 99-110.

PERIODICAL LITERATURE :

1) Reviews of Minnie M. Brashear's *Mark Twain, Son of Missouri* (1934).

654 LORCH, F. W. in *AL*, vol. 6, 460-463, Jan.

" She has done much to dispel the notion that Mark Twain's Missouri of the 1840's and 1850's was as culturally barren and oppressive as some critics have alleged... "

655 Anon. in *TLS*, Nov. 30, p. 779.

2) Reviews of Pattee's *Representative Selections* :

656 CLEMENS, Cyril. in *Commonweal*, vol. 22, 350-351, Oct. 11.
Pattee is taken to task for denying Mark Twain a place among " our few great literary masters " because he has no message.

657 DE VOTO, B. in *NEQ*, vol. 8, 427-430, Sept.

658 LORCH, F. W. in *AL*, vol. 7, 350-351, Nov.
Pattee spends too much time refuting Brooks's Freudian interpretation and is rather inconsistent when he concludes that Mark Twain is a " universal classic " after accusing him of being innocent of logic and fundamentally emotional.

659 Anon. in *TLS*, Nov. 30, p. 779.

3) Reviews of *Mark Twain's Wit and Wisdom* :

660 LORCH, F. W. in *AL*, vol. 7, 351, Nov.

661 LOVETT, R. M. in *NR*, vol. 85, 50-51, Nov. 20, " Mark Twain the American ".

662 Anon. in *New York Times Book Rev.*, Aug. 4, p. 5.

4) Reviews of *Mark Twain's Notebook* :

663 CANBY, H. S. in *Book of the Month Club News*, Nov., p. 15.

664 DE VOTO, B. in *New York Times Book Rev.*, Oct. 27, pp. 1, 22, " The Greatness of Mark Twain. "

665 Anon. in *TLS*, Nov. 30, p. 779.

5) Reviews of Wagenknecht's *Mark Twain, The Man and His Work* :

666 DE VOTO, B. in *New York Times Book Rev.*, Oct. 27, pp. 1, 22.

667 HAIGHT, G. S. in *YR*, vol. 25, 212-213, Autumn.

668 LOVETT, R. M. in *NR*, vol. 85, 50-51, Nov. 20.

669 Anon. in *TLS*, Nov. 30, p. 779.

* *
*

670 ALTICK, R. D. " Mark Twain's Despair, an Explanation in Terms of His Humanity. " *South Atlantic Quar.*, vol. 34, 359-367, Oct.
" It was the development of (the) normal human taste for materialism in Mark Twain, at the expense of his idealistic-intellectual-artistic side, that caused him ultimately to become a pessimist and a cynic. "

671 ARVIN, N. " Mark Twain : 1835-1935. " *NR*, vol. 83, 125-127, June 12.
" He is read not because he makes experience more intelligible... but because he cooperates with the desire to play hoo-

key. " Arvin as a socialist condemns him for his lack of " a revolutionary philosophy of comradeship ".

672 BINGHAM, Robert Warwick. " Buffalo's Mark Twain. " *Museum Notes, Buffalo Historical Society*, vol. 2, N°ˢ 4-6, 15 pp.

673 BORGES, Jorge Luis. " Una Vindicación de Mark Twain. " *Sur,* Año 5, n° 14, 40-46, Nov.

> Rejects Brooks's thesis.

674 CANBY, H. S. " Mark Twain : Anti-Victorian. " *SRL*, vol. 12, 3-4. 14, Oct. 12.

> Mark Twain was not suppressed, but oppressed. His oppression was religious and ethical.

675 CHARPENTIER, John. " Humour anglais et humour américain. A propos du centenaire de Mark Twain. " *Merc. de France*, vol. 264, 475-500, Dec.

676 CLEMENS, Cyril. " Mark Twain's Joan of Arc. " *Commonweal*, vol. 22, 323-324, July 26.

677 — " Scattered Letters of Mark Twain, together with Eulogistic Contributions for His Centennial. " *Missouri Hist. Soc. Glimpses of the Past*, vol. 2, 123-132, Nov.

678 COLUM, May M. " The Misunderstood Jester. " *Forum*, vol. 94, 277-278, Nov.

> A superficial discussion of Brooks's and Wagenknecht's views.

679 DICKINSON, A. D. " Huckleberry Finn is 50 years old, yes ; but is he respectable ? " *Wilson Bulletin for Librarians*, vol. 10, 180-185, Nov.

> About a letter which Mark Twain sent to the author, when the latter was a librarian in Brooklyn in 1905, to justify Huckleberry Finn whose so-called obscenity, he claimed, was nothing compared to that of the Bible.

680 DREISER, Theodore. " Mark the Double Twain. " *Eng. Jour.*, vol. 24, 615-627, Oct.

> Makes Twain in his own image : a pessimist and a determinist and a realist at heart.

681 DUNSMOOR, K. " Land of Tom and Huck. " *Scholastic*, vol. 27, 11-12, Nov. 23.

682 EMBERSON, Frances G. " Mark Twain's Vocabulary : A General Survey. " *Univ. of Missouri Studies*, vol. 10, n° 3, 1-53.

683 ESKEW, G. L. " Steamboating again on Mark Twain's River ". *Rotarian*, vol. 47, 25-28, 50, Nov.

684 FISCHER, Walter. " Mark Twain : Zu seinem 100 Geburtstage. " *Neueren Sprachen*, vol. 43, 471-480.

A good critical survey of Mark Twain's works. According to Fischer, Twain was neither a mere funny man, nor a deep pessimistic philosopher, but a good American pragmatist.

685 FOOTE, F. B. " A Mark Twain Problem — The Mysterious Paragraph. " *SRL*, vol. 12, 9, Oct. 26.

A passage of *The Mysterious Stranger* quoted by a San Francisco paper, but not to be found in the book. Cf. n° *710*.

686 HUGHES, R. " I Heard Mark Twain Laugh. " *Good Housekeeping*, vol. 101, 44-45, Nov.

687 LA COSSITT, Henry. " Hail to Hannibal, Honoring Mark Twain. " *New York Times Mag.*, Dec. 1, p 11, 16.

688 LAUTREC, Gabriel de. " Mark Twain. " *Merc. de France*, vol. 264, 69-82, Nov. 15.

Chiefly biographical, and, when critical, very superficial.

689 LEACOCK, S. " Mark Twain and Canada. " *Queen's Quar.*, vol. 42, 68-81, Feb.

On Mark Twain's visits to Canada.

690 LE BRETON, Maurice. " Un Centenaire : Mark Twain. " *RAA*, vol. 13, 401-419, June.

The author studies the reasons for Mark Twain's lack of success in France and then analyzes his Americanism. The America Mark Twain loved was that of his youth. He was essentially a Westerner, as De Voto claims. His realism was that of a dreamer. His humour now fanciful, now bitter and satirical, has been interpreted differently according to the temperament of the critics. Hence the different schools of Mark Twain criticism. This article itself is a brilliant synthesis of the various interpretations so far attempted.

691 LEMONNIER, Léon. " Les débuts d'un humoriste. " *RAA*, vol. 13, 401-419, Juin.

Insists on the duality of Mark Twain's genius.

692 — " Les Débuts d'un Humoriste. " *Grande Revue*, vol. 149, 76-88, Nov.

693 — " L'Enfance de Mark Twain. " *Revue de France*, vol. 15, 130-158, Nov.

694 MASTERS, Edgar Lee. " Mark Twain : Son of the Frontier. " *Am. Merc.*, vol. 36, 67-74, Sept.

Twain as the " super-reporter " of " the uncontaminated America of the West " whom his wife unfortunately tried to tame and refine. He was a pessimist at heart.

695 MEIGS, C. " Mark Twain. " *St. Nicholas*, vol. 63, 14-16, 50-51, Nov.

Tells his escape from Hannibal as a stowaway when a boy.

696 METZ, J. J. " Mark Twain Centennial. " *Industrial Arts and Vocational Education*, vol. 24, 364-365, Dec.

697 MONROE, Harriet. " On the Great River. " *Poetry*, vol. 46, 268-274, Aug.
   A trip down the Mississippi and a visit of Hannibal.

698 MORLEY, C. " Hunting Mark's Remainders. " *SRL*, vol. 13, 15-16, Nov. 2.
   In praise of *Huckleberry Finn*.

699 PAINE, A. B. " Unpublished Diaries of Mark Twain. " *Hearst's International*, vol. 99, 24-27, 134-136, Aug.

700 PARTRIDGE, Henry M. " Did Mark Twain Perpetrate Literary Hoaxes. " *Am. Book Collector*, vol. 6, 20-23, Jan., 50-53, Feb.
   The first instalment came out in the Dec. 1934 issue.

701 PHELPS, W. L. " Mark Twain. " *YR*, vol. 25, n. s., 291-310, Dec.

702 QUICK, Dorothy. " A Little Girl's Mark Twain. " *North Am. Rev.*, vol. 240, 342-348, Sept.

703 ROBBINS, L. H. " Mark Twain's Fame Goes Marching On : His Century Which Closes This Year Finds Him Still the Best-Loved and Most Widely Read of American Authors. " *New York Times Mag.*, April 21, pp. 4, 16.

704 ROBERTS, R. Ellis. " Mark Twain. " *Fortnightly Rev.*, n. s., vol. 138, 583-592, Nov.

705 SCHMITT, G. " Mark Twain Digs for Gold — One Act Play. " *Scholastic*, vol. 27, 9-10, Nov. 23.

706 SCHOENEMANN, F. " Mark Twain — ein Freund Deutschlands. " *Deutsche Allgemeine Zeitung*, Nov. 24.

707 STEWART, H. L. " Mark Twain on the Jewish Problem. " *Dalhousie Rev.*, vol. 14, 455-458, Jan.
   Mark Twain as an observer of anti-semitism in Germany.

708 UNDERHILL, I. S. " The Haunted Book : A Further Exploration Concerning Huckleberry Finn. " *Colophon*, n. s., vol. I, 281-291, Autumn.
   Biographical notes on the 1st edition.

709 VAN DOREN, Mark. " A Century of Mark Twain. " *Nation*, vol. 141, 472-474, Oct. 23.
   The contemporaries of Mark Twain enjoyed him as a humorist, but since 1910 he has become an object of thought and is now, considered an artist in prose.

710 WAGENKNECHT, E. " Mysterious Paragraph ; Reply. " *SRL* vol. 13, 29, Nov. 16.
   Cf. E. B. Foote's article above (nᵒ *685*). The reply does not solve the problem.

711 WISTER, Owen. " In Homage to Mark Twain. " *Harper's M.*, vol. 171, 547-556, Oct. (abridged in *Scholastic,* vol. 27, 6-7, Nov. 23).

Anecdotal. Also an analysis of Twain's pessimism.

712 Anon. " Mark Twain Centennial to be widely celebrated. " *Pub. W.*, vol. 127, 697, Feb. 9.

713 — " Mark Twain Centennial. " *Lit. Digest*, vol. 119, 31, April 20.

714 Anon. " Mark Twain in Canada. " *Queen's Quar.*, vol. 42, 272-274, May.

On Twain's visit to Canada in 1895.

715 — " Princes de l'humour : Alphonse Allais, Mark Twain. " *Annales Politiques et Littéraires*, vol. 160, 316-317, Sept. 25.

716 — " Mark Twain. " *SRL*, vol. 13, 8, Nov. 16.

717 — " Our Mark Twain. " *Scholastic*, vol. 27, 3, Nov. 23.

718 — " Chronology of the Life of Mark Twain. " *Ibid.*, 16, Nov. 23.

719 — " Ever This Twain Is Met. " *Lit. Digest*, vol. 120, 19, Nov. 30.

World-wide tributes paid on centenary of writer's birthday.

720 — " Mark Twain. " *TLS*, Nov. 30, pp. 779-780.

He was not a great creator, he was not a novelist, but he will survive as the author of *Tom Sawyer, Huckleberry Finn, Life on the Mississippi, Roughing It,* and portions of *The Gilded Age* and *Pudd'nhead Wilson.* " The humourist appears in them all, and yet it is less as a humourist than as a poet, a poet even in his humour, that one finally values him. "

721 — " The Mark Twain Commemoration. " *Columbia Univ. Quar.*, vol. 27, 357-378, Dec.

Includes an address by Prof. Campbell and " The Return of Huckleberry Finn " by C. Morley. The latter recognizes the importance of Brooks's and Mumford's interpretation of Mark Twain but reproaches them with approaching " a great humorist without exhibiting... the slightest ray of a sense of humor whatever ".

1936

BIOGRAPHIES AND BOOKS OF CRITICISM :

722 ADE, George. *Revived Remarks on Mark Twain*, also the address of John McCutcheon commemorating the centenary of Mark Twain's birth, compiled by George Hiram Brownell. Chicago, privately printed, 34 pp.

723 BENSON, Ivan. *Mark Twain in the West*. Sacramento, Calif., California State Printing Office, VII + 30 pp.

724 GRIMES, Absalom. *Absalom Grimes Confederate Mail-Runner*. New Haven, Yale Univ. Press.
> The first ed. of this book came out in 1926. The author represents himself as intimately associated with Mark Twain during " the campaign that failed ", but Mark Twain mentions him in his own account of this episode as a member of another company.

725 LEMONNIER, Leon. *La jeunesse aventureuse de Mark Twain*. Paris, Desclée de Brouwer et Co., 249 pp.
> A lively and entertaining book, which, however, contains no new information on Mark Twain.

726 O'CONNOR, Laurel. *Drinking with Mark Twain* : Recollections of Mark Twain and His Cronies as Told to Me. New York, Riemsolyk Bookservice, unnumbered pp.

INTRODUCTIONS AND PREFACES :

727 MARK TWAIN. *The Adventures of Tom Sawyer*, illustrated by Norman Rockwell, with an introduction by John T. Winterich. New York, The Heritage Press, London, The Nonesuch Press, 284 pp.

728 — *1601, or Conversation at the social fireside as it was in the time of the Tudors*, with notes on Mark Twain's 1601 and a check-

list of various editions and reprints compiled by Irvin Haas.
Chicago, Black Cat Press, 39 pp.

729 — *What is Man ?* with an introduction by S. K. Ratcliffe. London,
Watts & Co., xxxix + 114 pp.

730 BURRELL, J. A. *The Bedside Book of Famous American Short
Stories.* New York, Random House, xix + 1349 pp.
Includes "The Man That Corrupted Hadleyburg", pp. 260-298.

731 HUDSON, Arthur Palmer (ed.). *Humor of the Old Deep South.*
New York, Macmillan, xxvi + 548 pp.

732 LEACOCK, S. *The Greatest Pages of American Humor,* selected and
discussed by S. Leacock. Garden City, Doubleday, Doran & Co.,
x + 293 pp.
Pp. 127-153, selections from Mark Twain.

733 LOWE, Orton. *Our Land and Its Literature.* New York & London,
Harper & Brothers, xxxi + 666 pp.
Contains " The Jumping Frog. "

OTHER BOOKS DEALING WITH MARK TWAIN :

734 BOYNTON, Percy H. *Literature and American Life,* for Students
of American Literature. Boston, Ginn & Co., xiii + 933 pp.

735 NEUBAUER, Heinz. *Amerikanische Goldgräberliteratur* (Bret Harte,
Mark Twain, Jack London). Grossenheim i. Sa., H. Plasnick,
500 pp.

736 QUINN, Arthur Hobson. *American Fiction : An Historical and
Critical Survey.* New York & London, Appleton-Century Co.,
xxiii + 805 pp.
Pp. 243-256, " Mark Twain and the Romance of the South ",
an honest, commonplace critical survey.

737 TAYLOR, Walter Fuller. *A History of American Letters.* New York,
American Book Co., 460 pp.
A college handbook. On Mark Twain, pp. 262-274.

PERIODICAL LITERATURE :

1) Reviews of Wagenknecht's *Mark Twain, The Man and
His Work* (1935) :

738 BRASHEAR, M. M. in *Virginia Quar. Rev.,* " Mark Twain in Perspective ", vol. 12, 127-130, Jan.
Favourable.

739 De Voto, B. in *NEQ*, vol. 9, 332-338, June.

It is a significant fact that a professor like Wagenknecht should devote a whole book to Mark Twain who was considered as hardly a man of letters at all by the highbrows of his time. The xxth century is better attuned to his disillusionment and certain aspects of his americanism than the xixth.

740 Mc C. in *Catholic World*, vol. 142, 499-500, Jan.

741 Spiller, R. E. in *AL*, vol. 8, 96-98, March.

Torn between his loyalty to Paine and his respect for Brooks, Wagenknecht is more a mediator than a judge.

2) Review of Pattee's *Representative Selections* (1935) :

742 Mc C. in *Catholic World*, vol. 142, 499-500, Jan.

3) Reviews of *Mark Twain's Notebook* (1935) :

743 Clarke, E. J. in *Commonweal*, " Cynic and Humorist. " vol. 23, 415-416, Feb. 7.

744 Mc C. in *Catholic World*, vol. 142, 499-500, Jan.

Accuses Paine of trying to make Mark Twain acceptable to everybody in spite of his heretical views.

4) Review of Merle Johnson's *Bibliography* (1935) :

745 Randall, D. A. in *Publ. W.*, vol. 129, 917-918, Feb. 22.

* * *

746 Benson, Adolph B. " Mark Twain in Småland. " *American Swedish M.*, vol. 30, 4-6.

747 Burke, Richard. " Mark Twain : An Exhibition. " *New York Public Library Bull.*, vol. 40, 499-501, June.

748 Clemens, Cyril. " Mark Twain's Reading. " *Commonweal*, vol. 24, 363-364, Aug.

749 Coffin, Robert P. Tristram. " Poem to Mark Twain. " *Mark Twain Quar.*, Fall, p. 5.

750 Davidson, L. B. " He Fell in Love with a Picture. " *Reader's Digest*, vol. 28, 9-12, Jan.

i.e. with the picture of Olivia Langdon which her brother Charles showed him during the Quaker City cruise.

751 Ferguson, De Lancey. ,, The Uncollected Portions of Mark Twain's Autobiography. " *AL*, vol. 8, 37-46, March.

Points out a certain number of differences between the text published by Mark Twain himself in the *North Am. Rev.*, 1906-1907 and later in *Harper's M.* in 1922, and the text published in book form in 1924. There were unfortunate omissions and alterations.

752 FLANAGAN, J. T. " Mark Twain on the Upper Mississippi. " *Minnesota History*, vol. 17, 369-384, Dec.

On his trip to Minnesota, in the spring of 1882.

753 HAMADA, Masajiro. " Mark Twain's Conception of Social Justice. " *Studies in English Literature* (Japan), vol. 16, 593-616, Oct. .

Mark Twain as a champion of social justice. Naïve and superficial : " Samuel Clemens and Leo Tolstoï would have been as like as two peas, had Clemens only had ample side whiskers. "

754 LORCH, W. H. " Mark Twain's Orphanage Lecture. " *AL*, vol. 7, 453-455, Jan.

" The American Vandal Abroad ", Jan. 22, 1869 in Cleveland for the benefit of an orphanage on the invitation of Mrs. Fairbanks who was a member of the board of trustees.

755 MASTERS, E. L. " The House where Mark Twain was born. " *Mark Twain Quar.*, Fall, p. 5.

A poem.

756 MONTENEGRO, Ernesto. " Doble Personalidad de Mark Twain. " *Atenea* (Chili), Oct., 47-69.

A summary of Brooks's theory.

757 SAKHAROV, W. " Twain Exhibit in Russia. " *Library Jour.*, vol. 61, 157, Feb. 15.

758 SCHOENEMANN, Friedrich. " Mark Twain und Deutschland. " *Hochschule und Ausland*, Heft 1936, Jan. 37-43. (reprinted in *Auslese*, Heft, 1936, Feb.).

Summary of a commemorative speech delivered in Berlin in 1935.

759 — " Neue Mark Twain Studien. " *Neueren Sprachen*, vol. 44, 260-272.

A survey of recent Mark Twain criticism, with a strong political bias : reproaches Wagenknecht with making an insulting reference to Hitler in his book and accuses modern American literature of being debased by Jewish influences.

760 SCHULTZ, J. R. " New Letters of Mark Twain. " *AL*, vol. 8, 47-51. March.

Letters to Bayard Taylor.

761 SEAMAN, O. " To Mark Twain — A Poem. " *SRL*, vol. 13, 13, Feb. 29.

762 TARKINGTON, Booth. " Mark Twain and Boys. " *Mark Twain Quar.*, vol. I, Fall, 6-7.

763 WALKER, Franklin. " An Influence from San Francisco on Mark Twain's *The Gilded Age.* " *AL*, vol. 8, 63-66, March.

     Laura Hawkins's murder of Col. Selby, her trial and her acquittal on the ground of temporary insanity closely parallel the actual experiences of one Laura D. Fair of San Francisco whom Mark Twain may have known when he was living in Virginia City.

764 WINTERICH, J. T. " Mark Twain's Only Son. " *SRL*, vol. 14, 20, Oct. 3.

     A photograph of Langdon Clemens.

765 Anon. " He Kept His Nerve. " *SRL*, vol. 13, 8, Jan. 11.

     Mark Twain knew the seamy side of the Mississippi Valley, but, unlike Faulkner, Caldwell, etc., he did not lose his nerve and give up humanity.

766 — " Mark Twain's Favorite Music. " *Etude*, vol. 54, 661, Oct.

UNPUBLISHED THESES :

767 BENSON, Ivan. *The Western Development of Mark Twain,* a doctoral thesis for the Univ. of Southern California.

1937

BIOGRAPHIES AND BOOKS OF CRITICISM :

None.

INTRODUCTIONS AND PREFACES :

768 MARK TWAIN. *Letters from the Sandwich Islands Written for the Sacramento Union,* Introduction and conclusion by G. Ezra Dane, San Francisco, The Grabhorn Press, XII + 224 pp.

769 — *The Adventures of Tom Sawyer,* together with The Celebrated Jumping Frog of Calaveras County and Other Tales, 15 original illustrations. Reading, Pa., The Spencer Press, VIII + 310 pp.

770 — *The Prince and the Pauper,* illustrated by Robert Lawson. Chicago, Philadelphia, The John C. Winston Co., XV + 274 pp.

OTHER BOOKS DEALING WITH MARK TWAIN :

771 BLAIR, Walter. *Native American Humor.* New York, American Book Co., XV + 573 pp.

On Mark Twain, pp. 147-162 : an excellent study of Mark Twain relations with and superiority to Western and South-western humorists. Extracts from his works, pp. 515-561.

772 PRAZ, Mario. *Studi e Svaghi Inglesi,* Firenze (Florence), Sansoni, VIII + 348 pp.

Contains a stimulating essay on Twain, pp. 157-163.

PERIODICAL LITERATURE :

1) Review of Mark Twain's *Wit and Wisdom* (1935) :

773 L. in *Southwest Rev.,* vol. 22, 212, Winter.

2) Review of Mark Twain's *Notebook* (1935) :

774   H. N. in *Standard*, vol. 23, 217, March.

3) Review of L. Lemonnier's *La Jeunesse aventureuse de Mark Twain* (1936) :

774*   LE BRETON, Maurice in *EA*, vol. 1, 465, Sept.

* *
*

775   A. L. " Mark Twain on the Screen. " *SRL*, vol. 16, 10, June 12.
On the movie version of *The Prince and the Pauper*.

776   BABLER, O. F. " Mark Twain : An Aphorism. " *N & Q*, vol. 173, 45, July 17.
On the aphorism : " It is not always easy to bear another prosperity. Another man's, I mean. " (*Following the Equator*, Pt 2, Chap. 3.).

777   BENSON, Adolph B. " Mark Twain's Contacts with Scandinavia. " *Scand. Studies and Notes*, vol. 14, 159-167, Aug.

778   BLANCK, J. " Mark Twain's Sketches Old and New. " *Pub. W.*, vol. 132, 1740-1741, Oct. 30.
One of them " From Hospital Days " was not by him. Also an instance of unconscious plagiarism in *Following the Equator*.

779   BURTON, Richard. " Mark Twain in the Hartford Days. " *Mark Twain Quar.*, vol. I, n⁰ 4, p. 5, Summer.

780   CLEMENS, Cyril. " Mark Twain's Gold Hill Hold-Up. " *Rotarian*, vol. 51, 38-39, Nov.
A joke played on Mark Twain in 1866 in Gold Hill, Nevada.

781   CORYELL, I. " Josh, of the *Territorial Enterprise*. " *North Am. Rev.*, vol. 243, 287-295, June.
On Mark Twain in Virginia City.

782   FERGUSON, DeLancey. " The Petrified Truth. " *Colophon*, n. s., vol. 2, 189-196, Winter.
Like De Quille's Solar Armor, his Petrified Man hoax never enjoyed the success he later claimed for it.

783   HERRICK, Robert. " Mark Twain and the American Tradition. " *Mark Twain Quar.*, vol. 2, 8-11, Winter.
Mark Twain represents the true indigenous American tradition. Brooks cannot understand him. His criticism is born of European nostalgia and a spurious philosophy.

784   JOHNSON, Burges. " When Mark Twain Cursed Me. " *Mark Twain Quar.*, vol. 2, n⁰ 2, 8-9, 24.

785 Leisy, Ernest E. " Mark Twain's Part in *The Gilded Age.* " *AL*, vol. 8, 445-447, Jan.

" It appears that the strands of Warner and Mark Twain in this novel were more closely interwoven than had been supposed [by Paine]. "

786 Marcosson, Isaac F. " Mark Twain as Collaborator. " *Mark Twain Quar.*, vol. 2, n⁰ 2, 7, 24, Winter 1937-1938.

About an article on Henry Rogers.

787 Pabody, E. F. " Mark Twain's Ghost Story. " *Minnesota History*, vol. 18, 28-35, March.

On Mark Twain's appearance in Minneapolis with Cable on Jan. 24, 1885.

788 Robertson, Stuart. " Mark Twain in Germany. " *Mark Twain Quar.*, vol. 2, n⁰ 1, 10-12, Fall.

789 Rowe, Ida. " Mark Twain's Interest in Nature. " *Mark Twain Quar.*, vol. I, n⁰ 4, 7, 9-10, 14, Summer.

790 Swain, L. H. " Mark Twain as a Music Critic : A Case Study in Esthetic Growth. " *Furman Bull.*, vol. 19, 48-53, April.

791 Verdaguer, Mario. " Humorismo inglés e ironía yanqui. " *La Razón* (Panama), vol. 5, 2, July 3.

792 Waggoner, Hyatt H. „ Science in the Thought of Mark Twain. " *AL*, vol. 8, 357-370, Jan.

Mark Twain was influenced by the scientific thought of his time rather than by xviiith century thinkers, contrary to what M.M. Brashear tried to prove in her book.

793 Wood, Grant. " My Debt to Mark Twain. " *Mark Twain Quar.*, vol. 2, n⁰ 1, pp. 6, 14, 24, Fall.

His two favorite books : *Tom Sawyer* and *Huckleberry Finn*.

UNPUBLISHED THESES :

794 Neill, Annie B. *Mark Twain and the Arts ;* cf. summary in *Abstracts of Theses, Southern Methodist Univ.*, 25-26.

1938

BIBLIOGRAPHIES :

795 Lee, Alfred Pyle. *First and Other Editions of Samuel L. Clemens,* collected by the well-known bibliographer, Dr. Albert P. Lee of Philadelphia, with a few additions. New York, F. C. Duschnes, 31 pp.

BIOGRAPHIES AND BOOKS OF CRITICISM :

796 Benson, Ivan. *Mark Twain's Western Years,* together with hitherto unreprinted Clemens Western Items. Stanford Univ., Calif., Stanford Univ. Press & London, Oxford Univ. Press, x + 218 pp.

A Mark Twain was a mere amateur before he went West, he was a full-fledged author when he left it. The West made him.

797 Masters, Edgar Lee. *Mark Twain : A Portrait.* New York, Charles Scribner's Sons, 259 pp.

A caricature rather than a portrait ; a crude restatement of the Brooks theory ; holds *The Mysterious Stranger* to be Twain's masterpiece.

798 Ramsay, Robert L. & Emberson, Frances G. *A Mark Twain Lexicon.* Columbia, Mo., Univ. of Missouri Studies, vol. 13, n⁰ I, cxix + 278 pp.

INTRODUCTIONS AND PREFACES :

799 Mark Twain. *Letter to William Bowen, Buffalo, February Sixth, 1870,* Prefatory Note by Clara Clemens Gabrilowitsch, Foreword by Albert W. Gunnison. San Francisco, The Book Club of California, 11 pp.

800 — Letters from the Sandwhich Islands, Written for the Sacramento Union, Introduction and conclusion by G. Ezra Dane. Stanford

Univ. Press, & London, Oxford Univ. Press, xii + 224 pp.
Mark Twain embodied part of this material in *Roughing It.*

801 — *The Washoe Giant in San Francisco,* Collected and ed. with
an introduction by Franklin Walker. San Francisco, G. Fields,
143 pp.
The Washoe Giant, i.e. Mark Twain.

802 FRENCH, Joseph Lewis (ed.). *Sixty years of American Humor from
Mark Twain to Benchley.* A Prose Anthology. Garden City,
Garden City Publishing Co., x + 401 pp.
The first ed. was published in 1924. Cf. above n⁰ *323.*

OTHER BOOKS DEALING WITH MARK TWAIN :

803 PARKS, E. Winfield. *Segments of Southern Thought.* Athens, Ga.,
University of Georgia Press, ix + 392 pp.
Contains a chapter entitled " Mark Twain as Southerner ".

804 SEVERANCE, Emily A. *Journal* — *Letters of Emily A. Severance,*
ed. by Julia S. Millikin, Cleveland Gates Press, privately
printed, 221 pp.
A journal of the Quaker City cruise.

PERIODICAL LITERATURE :

1) Review of Hüppy's *Mark Twain und die Schweiz* (1935) :
805 LORCH, Fred W. in *AL,* vol. 9, 488-489, Jan.

2) Review of Ramsay and Emberson's *Mark Twain Lexicon :*
806 BLAIR, W. in *Univ. Rev.* (Univ. of Kansas City), " Mark Twain's
Way with Words ", vol. 5, 60-62, Autumn.

3) Reviews of E. L. Master's *Mark Twain : A Portrait :*
807 DE VOTO, B. in *SRL,* " Mark Twain : A Caricature of Mark Twain ",
vol. 17, 5, March 19.
A slating.

808 LORCH, Fred W. in *AL,* vol. 10, 373-376, Nov.
Masters interprets Mark Twain from a strictly proletarian
point of view.

809 WAGENKNECHT, E. in *New York Times Book Rev.,* May 8, p. 10.
Masters's book " is far from proving that Mark Twain deserves
to be cast into the outer darkness because forty years ago he
did not see clearly everything that Mr. Masters sees to-day "

4) Reviews of Benson's *Mark Twain's Western Years* :

810 MABBOTT, T. O. in *Commonvveal*, vol. 28, 302, July 8.

811 QUINN, A. H. in *Pacific Hist. Rev.*, vol. 7, 282-283, Sept.
Approves Mrs. Clemens's and Howells's influence on Mark Twain. What he wrote in the West was too often crude and vulgar.

812 WAGENKNECHT, B. in *New York Times Book Rev.*, June 19, p. 2.

5) Review of Mark Twain's *Letters from the Sandwich Islands* :

813 MABBOTT, T. O. in *Commonweal*, vol. 28, 480, Sept. 2.

*
* *

814 BLODGETT, Harold. " A Note on Mark Twain's *Library of Humor.* " *AL*, vol. 10, 78-80, March.
The first ed. was actually done by Howells and the 1906 one by Harper & Brothers.

815 DE VOTO, B. " Mark Twain Papers ; with excerpts from Twain's unpublished Outlines of History. " *SRL*, vol. 19, 3-4, 14-15, Dec. 10.

816 EASTMAN, Max. " Mark Twain's Elmira. " *Harper's M.*, vol. 176, 620-632, May.
Tries to prove that Elmira was very far from " those up-State towns... without traditions of moral freedom and intellectual culture " which Brooks and his supporters claimed it was.

817 FERGUSON, DeLancey. " Huck Finn Aborning. " *Colophon*, n. s., vol. 3, n° 2, 171-180, Spring.
After studying the original manuscript of *Huckleberry Finn* and the corrections made by Mark Twain, the author concludes : " Of the thwarted Swift invented by Mr. Brooks and his followers there is not a trace. "

818 JACOBS, W. W. " An Englishman's Opinion of Mark Twain ". *Mark Twain Quar.*, vol. 2, n° 4, 1-2, Fall.

819 JORDAN, Elizabeth. " A Silent Celebrety. " *Christian Science Monitor*, Nov. 4, p. 9.

820 KANTOR, M. " Boy in the Dark ; fantasy of the Mark Twain Country. " *Scholastic*, vol. 33, 6 +, Sept. 17.

821 LORCH, Fred W. " Mark Twain's Trip to Humboldt in 1861. " *AL*, vol. 10, 343-349, Nov.
Accuses him of behaving with levity when the Civil War broke out.

822 MacALISTER, Sir Ian. " Mark Twain, Some Personal Reminiscences. " *Landmark*, vol. 20, 141-147, March.

Chiefly on Mark Twain's popularity in England in the early nineties.

823 MOORE, J. B. " Mark Twain and Copyright. " *Mark Twain Quar.*, vol. 3, n⁰ 1, p. 3, Winter.

824 MORRIS, Courtland P. " The Model for Huck Finn. " *Mark Twain Quar.*, vol. 2, n⁰ 4, 22, 23, Summer-Fall.

The author sat for Kemble when he drew the illustrations of *Huckleberry Finn*.

825 MOTT, Howard S., Jr. " The Origin of Aunt Polly. " *Pub. W.*, vol. 134, 1821-1823, Nov. 19.

She was partly drawn from life, partly modelled on Benjamin Shillaber's Mrs. Ruth Partington.

826 NYE, Russel B. " Mark Twain in Oberlin. " *Ohio State Archaeological Quar.*, vol. 48, 69-73, Jan.

827 PUTNAM, Samuel. " The Americanism of Mark Twain. " *Mark Twain Quar.*, vol. 2, n⁰ 4, 13, 34, Fall.

828 QUICK, Dorothy. " My Author's League with Mark Twain. " *North Am. Rev.*, vol. 245, 315-329, Summer.

His friendship with a little girl ; shows how deeply he loved children in his old age.

829 REYNOLDS, H. " Mark Twain's Literary Beginnings. " *Christian Science Monitor*, Mag. section, p. 10. June 15.

830 ROADES, Sister M. T. " Don Quixote and *A Connecticut Yankee in King Arthur's Court*. " *Mark Twain Quar.*, vol. 2, n⁰ 4, 8-9, Fall.

831 TAYLOR, Walter F. " Mark Twain and the Machine Age. " *South Atlantic Quar.*, vol. 37, 384-396, Oct. (later reprinted in *Fifty Years of the South Atlantic Quarterly*, 1952, 397 pp.).

On Mark Twain's sympathy with the exploited in *The Gilded Age* and *A Connecticut Yankee*.

UNPUBLISHED THESES :

832 BAILEY, Mary Matilda. *Mark Twain and the Fine Arts*, cf. *Abstracts of Theses, Univ. of Pittsburgh Bulletin*, vol. 35, 28-34.

833 GAUDEK, Ida Rud. Math. *Persönliches Erleben in den Werken Mark Twains*, doctoral thesis for the Univ. of Vienna (cf. *AL*, vol. 21, 352, Nov. 1949).

1939

BIBLIOGRAPHIES :

834 Hellman, Florence S. *List of Writings by Mark Twain translated into certain foreign languages,* compiled by Florence S. Hellman, Washington, July 1939, 14 pp.

(U. S. Library of Congress, Division of Bibliography, Selected list of references, n° 1450, typewritten).

BIOGRAPHIES AND BOOKS OF CRITICISM :

835 Ade, George. *One Afternoon with Mark Twain.* Chicago, The Mark Twain Society of Chicago, 15 pp.

One afternoon in 1902.

836 Clemens, Cyril. *My Cousin Mark Twain,* with an introduction by Booth Tarkington, Emmaus, Pa., Rodale Press & London, Werner Laurie, xii + 219 pp.

Anecdotal and superficial.

837 Hemminghaus, Edgar H. *Mark Twain in Germany (1874 to date).* New York, Columbia Univ. Germanic Studies, n° 9, 170 pp.

The purpose of the book is " to present a somewhat clearly defined picture of the reception of Mark Twain by the German public and German critics ". Consists chiefly of a discussion of Schönemann's, Lüdeke's and W. Fischer's views.

838 Mendelson, M. *Mark Twain.* Moscow, Fskblksm Molodoya Gvardiya (Young Guard), 272 pp.

Cf. C. A. Manning's review in *AL,* Nov. 1948.

INTRODUCTIONS AND PREFACES :

839 Mark Twain. *Tom Sawyer,* with an introduction by Bernard De Voto, including as a prologue the " Boy's Manuscript " here first printed. Cambridge, Mass., Printed for the Members of the Limited Editions Club at the University Press, xxx + 340 pp.

According to the Editor, " Mark could not have written about boyhood as it appears in the works of S. Freud even he had thought of it that way, but there is no other evidence that he thought of it as otherwise than sexless... "

840 — *Conversation as it was at the fireside of the Tudors.* Embellished with an illuminating introduction, facetious notes and a bibliography by Franklin J. Meine. Chicago, Privately printed for the Mark Twain Society of Chicago, 80 pp.

841 MARK TWAIN. *Letters from Honolulu written for the Sacramento Union*, introduction by John W. Vandercock, Honolulu, T. Nickerson, xv + 101 pp.

842 — *The Prince and the Pauper*, ridotto e annotato da G. Tacconis. Turin, Società ed. internazionale (Scrittori inglesi e americani commentati per le scuole), 234 pp.

843 — *The Favorite Works of Mark Twain*, De Luxe Ed., New York, Garden City, Publishing Co., xxiv + 1178 pp.

Pp. ix-xii, a biographical summary by A. B. Paine.

Pp. xiii + xxiv, " In Homage of Mark Twain " by Owen Wister.

Contains *Life on the Mississippi*, *Huckleberry Finn*, *A Connecticut Yankee*, in their entirety and extracts from his other works.

OTHER BOOKS DEALING WITH MARK TWAIN :

844 SMITH, Bernard. *Forces in American Criticism*, A Study in the History of American Thought. New York, Harcourt, Brace & Co., x + 401 pp.

Scattered references to Mark Twain.

845 WALKER, Franklin D. *San Francisco's Literary Frontier*. New York, Alfred A. Knopf, xii + 400 + xxv.

PERIODICAL LITERATURE :

1) Reviews of Cyril Clemens's *My Cousin Mark Twain* :

846 BRASHEAR, M. M. in *AL*, vol. 11, 231-232, May (cf. n⁰ *847*).

847 CLEMENS, Cyril. " Reply to M. M. Brashear " *ibid.*, 296-297, Nov.

Protests against the unfairness of M. M. Brashear's review. (Cf. n⁰ *846*) claims that his book contains much new material.

848 De Voto, B. in *SRL*, vol. 19, 16, March 11.

A slating. Ridicules C. Clemens and accuses him of plagiarism. (Cf. nᵒ *849*).

849 Clemens, C. " Reply to Bernard De Voto. " *Ibid.*, p. 9, April 8.

Corrects a few mis-statements and exaggerations of De Voto. Cf. preceding article.

850 Anon. in *New York Times Book Rev.*, Feb. 5, p. 3.

" ... not a distinguished nor very valuable book, but it is lively and pleasantly familiar. "

851 — in *TLS*, Oct. 14, 587.

2) Reviews of Mark Twain's *Letters from the Sandwich Islands* (1938).

852 Campbell, O. J. in *AS*, vol. 14, 47-49, Feb.

" ... the linguistic interest to be found in these letters is not even that of an amateur scientist, but merely that of a humorist with an artist's interest in strange vocabularies. "

853 Horgan, P. in *YR*, vol. 28, 846-849, June.

854 Lorch, F. W. in *AL*, vol. 10, 511-513, Jan.

" ... these letters... present an important transition in Mark Twain's writing from the 'broad burlesque and sometimes crude satire which heretofore had been his principal stock in trade ' to the greater literary finish of *Innocents Abroad...* "

3) Reviews of Ramsay and Emberson's *Mark Twain Lexicon* (1938) :

855 Campbell, O. J. in *AS*, " A Mark Twain Lexicon ", vol. 14, 132-133, April.

" Meticulously accurate " from a linguistic point of view.

856 Greet, C. in *AL*, vol. 11, 233, May.

The Mark Twain Lexicon contains " 4342 entries for which Mark Twain gives the earliest recorded literary evidence ".

857 Holthausen, F. in *Angl. Bbl.*, vol. 50, 91-95.

858 Hulbert, J. R. in *JEGP*, vol. 38, 313-314.

The authors have a tendency to exaggerate the American character of Mark Twain's language.

858* Lemonnier, Léon in *EA*, vol. 3, 105, Jan.-March.

4) Review of Mark Twain's *Conversation as it was at the fireside of the Tudors :*

859 Davenport, B. in *SRL*, vol. 20, p. 19, July 1.

Disapproves of its publication.

5) Review of *The Washoe Giant in San Francisco* (1938) :
860 SMITH, G. H. in *AL*, vol. 10, 513-518, Jan.
The only value of these articles " lies in the fact that they were written by a man who became famous ".

6) Review of Benson's *Mark Twain's Western Years* (1938) :
861 HORGAN, P. in *YR*, vol. 28, 847-849, March.
Favourable.

*
* *

862 BLAIR, W. " Mark Twain, New York Correspondent. " *AL*, vol. 11, 247-259, Nov.
Mark Twain was correspondent for the *Alta California* in New York in 1867 before leaving on the Quaker City.

863 — " On the Structure of Tom Sawyer. " *MP*, vol. 37, 75-88, Aug.
Insists on Mark Twain's artistry : " If *Tom Sawyer* is regarded as a working-out in fictional form of... a boy's maturing, the book will reveal... a structure on the whole quite well adapted to its purpose. "

864 BROWNELL, G. H. " About Twain in Periodicals. " *Twainian*, vol. I, n⁰ 7, 4-5.

865 BUNKER, Blaise. " The Mark Twain Society. " *SRL*, vol. 20, 11-12, July 15.
On Cyril Clemens and his Society. Mildly humorous.

866 CLEMENS, Cyril. " Mark Twain's View of *1601*. " *SRL*, vol. 20, 9, Sept. 30.
Disapproves of the publication of *1601*.

867 COWIE, Alexander. " Mark Twain Controls Himself ; Reply to DeLancey Ferguson. " *AL*, vol. 10, 488-491, Jan.
Rejects the conclusions reached by Ferguson (*Colophon*, 1938) after studying the Buffalo Manuscript of *Huckleberry Finn*. Such a study does not prove anything according to him. By 1884 Mark Twain had not only accepted the checkrein of his wife and Howells, but had learned to adjust himself.

868 DE VOTO, B. " Mark Twain about the Jews. " *Jewish Frontier*, vol. 6, 7-9, May.

869 — " What Mark Twain Thought of *1601* ; An Unpublished Passage of Mark Twain's Autobiography. " *SRL*, vol. 20, 11, Oct. 14.
This passage shows that he was extremely fond and proud of it and would not turn in his grave if he knew it had been published again — contrary to what Cyril Clemens and others may think.

870 FERGUSON, DeLancey. " A Letter to the Editors of *AL* ; A Rejoinder. " *AL*, vol. 11, 218-219, May.

" Mark Twain was far from being a meek man. If he had felt as strongly on some matters as Mr. Brooks and Mr. Cowie suppose, he would have put up a fight on a few points at least, even if he yielded others for the sake of peace or respectability. "

871 — " The Case for Mark Twain's Wife. " *Univ. of Toronto Quar.*, vol. 9, 9-21 Oct.

In every day life it was always Mrs. Clemens that yielded. Besides, " somehow he accomplished more under censorship than was accomplished by contemporaries who had not the handicap of being married to Olivia Langdon ".

872 FULLER, M. " Mark Twain and the Middle Ages ; with reply by B. Davenport. " *SRL*, vol. 19, 9, Jan. 28.

A childish discussion.

873 GATES, William Bryan. " Mark Twain to His English Publishers. " *AL*, vol. 11, 78-80, March.

Business letters to Chatto & Windus.

874 GORDON, Charles W. " Meeting Mark Twain. " *Mark Twain Quar.*, vol. 3, n⁰ 2, pp. 17, 22, Spring.

875 ROERICH, Nicholas. " Mark Twain in Russia. " *Mark Twain Quar.*, vol. 3, n⁰ 2, p. 7, Spring.

876 THOMSON, O. R. Howard. " How Important is Mark Twain ? " *SRL*, vol. 19, 9, Janv. 7.

A letter to the editor. Thinks only *Tom Sawyer* and *Huckleberry Finn* will always be read + possibly *Following the Equator*.

877 VOGELBACK, Arthur L. " The Publication and Reception of *Huckleberry Finn* in America. " *AL*, vol. 11, 260-272, Nov.

Expressions of approbation were rare ; most critics received the book very coldly. They thought it offended the proprieties.

878 Anon. " Mark Twain's First Lecture Tour. " *Mark Twain Quar.*, vol. 3, n⁰ 3, 3-6, 24, Summer-Fall.

UNPUBLISHED THESES :

879 BAILEY, Mary M. *Mark Twain and the Fine Arts*, University of Pittsburgh, mentioned in *Doctoral Dissertations Accepted by American Universities*, compiled for the Association of Research Libraries, edited by Donald B. Gilchrist. New York, The H. W. Wilson Co., n⁰ 6, for 1938-1939, p. 96.

880 CARTER, Paul J. Jr. *The Social and Political Ideas of Mark Twain,* a Ph. D. Thesis for the Univ. of Cincinnati, mentioned *ibid.,* p. 93.

881 VOGELBACK, Arthur L. *The Literary Reputation of Mark Twain in America, 1869-1885,* Doctoral thesis for the Univ. of Chicago.

1940

BIOGRAPHIES AND BOOKS OF CRITICISM :

882 MOEHLE, Dr. Günter. *Das Europabild Mark Twains*, Neue Deutsche Forschungen, Band 275. Berlin, Junker und Dünnhaupt Verlag, 136 pp.

883 PROUDFIT, Isabel. *River-Boy ; The Story of Mark Twain,* illustrated by W. C. Nims. New York, J. Messner, 247 pp.

884 READ, Opie P. *Mark Twain and I.* Chicago, Reilly & Lee, 75 pp. A collection of jokes told by Mark Twain.

885 TAYLOR, Howard P. *Mark Twain and the Old " Enterprise " Gang ;* reminiscences of Howard P. Taylor and Steve Gillis. Holiday Greetings from the Watsons. San Francisco, The Grabhorn Press, 9 pp.

Letters written to Joseph T. Goodman on the occasion of Mark Twain's death, edited by Douglas S. Watson.

INTRODUCTIONS AND PREFACES :

886 MARK TWAIN. *Jim Smiley and His Jumping Frog,* illustrated by John T. McCutcheon and printed by the Pocahontas Press (Chicago), x + 19 pp.

887 — *The Adventures of Tom Sawyer,* retold in 96 pp. by Bennett Kline, illustrated by Henry E. Vallely. Racine, Wis., Whitman Publishing Co., 94 pp.

888 *Mark Twain in Eruption ;* hitherto unpublished pages about men and events, by Mark Twain, ed. and with an introduction by Bernard De Voto. New York and London, Harper & Brothers, xxviii + 402 pp.

Could be considered as the third volume of Mark Twain's *Autobiography.*

889 Mark Twain's Travels with Mr. Brown, collected and ed. with an introduction by Franklin Walker and G. Ezra Dane. New York, A. A. Knopf, 296 pp.

Letters written for the *Alta California* between the time he left San Francisco and his departure for the Holy Land.

OTHER BOOKS DEALING WITH MARK TWAIN :

890 BROOKS, Van Wyck. *New England : Indian Summer.* New York, E. P. Dutton, x + 557 pp.

Only a few references to Mark Twain. " ... one wonders why Mr. Brooks avoided a return to the problem of Mark Twain, during this period a New-Englander in many respects... Was the old battle wound still sore ? " (Robert Spiller, *AL*, vol. 12, p. 73).

891 GABRIEL, Ralph Henry. *The Course of American Democratic Thought.* New York, The Ronald Press, xi + 452 pp.

A few references to Mark Twain.

892 MENCKEN, H. L. *Happy Days, 1880-1892.* New York, Alfred A. Knopf, 313 pp.

On his discovery of *Huckleberry Finn* when a boy : " Its impact was genuinely terrific ", pp. 166-167, 170.

893 VAN DOREN, Carl. *The American Novel, 1789-1939 ;* Revised and enlarged edition. New York, Macmillan, vii + 406 pp.

The first ed. came out in 1921. On Mark Twain, cf. pp. 128-129, 137-162, 313-314.

PERIODICAL LITERATURE :

Review of *Mark Twain in Eruption :*

894 Anon. in *Time,* " Tired Volcano ", vol. 36, 80, Dec. 2.

* *

895 ABRAHAMS, R. D. „ At Hannibal, Mo. ; Poem. " *Sat. Evg. Post,* vol. 213, 66, Nov. 30.

896 BLANCK, Jacob. " The Gilded Age : A Collation. " *Pub. W.*, vol. 138, 186-188, July 20.

Purely bibliographical.

897 GAY, R. M. " The Two Mark Twains. " *Atlantic M.*, vol. 166, 724-726, Dec.

   i.e. the jester and the artist, what he was and what some critics think he should have been.

898 HIBLER, L. von. " Mark Twain und die deutsche Sprache. " *Anglia Zeitschrift für Englische Philologie*, vol. 65, nos 1-3, 206-213.

899 HUTCHERSON, Dudley R. " Mark Twain as a Pilot. " *AL*, vol. 12, 353-355, Nov.

   According to the testimony of several Mississippi pilots including Bixby, Mark Twain " was not a very good pilot because he lacked confidence in himself ".

900 KLETT, Ada M. " Meisterschaft, or the True State of Mark Twain's German. " *American-German Rev.*, vol. 7, no 2, 10-11, Dec.

901 LORCH, F. W. " A Note on Tom Blankenship (Huckleberry Finn). " *AL*, vol. 12, 351-353, Nov.

   One reads in the *Hannibal Daily Messenger* that he was sentenced to jail in 1861 for stealing turkeys and was later suspected of several robberies.

902 OLIVER, R. T. " Mark Twain's Views on Education. " *Education*, vol. 61, 112-115, Oct.

   He stressed the value of education but disliked the " rote-memory " methods of the schoolmasters of his day.

903 Anon. " Hannibal Crosses Mr. Farley ; Mark Twain Stamp. " *Commonweal*, vol. 31, 355, Feb. 16.

UNPUBLISHED THESES :

903* DAVIDSON, E. E. *Mark Twain and Conscience*, a doctoral thesis for the University of Missouri.

903** GIBSON, William M. *Mark Twain and William Dean Howells : Anti-Imperialists*, a doctoral thesis for the University of Chicago. (Cf. *1125*).

1941

BIBLIOGRAPHIES :

904 Clarke, Norman Ellsworth. *Huckleberry Finn Again; A Biblio-graphical Study*. Detroit, 14 pp.
   On the first edition of *Huckleberry Finn*.

BIOGRAPHIES AND BOOKS OF CRITICISM :

None.

INTRODUCTIONS AND PREFACES :

905 *Mark Twain's Letters to Will Bowen*, ed. by Theodore Hornberger. Austin, Texas, The University of Texas Press, 34 pp.
   Some data on Tom Sawyer. Will Bowen was one of Mark Twain's school-fellows at Hannibal.

906 Mark Twain. *Republican Letters*, ed. by Cyril Clemens, Foreword by Sir Hugh Walpole. Webster Groves, Mo., International Mark Twain Society, 51 pp.
   A collection of letters first published in the *Chicago Republican*, but very carelessly edited ; the original text has even occasionally been tempered with (cf. Fred W. Lorch, " A Reply to Mr. Clemens. " *AL*, vol. 16, 32-34, March 1944).

OTHER BOOKS DEALING WITH MARK TWAIN :

907 Hart, James D. *The Oxford Companion to American Literature*. New York, Oxford Univ. Press, viii + 888 pp.
   On Mark Twain, pp. 139-141.

PERIODICAL LITERATURE :

1) Review of Hemminghaus's *Mark Twain in Germany* (1939).

908 BLAIR, Walter in *AL*, vol. 13, 87, March.

2) Review of *Mark Twain in Eruption* (1940).

909 POCHMANN, Henry A. in *AL*, vol. 13, 173-176, May.

" ... whoever is familiar with his published works, including the two volumes of his *Autobiography* and A. B. Paine's *Biography*, will find little that is either genuinely novel or truly ' eruptive ' in the book. "

*
* *

910 BELLAMY, Gladys Carmen. " Mark Twain's Indebtedness to John Phoenix. " *AL*, vol. 13, 29-43, March.

Contrary to what De Voto may think, Mark Twain was indebted to John Phoenix at least for " The Petrified Man ".

911 BLEARDSIDES, Oliver. " Mark Twain's Characters Come from Real People. " *Mark Twain Quar.*, vol. 4, nº 4, 16-19, Summer-Fall.

912 CLEMENS, Cyril. " Mark Twain and Libel. " *SRL*, vol. 24, 9, Aug. 30.

Mark Twain was once sued for libel in 1883 by one C. C. Duncan whom he had attacked in the course of an interview.

913 DE VOTO, B. " Sam Clemens Tells A Story ; Excerpts from Mark Twain in Eruption. " *Scholastic*, vol. 38, 29-30, Feb. 10.

914 LORCH, F. W. " Mark Twain and the ' Campaign That Failed '. " *AL*, vol. 12, 454-470, Jan.

A vindication of Mark Twain's attitude at the beginning of the Civil War : he obeyed no base motives.

915 ORIANS, G. Harrison. " Walter Scott, Mark Twain and the Civil War. " *South Atlantic Quar.*, vol. 40, 342-359, Oct.

A refutation of the charges brought by Mark Twain against Walter Scott in *Life on the Mississippi*. According to him, Scott had been responsible for turning the South from a democratic into an aristocratic nation, thus causing the Civil War.

916 PARRY, A. " Mark Twain in Russia. " *Books Abroad*, vol. 15, 168-175, April.

On his popularity in Russia.

917 PRITCHETT, V. S. " *Huckleberry Finn* and the Cruelty of American Humor. " *New Statesman & Nation*, n. s. vol. 22, 113, Aug. 2.

The author finds nostalgia, but no pity in the book.

918 SLADE, W. G. " Mark Twain's Educational Views. " *Mark Twain Quar.*, vol. 4, n⁰ 4, 5-10, Summer-Fall.

919 STEWART, G. R. " Bret Harte upon Mark Twain in 1866. " *AL*, vol. 13, 263-264, Nov.

Report of a lecture delivered by Mark Twain in San Francisco. (*Springfield Republican*, Nov. 10, 1866).

920 TEMPLIN, E. H. " On Re-Reading Mark Twain. " *Hispania*, vol. 24, 269-276, Oct.

Very superficial and rather gratuitous : tries to define the Spanish flavor of Mark Twain's works.

921 WALKER, S. " Case of Mr. Whipple's Pants. " *New Yorker*, vol. 17, 58-61, Sept. 27.

Several fanciful endings for the story once told by Twain to I. Bacheller and published shortly afterwards in the *New York Sun* by Bob Davis.

922 WECTER, Dixon. " Mark Twain as Translator from the German. " *AL*, vol. 13, 257-263, Nov.

On Mark Twain's translation of Struwwelpeter. The older, more conventional Winston translation is generally preferred.

923 Anon. " Art of Saying No ; Mark Twain Refuses Permission to Dramatize Tom Sawyer. " *Reader's Digest*, vol. 38, 56, March.

924 Anon. " *Huckleberry Finn* in Public Domain. " *Pub. W.*, vol. 140, 2008, Nov. 29.

UNPUBLISHED THESES :

925 FLOWERS, Frank C. *Mark Twain's Theories of Morality*, a Ph. D. thesis for the Univ. of Louisiana (*Doctoral Dissertations*, n⁰ 8, p. 119).

1942

BIBLIOGRAPHIES :

926 A Check-List of the Mark Twain Collection Assembled by the late Willard S. Morse of Santa Monica, Calif., prepared by Ellen K. Shaffer & Lucille S. J. Hall; offered for sale by Dawson's Bookshop. Los Angeles, Calif., 92 pp.

BIOGRAPHIES AND BOOKS OF CRITICISM :

927 CLEMENS, Cyril. *Young Sam Clemens*, foreword by Hendrik Willem Van Loon and introduction by Grant Wood. Portland, Me., Leon Tebbetts, 282 pp.
    A collection of anecdotes rather than a biographical study.

928 MASON, Miriam E. *Mark Twain, Boy of Old Missouri*, illustrated by Paul Laune, Indianapolis, The Bobbs-Merrill Co., VII + 164 pp.

INTRODUCTIONS AND PREFACES :

929 MARK TWAIN : *The Adventures of Huckleberry Finn*, with an introduction by B. De Voto, Illustrated by Thomas Hart Benton. New York, The Limited Editions Club, LXVI + 396 pp.
    " The first ed. in which an effort has been made to establish the text. "

930 MARK TWAIN. *A Connecticut Yankee at King Arthur's Court*, with a foreword by John T. Winterich, illustrated by Warren Chappell. New York, The Heritage Press, xx + 319 pp.

931 Mark Twain Every Child Should Know. New York, Doubleday, Doran & Co., for the Parents' Institute, 280 pp.
    In other words, " The Prince and the Pauper. "

932 MARK TWAIN. *Letters in the Muscatine Journal*, ed. with an introduction by Edgar M. Branch. Chicago, The Mark Twain Association of America, 28 pp.

933 *Mark Twain at Work*, ed. by Bernard De Voto. Cambridge, Mass., Harvard Univ. Press, IX + 144 pp.

Contains early manuscript fragments of *Tom Sawyer* and *Huckleberry Finn* and an unpublished story playing with themes developed in *What is Man?* and *The Mysterious Stranger*. Abundant editorial comments.

OTHER BOOKS DEALING WITH MARK TWAIN :

934 BEARD, Charles A. & BEARD, Mary R. *The American Spirit :
A Study of the Idea of Civilization in the United States*, vol. IV in *The Rise of American Civilization*. New York, MacMillan, VII + 696 pp.

Pp. 49-51, " Mark Twain's Conception of Civilization " ; pp. 295-298, " Mark Twain and Walter Scott's Influence in the South " ; pp. 589-591, " Mark Twain's Hostility to Impe rialism ".

935 BLAIR, Walter. *Horse Sense in American Humor from Benjamin Franklin to Ogden Nash*. Chicago, Univ. of Chicago Press, XV + 341 pp.

Reprint of an earlier ed. (1937), published by the American Book Co. (xv + 573 pp.). On Mark Twain : pp. 1-2, 195-217 (a chapter entitled : " Mark Twain, Hank and Huck "), 272-274. Very superficial.

936 GORDON, G. S. *Anglo-American Literary Relations*. London, New York, Oxford Univ. Press, 119 pp.

On Mark Twain, pp. 99, 108-109. Insists on his early recognition in England.

937 TAYLOR, Walter F. *The Economic Novel in America*. Chapel Hill, N. C., XI + 378 pp.

On Mark Twain (especially on *The Gilded Age*), cf. pp. 116-147. There was no conflict between the artist and the business man within Mark Twain, " ... satirist, capitalist, and democrat worked toward the same object — that of enjoying the uses of the machine and lessening the abuses ".

PERIODICAL LITERATURE :

1) Review of Mark Twain's *Republican Letters* (1941) :

938 LORCH, F. W. in *AL*, vol. 13, 439-440, Jan.

2) Review of Mark Twain's *Letters to Will Bowen* (1941) :

939 POCHMANN, Henry A. in *AL*, vol. 14, 94-95, March.

3) Review of *Mark Twain at Work :*

940 MATTHIESSEN, F. O. in *NR*, vol. 107, 179, Aug. 10, " Twain into Clemens. "

Criticizes De Voto's bluster but acknowledges his judgment has deepened since *Mark Twain's America* and he has written a definitive note on the enforced expurgations.

* *

941 AUERNHEIMER, R. " Mark Twain and the Gestapo ; Man That Corrupted Hadleyburg Written in the Hotel Metropole of Vienna, now the Headquarters of the German Secret Police. " *Christian Science Monitor*, Mag. Section, 6, Oct. 10.

942 BERNARD, Harry. " Lettres Américaines. Filiations de Mark Twain. " *Revue de l'Université d'Ottawa*, vol. 12, 327-341, Juillet-Sept.

The author lists among Mark Twain's successors : E. L. Masters, with his *Mitch Miller*, Alvin Johnson with *Spring Storm*, James Still with *River of Earth* and M. R. Rawlings with *The Yearling.*

943 BLANCK J. " News from the Rare Book Sellers. " *Pub. W.*, vol. 142, 253, Dec. 26.

A letter thought by Paine to have been sent to T. B. Aldrich was first partially published in the *Pellet* to help raise funds for a Massachusetts Hospital.

944 BROWNELL, G. H. " A Question as to the Origin of the Name ' Mark Twain '. " *Twainian*, vol. I, nᵒ 2, 4-7, Feb.

The *Twainian*, like the *Mark Twain Quarterly*, specializes in Twainiana, but contains more valuable information. It was published previously to 1942, from Jan. 1930 to June 1941. But it was then only the organ of the Mark Twain Society of Chicago and contained almost no article of any interest. Cf. above nᵒ *864.*

945 CARTER, Paul. " Mark Twain and War. " *Twainian*, vol. I, nᵒ 3, 1-3, March.

946 DAVIDSON, W. E. " Mark Twain and Conscience. " *Ibid.*, vol. I, nᵒ 4, 1-5, April.

947 FEINSTEIN, George. " Vestigia in Pudd'nhead Wilson. " *Ibid.*, vol. I, nᵒ 5, 1-3, May.

On the literary imperfections Twain should have removed from *Pudd'nhead Wilson.* Cf. his 1946 article in *AL.*

948 Ferguson, DeLancey. „ Mark Twain's Comstock Duel : The Birth of a Legend. ” *AL*, vol. 14, 66-70, March.

The first version of this story (later taken up again by Paine in the *Biography*) appeared in *Tom Hood's Comic Annual*, 1873, under the title of “ How I escaped being killed in a duel ”.

949 Flack, Frank Morgan. “ Mark Twain and Music. ” *Twainian*, vol. 2, nᵒ 1, 1-4, Oct.

He made fun of it at first but came to respect it more and more and even to enjoy it.

950 Fuller, John Grant. “ Connecticut Yankee in King Arthur's Court ; dramatization of a novel by Mark Twain — abridged. ” *Scholastic*, vol. 40, 17-19, March 9.

951 Leisy, E. E. “ Mark Twain and Isaiah Sellers. ” *AL*, vol. 13, 398-405, Jan.

According to the author he did not borrow his pen-name from Isaiah Sellers.

952 Olson, J. C. “ Mark Twain and the Department of Agriculture. ” *AL*, vol. 13, 408-410, Jan.

Unpublished letters exchanged in 1895 with editorial comments.

953 Powell, L. C. “ Unpublished Mark Twain Letter. ” *AL*, vol. 13, 405-407, Jan.

A letter to Sir John Adams, Dec. 5, 1898.

954 Roberts, Harold. “ Sam Clemens : Florida Days. ” *Twainian*, vol. I, nᵒ 2, 1-3, Feb., nᵒ 3, 4-7, March.

On Mark Twain's stays at Florida, Mo. when a boy.

955 Tidwell, J. N. “ Mark Twain's Representation of Negro Speech. ” *AS*, vol. 17, 174-176, Oct.

His representation was “ both sincere and competent ”.

956 Vogelback, Arthur L. “ The Prince and the Pauper : A Study in Critical Standards. ” *AL*, vol. 14, 48-54, March.

“ ... critics approved of *The Prince and the Pauper* because, more than any other of Mark Twain's books up to that time, it complied with the tradition of correctness and imitation — with the genteel tradition. ”

957 Wood, G. “ Letter from Grant Wood. ” *SRL*, vol. 25, 11, Feb. 28.

A letter to Cyril Clemens on *Tom Sawyer* and *Huckleberry Finn*.

958 Anon. “ Varied Comment on the Origin of the Name Mark Twain. ” *Twainian*, vol. I’ nᵒ 5, 3-5, May.

959 — “ Musical Melange. ” *Ibid.*, vol. 2, nᵒ 2, 1-4, Nov.

UNPUBLISHED THESES :

960 BRANCH, Edgar Marquess. *The Literary Development of Mark Twain, 1852-1865,* a Ph. D. thesis for the Univ. of Iowa (*Doctoral Dissertations,* 1942, n⁰ 9, p. 106).

961 FLOWERS, Frank C. *Mark Twain's Theories of Morality,* Ann Arbor, Mich., University Microfilms, Publication n⁰ 418, XII + 223 pp. (a thesis for Louisiana State University).

961* HAYS, John Q. *The Serious Elements in the Writings of Mark Twain,* a doctoral dissertation for the University of California (Berkeley).

961** WAGER, Willis Joseph. *A Critical Edition of the Morgan Manuscript of Mark Twain's ' Life on the Mississippi ' ",* a doctoral dissertation for the University of New York.

1943

BIOGRAPHIES AND BOOKS OF CRITICISM :

962 BRANDT, Ralph Van Kirk Von. *Mark Twain*. Trenton, privately printed, 8 pp.
> Imaginary letters to and from Mark Twain.

963 FERGUSON, John DeLancey. *Mark Twain : Man and Legend*. Indianapolis, Bobbs-Merrill, 352 pp.
> The first full-length biography written since the Brooks-De Voto controversy. An excellent synthesis.

INTRODUCTIONS AND PREFACES :

964 MARK TWAIN. *Las Aventuras de Huck*, traducción directa del inglès y prólogo por Carlos Pereyra. Buenos Aires, Editorial Losada, 285 pp.

965 — *Tom Sawyer and Huckleberry Finn*, with an introduction by Christopher Morley, London, J. M. Dent & Sons, XII + 435 pp. (Everyman's Library).

966 — *Washington in 1868*, ed. with an introduction and notes by Cyril Clemens. Foreword by W. W. Jacobs, Webster Groves, Mo., International Mark Twain Society & London, T. W. Laurie, 55 pp.
> A series of articles published in the *Chicago Republican* from Feb. 8 to March 1, 1868.

OTHER BOOKS DEALING WITH MARK TWAIN :

967 STOVALL, Floyd. *American Idealism*, Norman, Okla. Univ. of Oklahoma Press, XII + 235 pp.
> On Mark Twain, pp. 112-116. Sees in him a typical adolescent. This lack of maturity was the source of his charm *(Huckleberry*

Finn) and of his weakness (the pessimism of *The Mysterious Stranger*).

PERIODICAL LITERATURE :

1) Review of *Mark Twain at Work* (1942) :

968 BLAIR, Walter in *AL*, vol. 14, 447-449, Jan.

Prefers De Voto's interpretation to that of Brooks, but thinks De Voto exaggerates the lack of cohesion of *Tom Sawyer* and *Huckleberry Finn*. (Cf. his own article on the structure of the former.)

2) Reviews of Ferguson's *Mark Twain : Man and Legend* :

969 PHELPS, W. L. in *Rotarian*, " Billy Phelps Speaking. " vol. 63, 40, July.

970 SPILLER, R. E. in *SRL*, " *Phenomenon of Mark Twain* ", vol. 26, 15, Aug. 7.

The author considers this book one of the best studies of Mark Twain.

*
* *

971 BROWNELL, G. H. " An ' Important Question Settled '. " *Twainian*, vol. 2, nº 5, 1-5, April.

Reprint of an article contributed by Mark Twain to the *Cincinnati Evg. Chronicle*, March 4, 1868.

972 — " From ' Hospital Days '. " *Ibid.*, vol. 2, nº 6, 1-5, March, nº 7, 4-6, April.

On an erratum in the 1st ed. of Mark Twain's *Sketches, New and Old*.

973 — " The Home of the Prodigal ,Son. " *Ibid.*, nº 7, April.

On a suppression made by Mark Twain in the original text of *Innocents Abroad*.

974 — " The Winner of the Medal. " *Ibid.*, nº 8, 1-4, May.

A story first published by Twain in *The American Union, A Fireside Journal*, vol. 38, nº 5, May 18, 1867.

975 — " Mark Twain's Eulogy on the ' Reliable Contraband '. " *Ibid.*, nº 9, 1-3, June.

Reprint of a story first published in *Packard's*, July 1869.

976 — " Twain's Version of Hamlet. " *Ibid.*, nº 9, 4-6, June.

On a parody of Hamlet written by Mark Twain.

977 BROWNELL, G. H. " Mark Twain's Tribute to Francis Lightfoot Lee. " *Ibid.*, vol. 3, nº 2, Nov. & nº 5, 4-5, Feb. 1944.

978 — " Mark Twain's Memory Builder. " *Ibid.*, vol. 3, n⁰ 3, 1-4, Dec.
On a memory training game patented by Mark Twain in 1885.

979 — " Here's Another of Those New-Found *Mercury* Tales. " *Ibid.*,
vol. 3, n⁰ 3, 4-5, Dec.

980 CLEMENS, Cyril. " The ' Birth of a Legend ' Again. " *AL*, vol. 15,
64-65, March.
According to him Mark Twain's account of his duel was true.
Several people bore witness to it. (A reply to DeLancey Ferguson's article in *AL*, March 1942).

981 — " Letter to the Editors. " *AL*, vol. 14, 430-431, Jan.
A reply to Lorch's review of Mark Twain's *Republican Letters*
in *AL*, Jan. 1942.

982 COWLEY, M. " Mencken and Mark Twain. " *NR*, vol. 108, 321-322,
March 8.
About Mark Twain's influence on Mencken.

983 FARRELL, J. T. " Twain's *Huckleberry Finn* and the Era He
Lived In. " *New York Times Book Rev.*, Dec. 12, 6, 37.
Emphasizes the democratic quality of the book.

984 FERGUSON, DeLancey. " Mark Twain's Lost Curtain Speeches on
the Plays ' Gilded Age ' and ' Ah Sin '. " *South Atlantic Quar.*,
vol. 42, 262-269, July.
Gives the text of two of these curtain speeches.

985 LILLARD, R. G. ,, Evolution of the ' Washoe Zephyr '. " *AS*,
vol. 18, 257-260, Dec.

986 TROXELL, G. McC. " Samuel Langhorne Clemens. " *Yale Univ.
Library Gazette*, vol. 18, 1-5, July.
On the Mark Twain collection in the Yale University Library.

987 WILLSON, Frank C. " That Gilded Age Again : An Attempt to
Unmuddle the Fifty-Seven Variants. " *Papers Bibliographical
Society of America*, vol. 37, 141-156.
On the original edition of *The Gilded Age*.

988 WIMBERLY, L. C. " Mark Twain and the Tichenor Bonanza. "
Atlantic M., vol. 172, 117, 119, Nov. (also in condensed form
in *Time*, vol. 42, 44-45, Nov. 1).
A humorous letter Mark Twain sent to the *New York Eveg.
Post* to ridicule a dispatch from California claiming that one
Tichenor had invented a marvellous process for extracting gold
from " gold-bearing " waters.

1944

BIBLIOGRAPHIES :

989 An Exhibition of the Works of Mark Twain, including manuscripts,
first editions and association items, at the Main Public Library,
April 30 through May 31, 1944, Sponsored by the Friends
of the Detroit Public Library. Detroit, Mich., 42 pp.

BIOGRAPHIES AND BOOKS OF CRITICISM :

None.

INTRODUCTIONS AND PREFACES :

990 MARK TWAIN. *Life on the Mississippi,* with an introduction by
Edward Wagenknecht and a number of previously suppressed
passages now printed for the first time, and edited with a note
by Willis Wager. New York, The Limited Editions Club,
XVIII + 418 pp.

OTHER BOOKS DEALING WITH MARK TWAIN :

991 DAVIS, Samuel P. *The Typographical Howitzer by Sam Davis* with
a foreword by Thomas P. Brown, Sacramento, Calif., The Meteo-
rite Press, VII + 8 pp.

Reprinted from the author's *Short Stories* published in San
Francisco in 1886.

PERIODICAL LITERATURE :

1) Reviews of Günter Möhle's *Mark Twains Europabild*
(1940) :

992 WEGELIN, Christof. in *AL*, vol. 16, 255-256.

A superficial and oversimplified study ; in particular, the author exaggerates Twain's racial affinity to England to the detriment of his political sympathy. Mark Twain saw in her a potential ally against imperialist Germany and barbarous Russia.

2) Review of Ferguson's *Mark Twain : Man and Legend*
(1943) :

993 BLAIR, W. in *AL*, vol. 16, 143-145, May.

A scholarly and well-balanced book.

* *
*

994 ADAMS, J. D. " Speaking of Books. " *New York Times Book Rev.*, April 30, p. 2, & May 14, p. 2.

On the Brooks-De Voto controversy.

995 BROWNELL, G. H. " Everybody's Friend. " *Twainian*, vol. 3, nᵒ 5, 1-4, Feb.

A Mark Twain letter to Josh Billings originally published in the *New York Weekly* and reprinted by Josh Billings in *Everybody's Friends*.

996 — " Mark Twain's Inventions. " *Ibid.*, vol. 3, nᵒ 4, 1-5, Jan.

997 — " What Ought He to Have Done ? " *Ibid.*, nᵒ 8, 1-4, May.

Some remarks by Mark Twain on child management.

998 — " About Mark Twain's Job on the *San Francisco Call*. " *Ibid.*, nᵒ 8, 4-6, May and vol. 4, nᵒ 6, 3-4, March 1945.

999 CLEMENS, Cyril. " Unique Origin of Mark Twain's Books. " *Missouri School Jour.*, vol. 40, 16, 18-19, Jan.

1000 — " George Bernard Shaw. " *SRL*, vol. 27, 15, Aug. 12.

A letter to the editor on Shaw's meetings with Mark Twain.

1001 — " Winston Churchill and Mark Twain. " *Hobbies*, vol. 49, 105-107, April.

On the different encounters of the two.

1002 DUDGEON, L. W. " Twainiana. " *Ibid.*, vol. 49, 98, July.

On the grandparents of Mark Twain.

1003 FARBER, Marjorie. " Poisoned Pens. " *New York Times Book Rev.*, April 23, p. 5.

Takes the defence of Brooks against De Voto in review of the latter's *Literary Fallacy*.

1004 GILDER, R. " Mark Twain Detested the Theatre. " *Theatre Arts*, vol. 28, 109-116, Feb.

1005 JONES, Joseph. " More Twain Found in *New York Weekly*. " *Twainian*, vol. 3, n° 6, 1-4, March.

A reprint with comments.

1006 LEWIS Sinclair. " Fools, Liars, and Mr. De Voto. " *SRL*, vol. 27, 9-12, April 15.

A savage personal attack on De Voto who had severely criticized the writers of the twenties in a little book entitled " The Literary Fallacy ", part of which had been published in the preceding issue of *SRL* under the title of " They Turned their Backs on America. "

1007 LILLARD, R. G. " Contemporary Reaction to ' The Empire City Massacre '. " *AL*, vol. 16, 198-203, Nov.

1008 LORCH, F. W. " A Reply to Mr. Clemens. " *AL*, vol. 16, 32-34, March.

On Cyril Clemens's edition of Mark Twain's *Republican Letters*. Cf. n° *906*.

1009 MAYBERRY, G. " Reading and Writing. " *NR*, vol. 110, 808, May 1st.

Praises " the clean-limbed, functional quality " of Mark Twain's prose.

1010 ORCUTT, W. D. " From My Library Walls. " *Christian Science Monitor*, Nov. 17, p. 7.

1011 QUAIFE, M. M. " Mark Twain's Military Career. " *Twainian*, vol. 3, n° 9, 4-7, June.

1012 RAYFORD, R. L. " Jumping Frog Jubilee. " *Am. Merc.*, vol. 59, 583-588, Nov.

The Jumping Frog Jubilee at Angel's Camp in 1929.

1013 WHEATHERLY, E. A. " Beau Tibbs and Colonel Sellers. " *MLN*, vol. 59, 310-313, May.

Beau Tibbs, a character in Goldsmith's *The Citizen of the World* may have been one of the models that Mark Twain used to draw Colonel Sellers in *The Gilded Age*.

1014 WEBSTER, S. C. " Mark Twain Business Man — Letters and Memoirs. " *Atlantic M.*, vol. 173, 37-46 (June), vol. 174, 72-80 (July), 71-77 (Aug.), 90-96 (Sept.), 100-106 (Oct.).

1015 WHITING, B. J. " Gugustucus, Royal Nonesuch and Other Hoaxes. " *South Folklore Quar.*, vol. 8, 251-275, Dec.

These hoaxes, of which one finds echoes in *Huckleberry Finn,* were common in the old South West.

1016 Anon. " Mark Twain ; Scenes from the Moving Picture. " *Scholastic,* vol. 44, 18-19, April 17.

1017 — " Mark Twain Lives All Over Again in New Film. " *Life,* vol. 16, 89-99, May 8.

A film on Twain's life.

1018 — " Gorki Incident ; An Unpublished Fragment by Mark Twain", *Slavonic Rev.,* vol. 22, 37-38, Aug.

A tale in which he tried to justify his attitude towards Gorki and prove that in Rome you must do as the Romans do.

1945

BIOGRAPHIES AND BOOKS OF CRITICISM :

1019 LILJEGREN, Sven E. *The Revolt Against Romanticism in American Literature as Evidenced in the Works of Samuel L. Clemens.* A. B. Lundequistka Bokhandeln, 60 pp.
Cf. below n° *1049*.

Emphasizes the seriousness, sadness and intellectual refinement of Mark Twain. Claims that " he began as a Romantic *at heart* and actually retained a *penchant* for Romanticism all his life... but went in for the reaction against literary Romanticism more violently than any of his companions. "

1020 PELLOWE, William C. S. *Mark Twain, Pilgrim from Hannibal.* New York, The Hobson Press, XIII + 301 pp.

" The aim of this book is to trace the unfolding of Mark Twain's personality, especially as he reacted to and expressed opinions upon the religious elements in the background and the currents of his time " (p. XII).

1021 ROESSEL, James. *Mark Twain, en odölig humorist.* Stockholm, Lindfors, 190 pp.

OTHER BOOKS DEALING WITH MARK TWAIN :

1022 CESTRE Charles. *La Littérature Américaine.* Paris, Armand Colin, 218 pp.

On Mark Twain, pp. 103-106. This is merely a text-book ; it contains only very succint comments on Mark Twain.

PERIODICAL LITERATURE :

Review of Cyril Clemens's *Young Sam Clemens* (1942).

1023 HORNBERGER, Theodore. in *AL*, vol. 17, 102, March.

" ... a useful crytallization of oral legend, not a biographical study... "

*
* *

1024 ADAMS, J. D. " Speaking of Books. " *New York Times Book Rev.*, June 17, p. 2 & June 24, p. 2.
On Mark Twain's travel books.

1025 ARMSTRONG, Rev. C. J. " Sam Clemens Considered Becoming a Preacher. " *Twainian*, vol. 4, nº 8, 1, May.

1026 BLANCK, J. " News from the Rare Book Sellers ; Mark Twain's *A Murder, a Mystery and a Marriage*, at last put in type. " *Pub. W.*, vol. 148, 620-621, Aug. 18.

1027 BROWNELL, G. H. " No Mystery about ' A Mystery Cleared Up. '. " *Twainian*, vol. 4, nº 8, 1-2, May.

1028 — " Why Mark Twain Registered His Name as a Trade Mark. " *Ibid.*, nº 7, 3-4, April.

1029 BROWNELL, G. H. " Mark Twain Tells of the Daring Deed of Prof. Jenkins and His Velocipede. " *Ibid.*, nº 5, 1-4, Feb., nº 6, 4, March.
Reprint with an introduction of a contribution of Mark Twain to the *Buffalo Express*, Aug. 26, 1869, of which he was part-owner at the time.

1030 — " Mark Twain Launched the Chicago Press Club of which George Ade Later Became a Member. " *Ibid.*, nº 6, 1-2, March.

1031 — " A Tale of Twain's Shipboard Poem ' Good-Bye ' or ' The Parting of the Ships ! ' " *Ibid.*, nº 9, June.

1032 CLEMENS, Cyril. " F. D. Roosevelt and Mark Twain. " *Dalhousie Rev.*, vol. 25, 339-341, Oct.
On the award of the Mark Twain gold medal to President Roosevelt.

1033 — " Winston Churchill and Mark Twain. " *Ibid.*, vol. 24, 402-405, Jan.

1034 — " Mark Twain's Exaggerated Death. " *Rotarian*, vol. 67, 58-59, Aug.
On the circumstances of Mark Twain's famous koke in 1897.

1035 — " They Knew Mark Twain. " *Hobbies*, vol. 50, 106-108, Sept.
" They " i.e. Shaw, Helen Keller, etc.

1036 — " New Light on Mark Twain's Virginia Ancestry. " *Ibid.*, 104-105, April.

1037 CLEMENS, Cyril. " Mark Twain's Ancestry. " *Mark Twain Quar.*, vol. 7, nº 2, pp. 8, 24, Winter-Spring 1945-1946.

1038 Cowley, M. " The Middle American Style : D. Crockett to E. Hemingway. " *New York Times Book Rev.*, July 15, pp. 3, 14.
From Crockett to Hemingway via Mark Twain.

1039 De Voto, B. " Mr. De Voto Explains As to Use of the Name Mark Twain. " *Twainian*, vol. 4, nᵒ 9, 2, June.
On the Mark Twain trade-mark.

1040 Feinstein, George. " Mark Twain's Regionalism in Fiction. " *Mark Twain Quar.*, vol. 7, nᵒ 2, pp. 7, 24, Winter-Spring, 1945-1946.

1041 Gibson, Charles Hammond. " My Last Impression of Mark Twain. " *Ibid.*, vol. 7, nᵒ 2, pp. 5-6.

1042 Gilder, Rodman. " Rodman Gilder Writes That One of These Two Twain Tales Is a Forgery. " *Twainian*, vol. 4, nᵒ 4, p. 4, Jan.

1043 Granger, Eugenie. " Mark Twain versus Publicity. " *Mark Twain Quar.*, vol. 7, nᵒ 2, p. 10, Winter-Spring, 1945-1946.

1044 Guest, Boyd. " Twain's Concept of Woman's Sphere. " *Ibid.*, vol. 7, nᵒ 2, 1-4, Winter-Spring. 1945-1946.

1045 Hall, Don E. " A Mark Twain Sales Tip. " *Ibid.*, p. 7.
A personal recollection.

1046 Hemminghaus, Edgar H. " Mark Twain's German Provenience. " *MLQ*, vol. 6, 459-478, Dec.

1047 Kinnaird, C. " Mark Twain's First Book. " *Am. Merc.*, vol. 60, 124, Jan.
The Jumping Frog, published thanks to the help of Charles Henry Webb, a journalist, inventor and adventurer.

1048 Lederer, Max. " Mark Twain in Vienna. " *Mark Twain Quar.*, vol. 7, nᵒ 1, 1-12, Summer-Fall.

1049 Liljegren, S. B. " The Revolt Against Romanticism in American Literature as evidenced in the works of Samuel L. Clemens. " *Studia Neophilologica*, vol. 17, 207-258. Cf. above nᵒ *1015*.

1050 Lorch, Fred W. " Mark Twain's Views on Western Indians. " *Twainian*, vol. 4, nᵒ 7, 1-3, April.

1051 O'Liam, D. " They Are Off at Angel's Camp ; Jumping Frog Jubilee of Calaveras County. " *Collier's*, vol. 115, 21, May 26.

1052 Wecter, Dixon. " Mark Twain and the West. " *Huntington Library Quart.*, vol. 8, 359-377, Aug.
On Mark Twain's life in the West ; chiefly anecdotal.

1053 Willson, Frank C. " Twain Spanks a Government Employee for Unofficial Employment. " *Twainian*, vol. 4, nᵒ 4, 2-4, Jan.

1054 — " Twain Tells How to Remove Warts and Tattoo Marks. "
Ibid., n⁰ 9, 3-4, June.

UNPUBLISHED THESES :

1055 Dickinson, Leon T. *Mark Twain's Innocents Abroad : Its Origin,
Composition, Popularity*, 224 pp. A Ph. D. thesis for the Univ.
of Chicago. (*Doctoral Dissertations*, 1945, n⁰ 12, p. 56).

BIBLIOGRAPHIES :

1056 BRANCH, E. M. " Chronological Bibliography of the Writings of Samuel L. Clemens to June 8, 1867. " *AL*, vol. 18, 109-159, May.

BIOGRAPHIES AND BOOKS OF CRITICISM :

1057 WEBSTER, Samuel C. *Mark Twain : Business Man.* Boston, Little, Brown & Co., XIII + 409 pp.

An answer to *Mark Twain in Eruption* (1940) and the accusations it contained against Charles H. Webster, the father of the author. Contains many hitherto unpublished Mark Twain Letters.

INTRODUCTIONS AND PREFACES :

1058 *The Portable Mark Twain*, ed. with an introduction by B. De Voto, New York, The Viking Press, VII + 786 pp.

Contains the complete text of *Huckleberry Finn* and *The Mysterious Stranger*, comprehensive selections from his other works and some hitherto unpublished letters.

1059 MARK TWAIN. *The Adventures of Tom Sawyer*, illustrated by Louis Slobodkin ; introduction by May Lamberton Becker, Cleveland and New York, The World Publishing Co., 302 pp. (Rainbow Classics).

A children's edition.

1060 MARK TWAIN. *The Prince and the Pauper*, preface by Mary E. Dillon. City of New York, Board of Education, VII + 248 pp.

1061 — *The Letters of Quintus Curtius Snodgrass*, ed. by Ernest

E. Leisy, Dallas, Tex. Univ. Press, Southern Methodist Univ., xii + 76 pp.

Letters originally published in the *New Orleans Crescent*, Jan.-March 1861, and attributed to Mark Twain by the editor.

1062 — *Qué es el hombre?* Con una introducción de S. K. Ratcliffe, Barcelona, Editorial Delfos, xxxix + 123 pp.

PERIODICAL LITERATURE :

Reviews of Samuel Charles Webster's *Mark Twain : Business Man :*

1063 FERGUSON, DeLancey. in *AL*, vol. 18, 169-170, May.

" ... some of Paine's most romantic details of the humorist's youth suffer a deflation which extends to the conclusions drawn from them by the psychoanalytical critics... "

1064 WOOD, J. P. in *SRL*, " All out of step but Mark ", vol. 29, 16-17, March 2.

1065 Anon. in *Time*, " Dear Charley ", vol. 47, 100-104, Feb. 11.

Mark Twain being a very poor business man, was entirely responsible himself for his business failure.

*
* *

1066 BIDEWELL, George Ivan. " Mark Twain's Florida Years. " *Missouri Historical Rev.*, vol. 40, 159-173, Jan.

The claim to a formative influence, in the development of Mark Twain, of Florida where he was born and later spent summer holidays on the farm of his uncle John Quarles, is more soundly grounded than is generally believed.

1067 BROWNELL, G. H. " The After Dinner Speaker's Best Friend : Mark Twain's Patent Adjustable Sepech. " *Twainian*, vol. 5, n⁰ 1, 1-3, Jan.-Feb.

1068 — " Maybe This Explains Why Mark Twain Left Nevada. " *Ibid.*, vol. 5, n⁰ 5, 2-3, Sept.-Oct.

Mark Twain, the author claims, left Nevada because former Confederate soldiers were to be disenfranchised.

1069 — " Two Hitherto Unknown Twain Tales Found in *New York Tribune*. " *Ibid.*, n⁰ 6, 1, Nov.-Dec.

Comments on Frank C. Willson's article in the May-June issue. Cf. below n⁰ *1086*.

1070 CASH, Thelma. " Mark Twain Goes West. " *Poet Lore,* vol. 52, n⁰ 3, 256-260.

On Mark Twain in Nevada.

1071 DE VOTO, B. " Easy Chair. " *Harper's M.,* vol. 192, 309-312, April.

The conflict within Mark Twain could not be healed and was the source of his humour.

1072 — " Fenimore Cooper's Further Literary Offenses. " *NEQ,* vol. 19, 291-301, Sept.

A hitherto unpublished continuation of " Fenimore Cooper's Literary Offenses ", with an introduction by De Voto.

1073 — " Letter from the Recording Angel. " *Harper's M.,* vol. 192, 106-109, Feb.

A hitherto unpublished sketch with an introduction by De Voto.

1074 FEINSTEIN, George. " Mark Twain's Idea of Story Structure. " *AL,* vol. 18, 160-163, May.

Mark Twain had a method in spite of his apparent methodlessness.

1075 FLACK, Frank Morgan. " About the Play ' Roughing It ' as Produced by Augustin Daly. " *Twainian,* vol. 5, n⁰ 4, 1-3, July-Aug.

1076 FREDERICK, J. T. " W. Allen White and Mark Twain. " *Rotarian,* vol. 68, 47-48, April.

A comparison.

1077 HOBEN, John B. " Mark Twain's *A Connecticut Yankee :* A Genetic Study. " *AL,* vol. 18, 197-218, Nov.

On the genesis and reception of the book.

1078 HOLLENBACH, John W. " Mark Twain, Story-Teller at Work. " *College English,* vol. 7, 303-312, March.

Mark Twain as a conscious and painstaking artist.

1079 HUSTVEDT, S. B. " The Preacher and the Gray Mare. " *Calif. Folklore Quar.,* vol. 5, 109-110, Jan.

On Chap. xxv of *Life on the Mississippi* and the Jonah folklore motif.

1080 JAMES, J. " Duke's Tooth-Powder Racket : A Note on *Huckleberry Finn.* " *MLN,* vol. 61, 468-469, Nov.

That racket really existed.

1081 LEDERER, M. " Einige Bemerkungen zu Adolf Wilbrandts *Der Meister von Palmyra.* " *MLN,* vol. 61, 551-555, Dec.

On the true character and meaning of the Austrian play. Cf. above n⁰ *219.*

1082 LEISY, Ernest E. " The Quintus Curtius Snodgrass Letters in the *New Orleans Crescent.* " *Twainian*, vol. 5, nᵒ 5, 1-2, Sept.-Oct.

1083 LOOMIS, C. Grant. " Dan De Quille's Mark Twain. " *Pacific Hist. Rev.*, vol. 15, 336-347.

On Mark Twain's friendship with Dan De Quille (William Wright) when he was on the staff of the *Virginia City Enterprise* in Nevada in 1862.

1084 LORCH, Fred W. " Mark Twain's Philadelphia Letters in the Muscatine Journal. " *AL*, vol. 17, 348-352, Jan.

Shows that some of these letters were partly copied from a newly published guide-book, *Philadelphia as it is in 1852* by R. A. Smith. Though Mark Twain's style in these letters is stereotyped and stilted, he avoided " many of the trite and euphemistic phrases of the author to whom he was indebted. " The letters were first published in book form in 1942.

1085 SHIRLEY, Philip. " Those Poems by Twain in *The Wasp* of San Francisco. " *Twainian*, vol. 5, nᵒ 3, 3-4, May-June.

1086 WILLSON, Frank C. " Twain's Tale, ' The Facts Concerning the Recent Important Resignation '. " *Ibid.*, 1-3.

Reprint of a humorous letter to the *New York Tribune* (Weekly), Jan. 1, 1868, with an introduction.

1087 WYMAN, Mary A. " A Note on Mark Twain. " *College English*, vol. 7, 438-442. April.

A parallel between Edmond Aubrey, the Paladin in *Joan of Arc* and Mark Twain ; they have many points in common.

UNPUBLISHED THESES :

1088 FEINSTEIN, George W. *Mark Twain's Literary Opinions*, a Ph. D. thesis for the Univ. of Iowa (*Doctoral Dissertations*, 1946, nᵒ 13, p. 59).

1089 RODNEY, Robert M. *Mark Twain in England ; A Study of the English Criticism of and Attitude towards Mark Twain : 1867-1940*, a Ph. D. thesis for the Univ. of Wisconsin (*Doctoral Dissertations*, 1946, nᵒ 13, p. 61), summed up in *Summaries of Doctoral Dissertations, Univ. of Wisconsin*, vol. 9, 491-493.

Contains very little information about the critical reception after 1910.

1947

BIBLIOGRAPHIES :

1090 Mark Twain : An Exhibition Selected Mainly from the Papers Belonging to the Samuel L. Clemens's Estate on Deposit in the Huntington Library. San Marino, Calif., 33 pp.

1091 Articles on American Literature Appearing in Current Periodicals 1920-1945. Durham, N. C., Duke University Press, x + 337 pp.
Pp. 127-138, a list of articles on Twain.

BIOGRAPHIES AND BOOKS OF CRITICISM :

1092 FREAR, Walter Francis. *Mark Twain and Hawaii.* Chicago privately printed, Lakeside Press, xiv + 519 pp.
A meticulous account of his four months stay in Hawaii.

1093 LEMONNIER, Léon. *Mark Twain.* Paris, A. Fayard, 269 pp.
A psychological study of the man and a critical survey of his works on the lines of Van Wyck Brooks's interpretation which the author follows very closely.

1094 LILJEGREN, Sven B. *The Revolt Against Romanticism in American Literature as Evidenced in the Works of Samuel L. Clemens,* Essays and Studies on American Language and Literature. Publications of the American Institute of the Univ. of Upsala, nᵒ 1, 60 pp.
An essay already published in 1945 in *Studia Neophilologica.* Cf. above nᵒ *1019* and nᵒ *1049.*

1095 MACK, Effie Mona. *Mark Twain in Nevada.* New York and London, Charles Scribner's & Sons, xiv + 398 pp.
According to this author, it was in Nevada that Mark Twain " incubated and in Virginia City that he became a full-fledged writer ".

INTRODUCTIONS AND PREFACES :

1096 MARK TWAIN. *The Adventures of Tom Sawyer* (introduction by Graham Hutton). London, Paul Eleck, 232 pp. (Camden Classics).

1097 — *The Adventures of Tom Sawyer*, Pagine scelte con note di Matilde Bargelli. Milan, C. Signorelli, 150 pp.

1098 — *The Adventures of Huckleberry Finn*, illustrated by Baldwin Hawes, introduction by May Lamberton Becker. Cleveland, World Publishing Co., 377 pp. (Rainbow Classics).

1099 RAHV, Philip. *The Discovery of Europe*, The Story of American Experience in the Old World, ed. with an introduction by Philip Rahv. Boston, Houghton Mifflin Co., xix + 743 pp.

Comments on Mark Twain, p. 237 and extracts from *The Innocents Abroad*, pp. 237-268.

OTHER BOOKS DEALING WITH MARK TWAIN :

1100 BROOKS, Van Wyck. *The Times of Melville and Whitman.* New York, P. Dutton, 489 pp.

On Mark Twain, pp. 283-300, 448-464 & *passim.* The author has not changed his mind since *The Ordeal of Mark Twain* and still interprets Twain as a split personality, but his judgments are fairer. He now sees in him a great folk artist and a " serio-comic Homer ". His former prejudice against the West has completely disappeared.

1101 WRITGHT, William. *The Big Bonanza.* An Authentic Account of the Discovery, History and Working of the World-Renowned Comstock Lode of Nevada, including the present condition of the mines situated thereon, sketches of the most prominent men interested in them, incidents and adventures connected with mining, the Indians, and the country... by Dan De Quille (William. Wright). Introduction by Oscar Lewis. New York, Alfred A. Knopf, xli + 439 pp.

Contains hitherto unpublished letters of Mark Twain.

PERIODICAL LITERATURE :

1) Review of *The Letters of Quintus Curtius Snodgrass* (ed. by Ernest E. Leisy) (1946) :

1102 LORCH, Fred W. in *AL*, vol. 19, 93-95, March.

These letters are important because they supply valuable material for a study of Mark Twain's early development.

2) Review of Lemonnier's *Mark Twain* :

1103 LE BRETON, Maurice. in *Langues Modernes*, 51e année, A 53-54, Sept.-Oct.

The reviewer considers it an excellent synthesis.

* *
*

1104 BERGLER, Edmund. " Exceptional Reaction to a Joke of Mark Twain. " *Mark Twain Quar.*, vol. 8, 11-18, Winter.

A Freudian explanation of the " shuddering silence " which followed Mark Twain's reference at the G. A. R. Convention in Chicago in 1879 to Gen. Grant " trying to find some way to get his big toe into his mouth " when a baby. Very far-fetched and betraying a complete lack of a sense of humor.

1105 BLANCK, J. " Best Seller of the 70's (Innocents Abroad). " *Pub. W.*, vol. 152, B 37, July 19.

1106 BOOTH, Bradford A. " Mark Twain's Friendship with Emma Beach. " *Mark Twain Quar.*, vol. 8, 4-10, Winter.

1107 — " Mark Twain's Friendship with Emmeline Beach. " *AL*, vol. 19, 219-230, Nov.

Emmeline Beach was one of the " Innocents Abroad. " This article contains a few unpublished letters of Mark Twain to her.

1108 BROWNELL, G. H. " About That Heliotype Portrait of Mark Twain in *Huckleberry Finn*. " *Twainian*, vol. 6, nº 1, 1-2, Jan.-Feb.

1109 — " Mark Orates on Death of Democratic Party in 1880. " *Ibid.*, 2-3.

1110 — " This German Biography Did not Contain Enough ' Frozen Truth ' to Satisfy Twain. " *Ibid.*, vol. 6, nº 2, March-April.

About an anonymous biographical sketch given in appendix to the last volume of a translation of his works published at Stuttgart by Lutz in 1898.

1111 — " Some Figures of the First Edition of *Tom Sawyer.* " *Ibid.*, p. 2.

1112 — " Twain ' Ciphers ' Loss from Postal Decree. " *Ibid.*, pp. 3-4.

1113 — " The First of Series II, American Travel Letters, in *Alta California.* " *Ibid.*, vol. 6, no 3, 1-3, May-June ; no 4, 4-6, July-Aug. ; no 5, 3-4, Sept.-Oct. ; no 6, 3-4, Nov.-Dec.

1114 BROWNELL, H. G. " That Picture of ' St. Louis Hotel ' in *Life on the Mississippi.* " *Ibid.*, vol. 6, no 4, 1-4, July-Aug.

1115 — " Fred J. Hall Tells the Story of His Connection with Charles L. Webster & Co. " *Ibid.*, vol. 6, no 6, 1-3, Nov.-Dec.

1116 CLEMENS, Cyril. " Twain's Southern Relative, Jeremiah Clemens. " *Mark Twain Quar.*, vol. 8, nos 3 & 4, p. 13, Spring-Summer.

1117 COAD, O. S. " Mrs. Clemens Apologizes for Her Husband. " *Journal Rutgers Univ. Library*, vol. 10, 29, Dec.

 Mrs. Clemens apologizes for her husband's failure to offer lunch to his guest, Theodore Stanton. He often skipped the midday meal.

1118 DE VOTO, B. " Those Two Immortal Boys. " *Woman's Day*, 38-39, 131-134, Nov.

 A critical analysis of *Tom Sawyer* and *Huckleberry Finn* composed by the author after listening to a " cheap and vulgar " radio dramatization of the former.

1119 DICKINSON, Leon Townsend. " Mark Twain's Revisions in Writing *The Innocents Abroad.* " *AL*, vol. 19, 139-157, May.

 Mark Twain revised the text of his letters to the *Alta California* to adapt it to the taste of an Eastern public.

1120 — " Marketing a Best-Seller : Mark Twain's *Innocents Abroad.* " *Papers of the Bibliographical Society of America*, vol. 41, 107-122, Second Quar. 1947.

 The book was sold by canvassing book-agents and not by book-sellers. Mark Twain and the American Publishing Co. engineered a remarkable promotion campaign.

1121 DONNER, Stanley T. " Mark Twain as a Reader. " *Quarterly Jour. of Speech*, vol. 23, 308-311, Oct.

 In his many public readings Mark Twain was very popular with audiences and earned considerable sums of money.

1122 DUGAS, Gaile. " Mark Twain's Hannibal. " *Holiday*, vol. 2, 102-107 + 136, April.

 Mark Twain's home town has become a shrine to American boyhood.

1123 FEINSTEIN, George W. " Mark Twain on the Immanence of Authors in their Writings. " *Mark Twain Quar.*, vol. 8, 13-14, Winter.

1124 FERMERSDORFF, Ellen H. " Mark Twain in Australia. " *Mark Twain Quar.*, vol. 8, nos 3-4, 20, Spring-Summer.
On Mark Twain's Stay in Australia.

1125 GIBSON, William M. " Twain and Howells : Anti-Imperialists. " *NEQ*, vol. 20, 435-470, Dec.
On their attitude at the time of the Boer War and the American campaign in the Philippines.

1126 GRANT, R. V. " The Word ' pulu '. " *AS*, vol. 22, 150-151, April.
A Hawaiian word which Mark Twain once used jocularly — or erroneously — to designate a Nevadan tree.

1127 HARRISON, James G. " A Note on the Duke in ' Huck Finn ' : The Journeyman Printer as a Picaro. " *Mark Twain Quar.*, vol. 8, 1-2, Winter.

1128 LAVERTY, Carroll D. " The Genesis of *The Mysterious Stranger*. " *Mark Twain Quar.*, vol. 8, 15-19, Spring Summer.
The germinal idea of *The Mysterious Stranger* was a moral tale of the same name in McGuffey's *Rhetorical Guide and Fifth Reader* (1841) by Jane Taylor, a fairly well-known English writer of stories for children.

1129 LORCH, Fred W. " Mark Twain's Sandwich Islands Lectures at St. Louis. " *AL*, vol. 18, 299-307, Jan.

1130 LOWELL, Charles J. " The Background of Mark Twain's Vocabulary. " *AS*, vol. 22, 88-98, April.
Many of the 600 odd words Mark Twain is credited with coining by R. L. Ramsay and F. G. Emberson in their *Mark Twain Lexicon* (1938) were in fact derived from the frontier usage of the day and can be found in passages of early Western periodicals quoted by the *Dictionary of American English*.

1131 PARSONS, Coleman O. " The Devil and Samuel Clemens. " *Va. Quar. Rev.*, vol. 23, 582-606, Autumn.
A study of Mark Twain's guilt complex which according to the author, was " rooted in his relations with Mother Jane and Brother Henry "), and of his sense of evil. Finally " denying the reality of sin, Clemens wrote off guilt and blamed God for the horrible affliction. "

1132 ROBINSON, Marie J. " Mark Twain Lecturer. " *Mark Twain Quar.*, vol. 8, 1-12, Spring-Summer.
His speaking style was outstanding because it was actually conversation, and his writing style is outstanding because it approximated his speaking.

1133 WECTER, Dixon. " Frank Finlay ; or, ' The Thameside Ten-
derfoot in the Woolly West '. " *Twainian*, vol. 6, n⁰ 4, 1-4,
July-Aug.

1134 — " The Love Letters of Mark Twain. " *Atlantic Monthly*,
vol. 180, 33-39 (Nov.), 66-72 (Dec.).

The author ridicules " the rather silly Freudian controversy "
about Mark Twain's relations with his wife and sees no signs
of that " ordeal which was supposed to have made him into
a kind of henpecked Rabelais. "

1135 Anon. " Much Fresh Mark Twain Material to be Made Available. "
Pub. W., vol. 151, 2433, May 10.

On new material to be published by Dixon Wecter.

1136 — " Unpublished Twain Letter. " *Mark Twain Quar.*, vol. 8,
19, Spring-Summer.

A letter to Henry Miller, general superintendent of the
Burlington Railroad (June 17, 1902) in answer to word that
a station had been named after him.

UNPUBLISHED THESES :

1137 BELLAMY, Gladys C. *Mark Twain as a Literary Artist*, a Ph. D.
thesis for the Univ. of Oklahoma (*Doctoral Dissertations*, 1947,
n⁰ 14, p. 83).

1137* DONNER, Stanley T. *The Speaking and Reading of Mark Twain*,
a doctoral dissertation for the Department of Speech of North-
western University. (Cf. *1121*.)

1138 MOORE, William E. *Mark Twain's Techniques of Humor*, a Ph. D.
thesis for George Peabody Institute, Nashville, Tennessee
(*Doctoral Dissertations*, 1947, n⁰ 14, p. 81).

1139 SCOTT, Arthur Lincoln. *Mark Twain as a Critic of Europe*, a
doctoral thesis for the Univ. of Michigan.

Cf. below, unpublished theses in 1948.

1948

BIBLIOGRAPHIES :

1139* Leary, Lewis (compilator). *Doctoral Dissertations in American Literature, 1933-1948*, reprinted from *AL*, vol. 20, n° 2, May 1948, pp. 169-230.

> This list supplements E. E. Leisy and Jay B. Hubbell's " Doctoral Dissertations in American Literature ", *AL*, vol. 4, pp. 419-465, Jan. 1933. A list of Ph. D. theses on Mark Twain will be found on p. 175.

1140 Spiller, Thorp, Johnson, Canby. *Literary History of the United States*. New York, Macmillan, 3 vols.

> Vol. III, pp. 442-450, contains a Mark Twain bibliography which includes a list of separate and collected works, edited texts and reprints, books of biography and criticism, periodical literature and primary sources.

BIOGRAPHIES AND BOOKS OF CRITICISM :

1141 Harnsberger, C. T. *Mark Twain at Your Fingertips*. New York, Beechhurst Press, xiv + 559 pp.

> Quotations from Mark Twain alphabetically arranged by subject matter. Foreword by Clara Clemens.

INTRODUCTIONS AND PREFACES :

1142 Mark Twain. *The Adventures of Huckleberry Finn*, illustrated by Donald MacKay. New York, Grosset & Dunlop, 431 pp. (Illustrated Junior Library).

1143 — *The Adventures of Huckleberry Finn*, with introductions by Brander Matthews and Dixon Wecter. New York, Harper's, xxv + 404 pp. (cf. 1918 ed.).

According to Wecter, " Today, when a tardily awakened national conscience has begun to regard race prejudices as the chief blemish on the face of American democracy, readers of *Huckleberry Finn* are struck more forcibly than those of a generation ago by the fact that its real hero is Nigger Jim " (p. xxiii).

1144 — *The Adventures of Huckleberry Finn*. Introduction by Lionel Trilling. New York, Rinehart, xxii + 293 pp. (cf. n° *1239*).

1145 — *Les Aventures d'Huckleberry Finn*, traduit de l'américain par Suzanne Nétillard, préface de Jean Kanapa, Paris, Éditions d'Hier et d'Aujourd'hui, vii + 288 pp.

The preface is a communist interpretation of Mark Twain. According to Kanapa, American capitalists tried to suppress the bolder and less orthodox works of Mark Twain. In Russia, on the contrary, Soviet critics have freely commented on his anti-imperialist views and he is one of the most popular writers.

1146 MARK TWAIN. *Life on the Mississippi*, with an introduction by J. W. Rankin. New York and London, Harper & Brothers, xxiv + 526 pp. (Harper's Modern Classics).

1147 — *The Prince and the Pauper*,· with an introduction by May Lamberton Becker. Cleveland, World Publishing Co., xiv + 274 pp.

A children's edition.

1148 — *A Connecticut Yankee in King Arthur's Court*, with an introduction by Carl Van Doren and illustrations by Honoré Guilbeau. New York, Heritage Press, vii + 269 pp.

1149 — *A Connecticut Yankee in King Arthur's Court*, adapted by Ruth T. King in collaboration with Elsa Wolf & Hilton D. King. New York, Globe Book Co., iii + 329 pp.

1150 *Mark Twain in Three Moods*, Three New Items of Twainiana edited by Dixon Wecter. San Marino, Calif. Friends of the Huntington Library, 32 pp.

Contains 1) part of a lecture on the Far-West.
2) " Chinese Labor " (in California, 1870).
3) A story told by Mark Twain to some friends at West Point in 1881.

OTHER BOOKS DEALING WITH MARK TWAIN :

1151 BRODIN, Pierre. *Les Maîtres de la Littérature Américaine*. Paris, Horizons de France, 491 pp.

On Mark Twain, pp. 267-306 and bibliography, pp. 472-480.

1152 Cowie, Alexander. *The Rise of the American Novel.* New York, American Book Co., xii + 877 pp.

On Mark Twain, pp. 599-652.

Mark Twain's " abounding vitality and natural freedom heartened scores of later writers, and his basic reliance on colloquial idioms acted as a proclamation of emancipation to countless slavish writers who, without his warrant, would not have dared to depart from the " literary " language of most of his contemporaries " (p. 612). The author also praises his realism and concludes : " If he was not a profound thinker, he was a skilled writer " (p. 635).

1153 Hyman, Stanley Edgar. *The Armed Vision.* New York, Alfred A. Knopf, xv + 417 + xxii pp.

Contains an excellent discussion of the Van Wyck Brooks-De Voto controversy (pp. 109, 113-118, 125, 141), and in particular a detailed study of the corrections made by Brooks in the second edition of *The Ordeal of Mark Twain.*

1154 Jones, Howard Mumford. *The Theory of American Literature.* Ithaca, N. Y., Cornell Univ. Press, 208 pp.

A criticism of the critics. Several references to Mark Twain.

1155 Spiller, Thorp, Johnson, Canby. *Literary History of the United States.* New York, Macmillan, 3 vols.

On Mark Twain, cf. vol. I, pp. 634-635 by Harold Blodgett (on Mark Twain's success abroad) ; vol. II, pp. 806-807 by Dixon Wecter (on Mark Twain as a publisher) ; pp. 837-838 by Willard Thorp (on Mark Twain's books on the Old World) ; pp. 917-939 by Dixon Wecter ; vol. III, pp. 442-450 (bibliography). Wecter rejects Brooks's interpretation, but proposes a Freudian explanation of his own based on the low sexual vitality of Mark Twain, who, according to Wecter, was out of his depth when he dealt with adult dilemmas and economic and social problems and was at home only when his subject was the report of his five senses or the championship of justice in the eternal conflict between bullies and " little folk. "

1156 Williams, Stanley T. *Tres Escritores Clasicos de la Literatura de los Estados Unidos,* translated by Filberto Gonzales. Mexico City, Instituto Mexicano-Norteamericano de Relaciones Culturales, 87 pp.

Contains the text of a lecture on Twain.

PERIODICAL LITERATURE :

1) Review of Frear's *Mark Twain and Hawaii* (1947) :
1157 WECTER, Dixon. in *SRL*, vol. 31, 18-19, Feb. 28.

" No comparable period of four months in Clemens's life has ever received this saturation treatment. " But was it worth it ? — It was there that Mark Twain discovered his talent for " word-painting ".

2) Review of M. Mendelson's *Mark Twain* (1939) :
1158 MANNING, Clarence W. in *AL*, vol. 20, 358-359, Nov.

" [This] book is a connected history of the spiritual and literary progress of a writer who is held back by the censorship of his wife and friends and who did not have the moral courage to break completely with a Europeanized and class society... All of Mark Twain's works... are fitted into the pattern that was laid down by Marx, Engels and Lenin... "

3) Review of *Mark Twain in Three Moods :*
1159 LEARY, Lewis in *AL*, vol. 20, 362, Nov.

4) Review of E. M. Mack's *Mark Twain in Nevada* (1947) :
1160 HART, James D. in *AL*, vol. 19, 379-380, Jan.

According to the reviewer the book is more about Nevada than about Twain. Some details are new, but Ivan Benson's *Mark Twain's Western Years* is crisper and more clearly conceived.

*
* *

1161 BROWNELL, H. G. " ' American Travel Letters ', Series II, Fifth of Series in *Alta California.* " *Twainian*, vol. 7, nº 1, 3-5, Jan.-Feb. (continued ; cf. 1947) ; nº 2, 3-6, March-April ; nº 3, 3-5, May-June ; nº 4, 3-4, July-Aug. ; nº 5, 3-4, Sept.-Oct. ; nº 6, 5-7, Nov. Dec.

1162 — " Mark Found He Already Knew the Tricks of Prof. Loisette's New Memories. " *Ibid.*, nº 2, 1-3, March-April.

1163 — " Twain's Tale of the Washoe Miner at ' The Reception at the President's '. " *Ibid.*, nº 4, 1-2, July-Aug.

1164 — " Twain's Scrapbook Praised for its Literary Excellence. " *Ibid.*, 5-6.

Reprint of an article on Mark Twain's scrapbook.

1165 BROWNELL, H. G. " Unknown Twain Speech at Elmira in 1879. "
Ibid., n⁰ 5, 5, Sept.-Oct.

1166 CLEMENS, Cyril. " Mark Twain's Story on the Siamese Twins. "
Hobbies, vol. 53, 139, Oct.

1167 COLEMAN, Rufus A. " Trowbridge and Clemens. " *MLQ*, vol. 9,
216-223, June.

1168 DeLANEY, Wesley A. " Twain's Last Visit to Bermuda Preceding
the Final Days of His Life. " *Twainian*, vol. 7, n⁰ 1, 1-3, Jan.-
Feb.

1169 — „ The Truth About That Humboldt Trip As Told by Gus
Oliver to A. B. Paine. " *Ibid.*, n⁰ 3, 1-3, May-June.
Gus Oliver was the " Oliphant " of *Roughing It* and " the
Uncomplaining Man " of *Innocents Abroad*.

1170 DUFFY, Charles. " Mark Twain Writes to Howells. " *Mark Twain
Quar.*, vol. 8, n⁰ 2, 4, Summer-Fall.
An unpublished letter.

1171 EIDSON, John Olin. " Innocents Abroad, Then and Now. "
Georgia Rev., vol. 2, 183-192, Summer.
On the attitude towards European culture of American sold-
iers of World War II. It was similar to that of Mark Twain.

1172 FEINSTEIN, G. W. " Twain as a Forerunner of Tooth-and-Claw
Criticism. " *MLN*, vol. 63, 49-50, Jan.
Twain was a forerunner of Mencken, Shaw, De Voto, all of
them admirers of his on their own admission.

1173 FIEDLER, Leslie. " Come back to the Raft Ag'in, Huck Honey ! "
Partisan Rev., vol. 15, 664-671, June.
On the negro and the homosexual in American society and
in *Huckleberry Finn*.

1174 FLOWERS, Frank C. " Mark Twain's Theories of Morality. "
Mark Twain Quar., vol. 8, p. 10, Summer-Fall.

1175 GIBSON, William Merriam. " Mark Twain and Howells : Anti-
Imperialists. " *NEQ*, vol. 21, 435-470, Dec.
(Part of a thesis for the Univ. of Chicago).

1176 HARNSBERGER, Caroline Thomas. " Bernard Shaw Welcomes the
Author of ' Mark Twain at Your Fingertips '. " *Twainian*,
vol. 7, n⁰ 6, 1-2, Nov.-Dec.
About the author's visit to G. B. Shaw.

1177 HOLLOWAY, T. E. " Mark Twain's Turning Point. " *Mark Twain
Quar.*, vol. 8, n⁰ 2, 1-3, Summer-Fall.
On the influence of the Joan of Arc legend on Mark Twain's
career.

1178 Hutcheson, Austin E. " Twain Letter to Bob Howland Asks About Good Audience for Carson City Lecture. " *Twainian*, vol. 7, n⁰ 5, 1-2, Sept.-Oct.

1179 Hutcheson, Austin E. " Twain Was ' News ' to Other Newspapers While a Reporter on the *Enterprise*. " *Twainian*, vol. 7, n⁰ 6, 3-4, Nov.-Dec.

1180 McKeithan, D. M. " A Letter from Mark Twain to Francis Henry Skrine in London. " *MLN*, vol. 63, 134-135, Feb.

A hitherto unpublished letter dated Jan. 7, 1902, in which Twain comments on Kipling.

1181 — " More About Mark Twain's War With English Critics of America. " *Ibid.*, 221-228, April.

Meant to supplement Hoben's article in *AL*, Nov. 1946, pp. 197-218 ; in the author's opinion, *The Prince and The Pauper* was already in many respects an attack on monarchy, especially in so far as it shows " the impossibility of distinguishing between the pauper and the prince except by their clothing. "

1182 — " Occasion of Mark Twain's Speech on Foreign Critics. " *PQ*, vol. 27, 276-279, July.

It was a reply to Matthew Arnold's *Civilisation in the United States* and Sir Lepel Henry Griffin's *The Great Republic*.

1183 Mendelson, M. " Mark Twain Accuses. " *Soviet Literature*, May, 151-161.

Mark Twain as a courageous denunciator of American imperialism.

1184 Russell, Lillis L. " Americanism as Typified by Mark Twain. " *Mark Twain Quar.*, vol. 8, 14-15, Summer-Fall.

1185 Schmitt, G. " Mark Twain Digs for Gold : Radio Play. " *Scholastic*, vol. 52, 23-25, May 10.

1186 Squires, J. Radcliffe. " Mark Twain. " *Accent*, vol. 9, 32-33, Autumn.

An interpretation in verse, but rather obscure.

1187 Strong, Phil. " Mark Twain Cruise : Aboard a Modern River Boat, with Sam Clemens's Shade at the Wheel. " *Holiday*, vol. 5, 56-62, 86-87, 90, 92, 93, 95, 97, April.

1188 Vogelback, Arthur L. " Mark Twain : Newspaper Contributor. " *AL*, vol. 20, 111-128, May.

In the decade following *Innocents Abroad*, Twain was an " incorrigible writer of letters to the press " as if he had wanted to show that he was not only a humourist but also a serious writer interested in serious subjects.

1189 WECTER, Dixon. " Mark Twain's River. " *Atlantic Monthly*, vol. 182, 45-47, Oct.

A trip down the Mississippi on a tow-boat in 1947.

1191 — " Mark Twain's Love Letters. " *Ibid.*, vol. 181, 83-88, Jan. (begun in 1947) — excerpts to be found in *Scholastic*, vol. 51, 20, Jan. 19.

1192 WEISINGER, Mort. " Listen ! Mark Twain Speaking. " *Sat. Evg. Post*, vol. 221, n⁰ 1, 12, July 3.

Discloses that the Voice Library at Yale Univ. contains a record of Mark Twain's voice.

1193 WILLIAMS, Mentor L. " Mark Twain's Joan of Arc. " *Michigan Alumnus Quart. Rev.*, vol. 54, 243-250, May 8.

Why Mark Twain thought that *Joan of Arc* was his best book.

1194 WILSON, Robert H. " Malory in the *Connecticut Yankee*. " *Univ. of Texas Studies in English*, vol. 27, 185-205, June.

Mark Twain used Malory's *Morte d'Arthur* both " intensively and cleverly " following it more closely than is generally realized.

1195 WORKMAN, Mims Thornburgh. " The Whitman-Twain Enigma. " *Mark Twain Quar.*, vol. 8, 12-13, Summer-Fall.

Why did Whitman never praise or mention Mark Twain ? The author does not know the answer. It is to be found in *With Walt Whitman in Camden*. Speaking of Mark Twain, Whitman once declared to Horace Traubel the confident of his old age : " I think he mainly misses fire : he might have been something but he never arrives. " (Quoted by Newton Arvin ; cf. n⁰ *671*, p. 125 A).

1196 Anon. " Twain's Trustees Bring Suit .to Halt Publication of Story. " *Pub. W.*, vol. 153, 233, Jan. 17.

That story was *A Murder, a Mystery and a Marriage*, written in 1876, and not meant for publication according to the trustees.

1197 — " Owner of Mark Twain Manuscript Free to Publish Story. " *Ibid.*, 320, Jan. 24.

1198 — " Unpublished Twain Letters. " *Mark Twain Quar.*, vol. 8, 13, Summer-Fall.

Letters to a certain Frank, March 26, 1897.

UNPUBLISHED THESES :

1199 ANDREWS, Kenneth R. *Mark Twain's Hartford*, a doctoral thesis for the Univ. of Illinois. (Cf. *AL*, vol. 21, Nov. 1949, p. 349).

1200 Scott, Arthur Lincoln. *Mark Twain as a Critic of Europe*, Ann Harbor, Mich., Microfilm of typewritten manuscript made in 1948 by University Microfilms (Publication n⁰ 1073), x + 274 pp. — a thesis for the Univ. of Michigan, summed up in *Microfilm Abstracts*, vol. 8, n⁰ 2, 107-108, 1948.

1200* Young, Philip. *Ernest Hemingway and Huckleberry Finn : A Study in Continuity*, a doctoral dissertation for the University of Iowa (cf. p. 60, n. 2).

1949

BIOGRAPHIES AND BOOKS OF CRITICISM :

1201 CLEMENS, Cyril. *Mark Twain and Franklin D. Roosevelt.* Webster Groves, Mo., International Mark Twain Society, 20 pp.

A reprint of the interview which the author published in 1930 in *Tributes to Mark Twain.*

INTRODUCTIONS AND PREFACES :

1202 MARK TWAIN. *Tom Sawyer,* adapted by Albert O. Berglund; illustrated by Seymour Fleishman. Chicago, Scott, Foresman, x + 324 pp.

1203 — *The Adventures of Tom Sawyer,* together with The Celebrated Jumping Frog of Calaveras County and Other Tales, with 16 original illustrations by Dave Mink. Chicago, Fountain Press, ix + 310 pp. (World's Greatest Literature).

1204 *Mark Twain to Mrs. Fairbanks,* edited by Dixon Wecter. San Marino, Calif., The Huntington Library Publications, xxx + 286 pp.

Next to his wife, no woman played so vital a part in Mark Twain's transformation from " the wild humorist of the Pacific Slope " into a great writer as Mrs. Fairbanks. These hitherto unpublished letters shed light on his development, particularly during the years between his coming out of the West in 1867 and his settling in Hartford, a decisive period in his evolution.

1205 *The Love Letters of Mark Twain,* edited by Dixon Wecter New York, Harper & Brothers, 374 pp.

These hitherto unpublished letters show step by step how Mark Twain and Olivia Langdon fell deeply and permanently in love. They cover the period from 1868 when their courtship began until her final illness in the spring of 1904.

1206 Pochmann, Henry A. & Allen, Gay W. *Masters of American Literature*. New York, Macmillan, 2 vols.

In vol. 2, pp. 436-441, an excellent introduction to Mark Twain and a selected bibliography; pp. 441-478, extracts from his works which include a long passage from *The Man That Corrupted Hadleyburg*.

OTHER BOOKS DEALING WITH MARK TWAIN :

1207 Bompiani. *Dizionario Letterario Bompiani delle Opere e dei Personaggi di tutti i tempi e di tutte letterature*. Milan, Bompiani, 1949-1950.

Contains articles on Mark Twain's works in vol. I, IV, VI & VII.

1208 Koht, Halvdan. *The American Spirit in Europe : A Survey of Transatlantic Influences*. Philadelphia, Univ. of Pennsylvania Press, ix + 289 pp.

Cf. pp. 226-228 on Mark Twain's Reception in Europe.

1209 Wann, Louis. *The Rise of Realism, American Literature from 1860 to 1900*. New York, Macmillan, xv + 874 pp.

Pp. 379-456, extracts from Mark Twain's works, pp. 845-846, a biographical and critical sketch.

PERIODICAL LITERATURE :

1) Reviews of *Mark Twain's Letters to Mrs. Fairbanks* :

1210 Halsband, R. in *SRL*, " Clemens and his other mother. " Vol. 32, 17, Oct. 22.

Praises Dixon Wecter's editing.

1211 Anon. in *TLS*, Nov. 18, p. 752.

2) Review of *Mark Twain's Love Letters* :

1212 Williamson, Samuel T. in *New York Times Book Rev.*, Nov. 18, 53.

The interest of these letters " is their effect on the Van Wyck Brooks-Bernard De Voto shadowboxing... " They " should be kerosene poured on a smouldering controversy. Somebody is sure to write another bad book. " This prophecy has not come true so far.

3) Review of Frear's *Mark Twain and Hawaii* (1947) :

1213 Leisy, Ernest E. in *AL*, vol. 21, 251-252, May.

* *
*

1214 Brynes, Asher. " Boy-Men and Men-Boys. " *YR*, vol. 38, 223-233, Winter.

On the best-sellers for boys written by Twain, Aldrich and Peck.

1215 Carpenter, E. H., Jr. " Millions in It. " *Pacific Hist. Rev.*, vol. 18, 110-111, Feb.

A letter of Mark Twain to the *New York Evg. Post*, Sept. 17, 1880, on gold-bearing water in California.

1216 Chamberlain, T. G. " Mark Twain's Trustees : with reply to C. Clemens. " *Nation*, vol. 168, 224-225, Feb. 19.

Denies Cyril Clemens (who had claimed to be " the greatest living authority on Mark Twain "), the right to publish the official edition of Mark Twain's letters.

1217 Clemens, Cyril. " Mark Twain's Opinion of the Human Body. " *Hobbies*, vol. 54, 140, April.

1218 — " Harry S. Truman : Mark Twain Enthusiast. " *Dalhousie Rev.*, vol. 29, 198-200, July.

1219 — " The President : Mark Twain Enthusiast. " *Hobbies*, vol. 54, 139, May.

1220 Dickinson, L. T. " The Sources of *The Prince and the Pauper*. " *MLN*, vol. 64, 103-106, Feb.

Mark Twain used J. Hammond Trumbull's *The True Blue Laws of Connecticut and New Haven and the False Blue Laws* + a xviith century English book, Richard Head and Francis Kirkman's *The English Rogue*. In them he found the documentation he needed, but they were not really sources.

1221 Kanapa, Jean. " Mark Twain ", premier classique de l'Amérique. *Lettres Françaises*, Janv. 6.

1222 Long, E. H. " Sut Lovingood and Mark Twain's *Joan of Arc*. " *MLN*, vol. 64, 37-39, Jan.

The comic episode in chapter xxxvi about Uncle Laxart and the bull is based on a yarn told by Sut Lovingood, a Western humorist.

1223 Lorch, Fred W. " 'Doesticks' and *Innocents Abroad*, (with texts of two letters to Mark Twain). " *AL*, vol. 20, 446-449, Jan.

Two letters to Mortimer Neal Thomson, " Doesticks ", dated 1870, which show that, contrary to Paine's opinion, Mark Twain intended to write a book about his Quaker City trip even prior to his departure.

1224 PETERSEN, Svend. " Splendid Days and Fearsome Nights. "
Mark Twain Quar., vol. 8, 3-8, 15, Winter-Spring.
On anachronisms in Mark Twain's works.

1225 SLATER, J. " Music at Col. Grangerford's : A Footnote to *Huckleberry Finn* " *AL*, vol. 21, 108-111, March.

1226 WALSH, Elizabeth P. " A Connecticut Yankee of Our Lady's
Court. " *Catholic World*, vol. 169, 91-97, May.

1227 WEST, Ray B., Jr. " Mark Twain's Idyl of Frontier America. "
Univ. of Kansas City Rev., vol. 15, 92-104, Winter.
On *Huckleberry Finn*, " an idyl of American boyhood. "

1228 Anon. " Mark Twain's Unfinished Manuscript. " *New Yorker*,
vol. 24, 15-16, Jan. 29.
About the publication of *A Murder, A Mystery and a Marriage*
which the Mark Twain estate refused to allow. Cf. above
nos *1196-1197*.

1229 — " University of California to Get Mark Twain Papers. "
Pub. W., vol. 156, 2281, Dec. 3.

1950

BIBLIOGRAPHY :

1229* ENGLEKIRK, John E. *A Literatura Norteamericana no Brasil,*
Privately printed in Mexico. Distributed by Author (Tulane
University), 185 pp.

A bibliography of American works translated and published
in Brazil. An historical introduction discusses Brazilian interest
in American authors, in Mark Twain among others.

BIOGRAPHIES AND BOOKS OF CRITICISM :

1230 ANDREWS, Kenneth R. *Nook Farm — Mark Twain's Hartford
Circle.* Cambridge Mass., Harvard Univ. Press, xii + 288 pp.

The gentility of Hartford was far more flexible than is
generally believed. The narrowness, complacence, sterility and
Grundyism sometimes thought to have prevented Mark Twain
from attaining his full stature are nowhere in evidence in
Nook Farm, according to the author. Some of Twain's neigh-
bours even shared his spiritual unrest. There was no conflict
with his environment.

1231 BELLAMY, Gladys Carmen. *Mark Twain as a Literary Artist.*
Norman, Okla., Univ. of Oklahoma Press, 396 pp.

The author undertakes to show that Mark Twain was much
more the conscious craftsman than is generally believed. His
mind was torn by a violent mental conflict which distorted
much of his work, but through years of practice he evolved
methods by which he could achieve artificially the serenity
and detachment required by art.

1232 BRANCH, Edgar Marquess. *The Literary Apprenticeship of Mark
Twain,* with selections from his apprentice writing. Urbana,
Ill., Univ. of Illinois Press, xiv + 325 pp.

A detailed study of Mark Twain's early writings from
boyhood to the sailing of the Quaker City. One of the author's

conclusions is that contrary to De Voto's opinion Nevada
journalism had a harmful influence on his evolution : " ... much
of what he learned in Washoe went into his mature work
— often to its detriment... its very presence was often a mark
of literary immaturity. "

1233 HORNSTEIN, Simon. *Mark Twain.* Paris, Renée Lacoste & Co.,
185 pp.

The sub-title " La faillite d'un idéal " clearly indicates that
the author follows Brooks's interpretation, but in spite of this
bias the book is a well-documented and adequate critical
survey of Mark Twain's works. p. 177, the author tries to explain
the reasons for Twain's relative lack of success in France.
Pp. 182-184, a bibliography of French translations and
adaptations.

INTRODUCTIONS AND PREFACES :

1234 MARK TWAIN. *The Adventures of Huckleberry Finn,* with an introduction by T. S. Eliot. New York, Chanticleer Press, XVI
+ 292 pp.
Cf. introduction pp. 60-61.

1235 MARK TWAIN. *Life on the Mississippi,* with an introduction by
Dixon Wecter. New York, Harper & Brothers, XVI + 526 pp.

1236 *Comstock Bonanza;* Rare Western Americana of Mark Twain,
Bret Harte, Sam Davis, James W. Gally, Dan de Quille,
Joseph T. Goodman, J. Ross Browne, Fred Hart, collected
and edited by Duncan Emrich. New York, The Vanguard
Press, 363 pp.

OTHER BOOKS DEALING WITH MARK TWAIN :

1237 CAHEN, Jacques Fernand. *La Littérature Américaine.* Paris,
Presses Universitaires (Collection Que Sais-Je ?), 128 pp.
On Mark Twain, pp. 42-47 ; the author criticizes him severely
for his lack of taste, but praises him as the first American
realist with *Life on the Mississippi, Tom Sawyer* and *Huckleberry Finn.*

1238 HART, James D. *The Popular Book; A History of America's
Literary Taste,* New York, Oxford University Press, 351 pp.
Passim on the sales of Mark Twain's books in his lifetime.

1239 Trilling, Lionel. *The Liberal Imagination.* New York, The Viking Press, xvi + 303 pp.

Contains an essay on *Huckleberry Finn,* pp. 104-117, already published in 1948 as an introduction to Twain's book. The author considers *Huckleberry Finn* " one of the world's great books and one of the central documents of American culture ", " an almost perfect work " in form as well as in style. In his opinion, Mark Twain was a conscious artist and even occasionally a conscientious craftsman.

Cf. Introd. last p., n. 3.

PERIODICAL LITERATURE :

1) Review of *Mark Twain to Mrs. Fairbanks* (1949) :

1240 Dickinson, Leon T. in *AL*, vol. 22, 202-203, May.

Though the editor (Dixon Wecter) does not re-open the question of the female-dominated Mark Twain, " it is clear that he believes Mrs. Fairbank's influence to have been for the best, as it probably was ".

2) Reviews of Branch's *The Literary Apprenticeship of Mark Twain :*

1241 Ferguson, DeLancey. in *AL*, vol. 22, 362-363, Nov.

The author accepts some of Paine's most egregious blunders and in the major portion of the book his criticism seems too detailed for the very slender merit of the writing he examines, but it reaches a high level in the closing section where he analyzes the thematic structure of *Huckleberry Finn.*

1242 Thompson, Lawrance. in *New York Times Book Rev.,* July 2, p. 4.

The reviewer claims that, contrary to E. M. Branch's opinion, no " logic of development " can be found in Twain's work because he was essentially an improviser.

3) Reviews of Bellamy's *Mark Twain as a Literary Artist :*

1243 Redding, Saunders. in *Am. Scholar*, vol. 20, 118-122, Winter 1950-1951.

According to this reviewer, the proof Miss Bellamy adduces " as to Twain's conscious artistry... is not always quite valid ".

1244 Wallace, E. in *SRL*, " Beloved Jester's Many Moods ", vol. 33, 30, Sept. 23.

Very favourable.

1245 WHICHER, George F. in *New York Times Book Rev.*, Aug. 13, p. 6.

" In placing her emphasis squarely on the development of Mark Twain as a literary artist, Miss Bellamy... has set the appropriate keystone on the arch of Mark Twain criticism. "

4) Reviews of Andrews's *Nook Farm — Mark Twain's Hartford Circle :*

1246 GEISMAR, Maxwell. in *New Work Times Book Rev.*, Oct. 8, p. 5.

Geismar thinks that Andrews minimizes the central tragedy in Mark Twain's life by assigning his increasing bitterness merely to the psychoanalytic couch.

1247 WINTERICH, J. T. in *SRL*, " Clemens and Colony in the Hartford Days ", vol. 33, 26-27, Oct. 14.

Very favourable. The hero of the book is Joe Twichell and the heroine Mrs. Clemens whose detractors are taken to task.

5) Review of T. S. Eliot's edition of *Huckleberry Finn :*

1248 Anon. in *TLS*, " The Boy and the River. " Nov. 10, p. 708.

" Mr. Eliot does not betray, in his very grown-up introduction, whether he remembers being " a boy once. Mark Twain outdoes almost all writers : " He remembers being not one boy, but two. "

6) Review of Mark Twain's *Un Yankee à la Cour du Roi Arthur.*

(traduction d'Odette Ferry et J. de Plunkett. Paris, Bruxelles, Éditions de la Paix, 335 pp.).

1249 DECAUNES, Luc, in *Paru*, n° 62, p. 68, Juillet.

A vulgar and boring novel according to the reviewer.

*
* *

1250 ALKUS, M. " Comet of Destiny. " *Coronet*, vol. 28, 159 pp., Aug.

1251 BLANCK, Jacob. " In Re *Huckleberry Finn.* " *New Colophon*, vol. 3, 153-159, 1950.

A bibliographical study of the different editions.

1252 BOOTH, Bradford. " Mark Twain's Comments on Holmes's *Autocrat.* " *AL*, vol. 21, 456-463, Jan.

According to the author, Holmes may have exerted a certain influence on the development of Twain's humor after *Innocents Abroad*. By way of proof, Bradford Booth quotes the marginalia in the copy of the *Autocrat* which Twain used in 1869 while courting Livy.

1253 BRANCH, Edgar M. " The Two Providences : Thematic Forms in *Huckleberry Finn.* " *College English,* vol. 11, 188-195, Jan.

The two conceptions of heavenly providence held by Miss Watson and Widow Douglas become the struggle between intuitive and conventional morality within Huck's conscience. The duality is implicit even in the style of the novel.

1254 CLEMENS, Cyril. " Hervey Allen and Mark Twain. " *Hobbies,* vol. 55, 120, April.

On Hervey Allen's fondness for Mark Twain's books.

1255 — " Margaret Mitchell and Mark Twain. " *Ibid.,* 140, Oct.

1256 — " Collecting Mark Twain, Eugene Field and Harry Truman. " *Ibid.,* 141, Nov.

1257 — " Shaw and Twain. " *Christian Science Monitor,* Dec. 5.

A letter to the editor on Shaw's meetings with Mark Twain.

1258 CUNLIFFE, Marcus. " The Boy and the River. " (A letter to the editor). *TLS,* Nov. 17, p. 727, & Dec. 8, p. 785.

On the origin and meaning of Mark Twain's pseudonym. The reviewer answered, *ibid.,* p. 747, Nov. 24 & p. 785, Dec. 8.

1259 EDWARDS, Peter G. " The Political Economy of Mark Twain's Connecticut Yankee. " *Mark Twain Quar.,* vol. 8, 2, 18, Winter.

1260 FATOUT, Paul. " Mark Twain Lectures in Indiana. " *Indiana Magazine of History,* Year 1950, 363-367, Dec.

On Mark Twain's lectures in Indianapolis and Logansport in 1872.

1261 FRANCIS, Raymond L. " Mark Twain and H. L. Mencken. " *Prairie Schooner,* vol. 24, 31-40, Spring.

On similarities between the two writers.

1262 KITZABER, Albert F. " Götterdämmerung in Topeka : The Downfall of Senator Pomeroy. " *Kansas Hist. Quar.,* vol. 18, 243-278, Aug.

A detailed account of the exposure and conviction of Senator Pomeroy in 1873 with references to Mark Twain's use of the incident in *The Gilded Age.*

1263 LORCH, Fred W. " Mark Twain's Lecture from *Roughing It.* " *AL,* vol. 22, 290-307, Nov.

A reprint, with an introduction, of the text of that lecture which Mark Twain gave in 1871 during an extensive lecture tour organized by Redpath, proprietor of the Boston Lyceum Bureau.

1264 MICHEL, Robert. " The Popularity of Mark Twain in Austria. " *Mark Twain Quar.,* vol. 8, 5-6, 19, Winter.

1265 MOFFETT, Wallace B. " Mark Twain's Lansing Lecture on *Rough-ing It.*" *Michigan Hist. Mag.*, vol. 34, 144, 170, June.

An account of the circumstances of Mark Twain's talk at Lansing on Dec. 14, 1871 and a reprint of the lecture.

1266 SCHOFIELD, Kenneth B. " The Boy and the River." (A letter to the editor.) *TLS*, Dec. 8, p. 785. Cf. above under Cunliffe.

1267 TROMMER, Marie. " *Tom Sawyer* and the Missing Cat Chapter. " *Mark Twain Quar.*, vol. 8, 3-4, Winter.

On a cat story included in the Russian edition of *Tom Sawyer* which the author read when a child.

1268 WINKLER, John A. " Tom Sawyer's Town — A Sketch. " *Twainian*, vol. 9, n⁰ 3, 1, 4, May-June & n⁰ 4, 3-4, July-Aug.

UNPUBLISHED THESIS :

1268 *ERVIN, Jean C. " *Mark Twain, Speechmaker.* " University of Missouri, Department of Speech.

1951

BIBLIOGRAPHIES :

1269 *O'Connor Auction List*, Mark Twain Library Auction, April 10th, 2005 North La Brea Ave., O'Connor Auction Studios, 7949 Sunset Boulevard, Hollywood 46, Calif.

1270 *Zeitlin and Ver Brugge List*, Books from the Library of Mark Twain, also articles from his home purchased at the sale of the Library of his daughter, Clara Clemens Samassoud, April 10-14, 1951, Zeitlin and Ver Brugge, Booksellers, 815 North La Cienega, Los Angeles, Calif., List n⁰ 132, May 1951.

Both lists help to determine the extent of Mark Twain's reading.

BIOGRAPHIES AND BOOKS OF CRITICISM :

1271 Canby, Henry S. *Turn West, Turn East.* — *Mark Twain and Henry James.* Boston, Houghton Mifflin Co., 318 pp.

1272 Gilkey, Robert. *Mark Twain Voyageur et son Image de l'Europe.* Paris, xiv + 327 pp. (a doctoral dissertation for the University of Paris — mimeographed).

INTRODUCTIONS AND PREFACES :

1273 Mark Twain. *The Adventures of Tom Sawyer*, adapted by Erwin H. Schubert, edited by Delpha Hurlburt. New York, Globe Book Company, viii + 219 pp.

PERIODICAL LITERATURE :

1) Review of *Mark Twain's Love Letters* (1949) :

1274 Dickinson, Leon T. in *AL*, vol. 22, 524-525, Jan.

This book does not solve the problem of Mrs. Clemens's censorship. Letters to and from her reveal her " no more and no less a blight on the flowering of his genius than we have supposed ".

2) Review of Bellamy's *Mark Twain as a Literary Artist* (1950) :

1275 BLAIR, Walter in *AL*, vol. 22, 521-524, Jan.
The reviewer thinks that the author has paid more attention to the thought than to the form and feels " she might have given useful emphasis to the fact that Twain, tame as he may seem today, was considered in his own day a violent smasher of taboos ". He also criticizes her for considering *Following the Equator* the greatest of Twain's travel-books and for ranking *Captain Stormfield's Visit to Heaven* with *Huckleberry Finn.*

3) Reviews of Andrews's *Nook Farm — Mark Twain's Hartford Circle* (1950) :

1276 BLAIR, Walter. in *AL*, vol. 23, 258-259, May.

1277 Anon. in *TLS*, " New England Intellectuals. " Feb. 16, p. 95.
" The completeness of Mr. Andrews's survey is impressive, but his manner is objective even to dryness. "

4) Review of Canby's *Turn West, Turn East — Mark Twain and Henry James* :

1278 EDEL, Leon. in *New York Times Book Rev.*, Nov. 11, p. 8, " Two Innocents at Home ".

1279 GRAY, J. in *SRL*, vol. 34, 27, Dec. 1, " Interpreting Genius ".

*
* *

1280 BARSAMIAN, Kenneth J. " Mark Twain's Mudhen Victory. " *Mark Twain Quar.*, vol. 9, 12-13, Winter.

1281 BLUMFIELD, R. D. " Twain note. " *Hobbies*, vol. 56, 152, Dec.

1282 BURNAM, Tom. " Mark Twain and the Paige Typesetter : A Background of Despair. " *Western Humanities Rev.*, vol. 6, 29-36, Winter 1951-1952.
According to the author, Paige's failure had more bearing on Mark Twain's pessimism than is generally realized.

1283 BURNET, Ruth A. " Mark Twain in the Northwest — 1895. " *Pacific Northwest Quar.*, vol. 42, 187-202, July.

1284 CANBY, H. S. " Hero of the great knowhow : Mark Twain's machine-age Yankee. " *SRL*, vol. 34, 7-8, Oct. 20.

1285 CARDWELL, Guy A. " Mark Twain's Hadleyburg. " *Ohio State Archaeological and Historical Quar.*, vol. 60, 257-264, July.
Hadleyburg, according to Cardwell, was purely imaginary

and anyway it was certainly not Oberlin, Ohio, as had been suggested (nº *826*).

1286 CLEMENS, Cyril. " Mark Twain is entertained by Edward VII. " *Hobbies*, vol. 56, 138, March.

1287 — " Missing Mark Twain Manuscript. " *Mark Twain Quar.*, vol. 9, nº 1, p. 13, Winter (also in *Hobbies*, vol. 56, 136, May). On the manuscript of *The Prince and the Pauper*.

1288 — " Mark Twain and his corncob. " *Hobbies*, vol. 56, 160, June.

1289 COLLINS, L. " Postcards on Mark Twain and Tom Sawyer. " *Hobbies*, vol. 56, 150-152, Nov.

1290 COMMAGER, H. S. " Golden West : based on *Roughing It*. " *Scholastic*, vol. 57, 10-11, Jan. 3.

1291 DOUGLAS, Robert. " The Pessimism of Mark Twain. " *Mark Twain Quar.*, vol. 9, nº 1, 1-4, Winter.

1292 EKSTROEM, Kjell. " Extracts from a diary kept by Ozias W. Pond during the Clemens-Cable tour of readings in 1885. " *Archiv für das Studium der Neueren Sprachen*, vol. 188 (103rd Year), 109-113, May.
O. W. Pond acted as Mark Twain's and Cable's manager during the tour.

1293 ELIOT, T. S. " Huckleberry Finn. " *Bonniers Litterära Magasin* (Sweden), vol. 20, 751-756, Dec.
Cf. above nº *1234*.

1294 FRANCIOSA, Massimo. " I meriti nascosti di Mark Twain narratore. " *La Fieria Letteraria*, nº 25, pp. 4, 7, June 24.
On Mark Twain's consummate skill as a storyteller.

1295 HERZL, Dr. Theodor. " Mark Twain in Paris. " *Mark Twain Quar.*, vol. 9, nº 1, 16-18, Winter.

1296 JONES, Alexander E. " Heterodox thought in Mark Twain's Hannibal. " *Arkansas Historical Quar.*, vol. 10, 244-257.

1297 McGOWAN, Gault. " Mark Twain and Heidelberg. " *Mark Twain Quar.*, vol. 9, nº 1, p. 30.

1298 STRONG, Leah A. " Mark Twain on Spelling. " *AL*, vol. 23, 351-359, Nov.
Text of a preliminary speech at a spelling-bee held at Hartford, reprinted from the *Hartford Courant*, May 13, 1875.

1299 TIGERT, John. " Mark Twain, Man of the People, Amidst Pomp and Circumstance at Oxford University. " *Mark Twain Quar.*, vol. 9, 10-11, Winter.

1300 TRAINOR, Juliette A. " Symbolism in *A Connecticut Yankee in King Arthur's Court*. " *MLN*, vol. 66, 382-385, June.

According to J. A. Trainor, the two giants whom Launcelot encounters at the beginning of the book represent the Catholic Church and monarchy.

1301 WAGENKNECHT, E. " Twain, A Literary Lincoln. " *SRL*, vol. 34, 25-26, Jan. 20.

Mark Twain is read more and more. He survives both as a writer and a legend, a rare combination.

1302 WIGGINS, Robert A. " The Original of Mark Twain's *Those Extraordinary Twins.* " *AL*, vol. 23, 355-357, Nov.

The originals were probably the Tocci twins, who made public appearances in the U. S. in the winter of 1891. Mark Twain may have read about them in the Dec. 1891, *Scientific American.*

1303 WILLIAMS, Cecil B. " Mark Twain, American Paradox. " *Bulletin of Oklahoma Agric. and Mech. College*, vol. 48, 14-20, Sept. 30.

1304 Anon. " Recent Acquisitions. " *Princeton University Library Bulletin*, vol. 12, 217-218, Summer 1951.

On the acquisition of the Thomas L. Leeming collection of Mark Twain manuscripts and first editions.

1305 Anon. " Mark Twain and Anthony Trollope, Equestrians. " *Mark Twain Quar* , vol. 9, 14-15, Winter.

1306 — " Mark Twain, J. Swift e Alphonse Daudet presentati ai ragazzi. " *La Feria Letteraria*, n⁰ 49, p. 8, Dec. 10.

UNPUBLISHED THESES :

1307 CUMMINGS, Sherwood. " *Mark Twain's Attitude towards Science.* " University of Wisconsin.

1307* FRIED, Martin B. " *The Sources, Composition and Popularity of Mark Twain's Roughing It.* " University of Chicago.

1952

BIOGRAPHIES AND BOOKS OF CRITICISM :

1308 WECTER, Dixon. *Sam Clemens of Hannibal.* Boston, Houghton, Mifflin, 335 pp.

A fragment of what might have been the definitive biography of Mark Twain, had not the author died in 1951, before its completion. As a result, this book takes the humorist only to the age of 18. It contains much new information, but will not appreciably alter the generally accepted conception of Mark Twain's personality.

INTRODUCTIONS AND PREFACES :

1309 MARK TWAIN. *Report from Paradise*, ed. by Dixon Wecter, with drawings by Charles Locke. New York, Harper & Bros., 94 pp.

A description of heaven which, in Mark Twain's thought, was meant to " debunk " the traditional conception of paradise. *Captain Stormfield's Visit to Heaven*, which appeared in his lifetime, was a fragment of this fragmentary manuscript.

OTHER BOOKS DEALING WITH MARK TWAIN :

1310 BROOKS, Van Wyck. *The Confident Years — 1895-1915.* New York, E. P. Dutton & Co., 627 pp. or London, J. M. Dent and Sons, VIII + 374 pp.

Surprisingly enough, this book contains only scattered allusions to Mark Twain.

PERIODICAL LITERATURE :

1) Review of *Mark Twain to Mrs. Fairbanks* (1949) :

1311 LEISY, Ernest E. in *MLQ*, vol. 13, 108-109, March.

2) Review of Wecter's *Sam Clemens of Hannibal* (1952) :

1312 FERGUSON, DeLancey in *New York Times Book Rev.*, Aug. 31, p. 3, " When Mark Was Young. "

1312* MEYER, George W. in *American Scholar*, " Days of Innocence. " Vol. 22, 112-114, Winter 1952-53.

3) Review of Canby's *Turn West, Turn East : Mark Twain and Henry James* (1951) :

1313 GIBSON, William M. in *AL*, vol. 24, 253-254, May.

4) Review of *Comstock Bonanza*, coll. and ed. by Duncan Emrich (1950) :

1314 DAVIDSON, Levette J. in *AL*, vol. 24, 107-109, March.

5) Review of Mark Twain's *Report from Paradise* :

1315 FERGUSON, DeLancey in *New York Times Book Review*, vol. 57, nº 36, p. 12, Sept. 7.

6) Review of R. Gilkey's *Mark Twain Voyageur et son Image de l'Europe* (1951) :

1316 NATHAN, Monique. in *Critique*, vol. 8, 893-894, Oct.

*
* *

1317 BLAIR, Walter. " Last of the Jongleurs. " *SRL*, vol. 35, 9-10, Aug. 30.

1318 BUTTERFIELD, Roger. " Roger Butterfield Forwards ' Enterprise ' Mark Twain Item Unknown to Experts. " Virginia City (Nev.). *Territorial Enterprise*, Aug. 1, p. 3.
This item is a letter dated March 3, 1873, in which Mark Twain endorses White's patent fly and mosquito net frames.

1319 CARDWELL, Guy A. " Mark Twain's ' Row ' with George Cable. " *MLQ*, vol. 13, 363-371, Dec.
According to the author, there was friction between the two men, but it never amounted to a " row " contrary to what other critics have claimed. (Cf. *1326*).

1320 CLEMENS, Cyril. " Sam Clemens into Mark Twain. " Virginia City (Nev.). *Territorial Enterprise*, vol. 98, May 2, p. 6.

1321 CUFF, Robert Penn. " Mark Twain's Use of California Folklore in His Jumping Frog Story. " *Jour. of American Folklore*, vol. 65, 155-158, April-June.

1322 FUSSELL, E. S. " The Structural Problem of ' The Mysterious Stranger '. " *Studies in Philology*, vol. 49, nº 1, Jan.

1323 HARDING, Walter. " A Note on the Binding of the First Edition of ' Huckleberry Finn '. " *Bibl. Soc. Univ. of Virginia News Sheet*, n⁰ 20, 1-2, March.

1324 HINZ, John. " Huck and Puck : , Bad Boys in American Fiction. " *South Atlantic Quar.*, vol. 51, 120-129, Jan.

1325 JOHNSON, Burgess. " A Ghost for Mark Twain. " *Atlantic Monthly*, vol. 189, n⁰ 5, 65-66, May.

> The author, when serving as one of the junior editors in the book department of Harper & Bros., revised the *Mark Twain Library of Humor*, but received no share of the royalties and no recognition on the title page.

1326 LORCH, Fred W. " Cable and His Reading Tour with Mark Twain in 1884-1885. " *AL*, vol. 23, 471-486, Jan.

1327 — " Mark Twain's ' Artemus Ward ' Lecture on the Tour of 1871-1872. " *NEQ*, vol. 25, 327-343, Sept.

1328 — " A Note on Mark Twain's Lecture on the Far-West. " *AL*, vol. 24, 377-379, Nov.

> According to the author, it is " Highly probable... that the lecture fragment which Mr. Wecter printed in *Mark Twain in Three Moods*, was part of ' The Curiosities of California ' lecture which he prepared in 1869 but never used. "

1329 ROADES, Sister Mary Teresa. " Was Mark Twain Influenced by the Prolog to ' Don Quixote ' ? " *Mark Twain Quar.*, vol. 9, 4-6, Winter.

> Cf. n⁰ˢ *287* & *411*.

1330 SANTAYANA, George. " Tom Swayer and Don Quixote. " *Ibid.*, vol. 9, 1-3.

> Cf. Preceding article.

1331 SCHWARTZ, Edward. " Huckleberry Finn : The Inward Thoughts of a Generation. " *Mark Twain Quar.*, vol. 9, 11-16, 23, Winter.

1332 YOUNG, J. H. " Anna Dickinson, Mark Twain and Bret Harte. " *Pennsylvania Magazine of History and Biography*, vol. 76, 39-46, Jan.

> Mark Twain as seen by Anna Dickinson, " Queen of the Lyceum Stage ".

UNPUBLISHED THESES :

1333 KRUMPELMANN, John T. *Mark Twain and the German Stage* a doctoral dissertation for Louisiana State University.

INDEX

The numbers in thick type refer to pages in the introduction, those in ordinary type to entries in the bibliography.

A

B

— as a boy, **25-26**, **36-37**, **47-48**, 175, 347, 429, 446, 594, 693, 695, 927, 1308, 1312.
— at Buffalo, 672.
— and the burglar, 273.
— as a businessman, 64, 1057, 1063-1065.
— in California, 16-62, 66, 271, 438, 862, 889, 1150, 1161, 1321, 1328.
— in Canada, 689, 714.
— in Carson City, 499, 1178.
— in Cleveland, 754.
— on the Comstock, 428, 610, 948, 980, 1101, 1236, 1314.
— and copyrights, 417, 823.
— and dialect, 423, 955.
— on education, 902, 918, 997.
— at Elmira, **52**, 8, 637, 816, 1165.
— in England, 52, 81, 472, 822, 936, 1089.
— *Enterprise* (as a journalist on the staff of the), 128, 885, 1179.
— in Europe, 111, 247, 882, 992, 1099, 1139, 1155, 1200, 1208.
— and Mrs. Fairbanks, 754, 1204, 1240.
— his financial difficulties, 64, 195.
— at Florida (Mo.), 350, 954, 1066.
— and France, **16**, 57.
— as a freemason, 445.
— and the German language, 898, 900, 922, 1046.
— and Germany, 57, 706, 758, 788, 837, 908.
— girls (his friendship with little), 127, 139, 828.
— in Gold Hill (Nevada), 780.
— his grandparents, 1002, 1036, 1037.
— Grant's Memoirs, 131.
— at Hannibal, 152, 208, 408, 458, 460, 494, 561, 651, 687, 691, 692, 695, 697, 895, 901, 903, 905, 1122, 1296.
— at Hartford, **52**, 258, 274, 603, 779, 1199, 1230, 1246-1247, 1298.
— in Hawaii, 187, 1092, 1126.
— and Heidelberg, 1297.
— in Honolulu, 271.
— in Humboldt County, 821, 1169.
— Humour, 65*, 118, 119, 176, 197, 200, 201, 202, 203, 234, 241, 250, 268, 301, 311, 315, 358, 370, 427, 517, 518, 524, 624, 675, 715, 771, 791, 802, 917, 1021, 1138.
— in Indiana, 1260.
— as an inventor, 383, 996.

— in Iowa, 470.
— in Italy, 233.
— on Jackass Hill, 409, 625.
— and the Jews, 320, 707, 868.
— at Keokuk, 430, 470.
— at Lansing, 1265.
— his last years, 523.
— as a lecturer, 878, 1132, 1268*.
— his literary opinions, 1088.
— and the memory-builder, 978.
— in Minnesota, 752, 787.
— on the Mississippi, 86, 452, 456, 683, 697, 752, 1187, 1189.
— in Missouri, 164, 318, 350, 493, 542, 601, 654, 899, 928.
— on morality, 925, 1174.
— at Muscatine, 470, 1084.
— and music, 284, 766, 790, 949, 959.
— and nature, 788.
— in Nevada, **51**, 62, 126, 128, 129, 141, 155, 196, 321, 409, 428, 456, 480, 618, 735, 780, 1068, 1070, 1095, 1101, 1160, 1185.
— in Newark, 627.
— in New York, 862.
— in the Northwest, 1283.
— in Oberlin (Ohio), 826, 1285.
— as an occultist, 628.
— as an orator, 79, 308, 984.
— at Oxford, 1299.
— on the Quaker City, 804.
— and the Paige typesetter, 1282.
— in Paris, 1295.
— his pessimism, **27**, **42**, 95, 188, 294, 295, 307, 326, 327, 670, 680, 684, 711, 1291.
— in Philadelphia, 1084.
— his philosophy, 140, 153, 190, 191, 320.
— as a pilot, 173, 452, 456, 491, 899.
— as a printer, 189.
— his pseudonym, **37**, 590, 944, 951, 958, 1028, 1039, 1258, 1266.
— as a psychologist, 617.
— as a publisher, 47, 156, 1155.
— as a radical, 359.
— as a reader, 1121.
— as a reporter, 81, 128, 171, 247, 430, 1188.
— and Russia, 757, 838, 875, 916.
— in San Francisco, 66, 171, 763, 801, 845, 889, 919, 998, 1085.
— in Scandinavia, 746, 777.
— and science, 792, 1307.
— his scrapbook, 1164.